Eisenhower

Louis Galambos

EISENHOWER
Becoming the Leader of the Free World

Johns Hopkins University Press *Baltimore*

Johns Hopkins University Press
2715 North Charles Street
Baltimore, Maryland 21218-4363
www.press.jhu.edu

Library of Congress Cataloging-in-Publication Data

Names: Galambos, Louis.
Title: Eisenhower : becoming the leader of the free world / Louis
    Galambos.
Description: Baltimore : Johns Hopkins University Press, 2018. |
    Includes bibliographical references and index.
Identifiers: LCCN 2017030371| ISBN 9781421425047 (hardcover :
    alk. paper) | ISBN 9781421425054 (electronic) | ISBN 1421425041
    (hardcover : alk. paper) | ISBN 142142505X (electronic)
Subjects: LCSH: Eisenhower, Dwight D. (Dwight David), 1890–1969. |
    Presidents—United States—Biography. | United States—Politics
    and government—1953–1961. | Generals—United States—
    Biography. | World War, 1939–1945—Biography.
Classification: LCC E836 .G35 2018 | DDC 973.921092 [B]—dc23
LC record available at https://lccn.loc.gov/2017030371

A catalog record for this book is available from the British Library.

Frontispiece: The Eisenhower family. From left to right: Dwight,
father David, Arthur, Earl, Milton with long hair, Edgar, mother
Ida, and Roy.

*Special discounts are available for bulk purchases of this book. For
more information, please contact Special Sales at 410-516-6936 or
specialsales@press.jhu.edu.*

Johns Hopkins University Press uses environmentally friendly book
materials, including recycled text paper that is composed of at least
30 percent post-consumer waste, whenever possible.

To all of my students, graduate and undergraduate, over the years

Contents

Preface

We all have a story to tell. It's the story we tell about ourselves and our lives. We tell it to ourselves over and over again, and we tell parts of the story to those who are closest to us—our girlfriends or boyfriends, our husbands or wives, our colleagues, our bosses, and those who work for us. We seldom try to tell the whole story because it is very long and terribly detailed. The details may or may not be true. But the stories are nevertheless important because they explain what we do and are crucial to understanding our lives. Our story keeps growing and changing as our lives unwind. Then the story begins to work toward an inevitable conclusion most of us would rather not acknowledge.

Dwight David "Ike" Eisenhower had a story to tell about his life, a story that changed several times over his long and remarkable career as a military and political leader. His personal story about Ike—that is, his identity—changed decisively seven times as his career unfolded. His status changed, as did his responsibilities, challenges, and reputation. Each change made him a somewhat different person and a different leader, and the major goal of this book is to get at what was changing him, how he was changing, and how it impacted his ability to lead.

Some of the changes in Ike's career were "Machiavellian moments."[1] Some of these involved his encounters with the "employment of cunning and duplicity in statecraft or in general conduct" by others.[2] In the two most memorable occasions, he was surprised to find himself the target of this conduct. As he and his leadership style matured, he would find a few occasions to deploy his own cunning and even a touch of duplicity in an effort to achieve his objectives. He of course masked these changes in his leadership behind a sunny, down-home persona and a justly famous smile.

The smile alone, however, was not going to carry him through the dramatic transformations that took place in America and much of the world between the 1890s, when he was a child, and 1961, when he retired from the presidency. His early life played out in the sort of small-town, bucolic setting that was a central characteristic of America for three centuries. Mark Twain's wonderful stories captured the spirit and some of the contradictions of that society and the people who lived in the surrounding farm country. By the late nineteenth century, small-town, agrarian values were deeply planted in the national psyche, but the second agricultural revolution and rapid urbanization in the twentieth century steadily ground away at the demographic, economic, and social base of that culture.[3] By 1960, more than 60 percent of the population lived in the suburbs or the central city in one of the country's sprawling metropolitan areas.[4] Great corporate farms dominated the markets for agricultural commodities. Businesses such as General Motors were larger, economically speaking, than most of the world's nations. Technological and scientific developments drove some of these important transformations. Mechanical, electrical, and chemical innovations changed the way Americans got from one place to another, heated and lighted their homes, prevented and treated their illnesses, produced and distributed their essential goods and services, and enjoyed their leisure time.

All of these developments were accelerated by the rise of the professions, which became centers of expertise and important pathways to social mobility. This made access to education even more important than it had been in the nineteenth century. In 1890, the three leading American professions were still law, medicine, and the clergy, but by 1960, more than 11 percent of the workforce had some claim to professional status. From chemical engineers to biological scientists, from statisticians and psychologists to nutritionists, physicists, and accountants, the professions had changed American life and were continuing to splinter into increasingly specialized occupations.

One of the professions that changed significantly was the military—the profession for which young Ike was trained. It had been a widely disrespected and stunted source of careers in the 1890s, but by the 1960s it was a formidable presence in American life, an institution of central importance to US public policy and to those millions of Americans deeply concerned about Cold War national security. Throughout the twentieth century, the professional soldier worked in and was controlled by a formidable bureaucracy. The military officer was thus more like a clergyman than a private-practice lawyer, more like a professional business manager than a doctor or dentist. Whatever his rank, the soldier was obliged to adjust to awesome technological changes in the weapons of war—the machine gun, the tank, the truck, the jeep, the airplane, radar, sonar, the missile, and finally atomic and nuclear bombs. All decisively altered the way soldiers fought or prepared to fight. Little wonder that a successful officer might by 1961 have an advanced degree in engineering or another discipline. The warrior model was not entirely outdated, but it was increasingly the exception, not the rule. When a leading officer could become secretary of state, something dramatic had changed in the US Army's role at home and America's role in the world.

Indeed, the global balance of power had shifted in decisive ways five times between the late nineteenth century and Ike's retirement. The rise of Germany and its fall in World War I were followed by the reassertion of German power and the rise of Japan in the 1930s. Another defeat in World War II brought down both Germany and Japan and left the Soviet Union and the United States facing each other in a global struggle for supremacy. By that time, an America that had faced inward for more than a century had moved out into the world, exercising its power and influence in foreign wars and several major revolutions. The United States—like all of the nations that experienced industrial revolutions—acquired the new possessions and client states that were customary features of an emerging empire. During the Cold War, America and its allies were arrayed against the Soviet Empire and its communist dominions. By the 1950s, the mainland United States was threatened for the first time since 1815 with a direct and destructive attack by hostile nations. America's leaders were, with ample justification, fearful of a surprise assault with missiles and nuclear weapons.

At home, the United States was experiencing a series of decisive internal political changes. Like all capitalist nations, America had to

cope with an economy that was never at rest. Waves of growth were followed every two decades or so by serious depressions. The worst collapse, the Great Depression of the 1930s, prompted the nation to
extend the power and reach of its national administrative state. The
foundation for the welfare and regulatory programs of the New Deal
had been laid in the Progressive Era, prior to World War I. But the political innovations of the thirties were more dramatic and far-reaching
than anything the country had experienced since the adoption in 1787
of the Constitution.

Following the stock market crash in 1929, many Americans sought
through their local, state, and federal governments to provide security
and equity for those citizens who did not share equally in the opportunities, prosperity, and power associated with the nation's expansion. During the post–World War II decades, major changes also took place in the
roles of women and people of color. Like all of the world's capitalist countries, the United States created and then had to learn how to manage a
bureaucratic administrative state to implement its new policies. Between 1890 and 1961, the nation added formidable welfare and regulatory institutions to its existing array of promotional and security
bureaucracies.

In the following pages, I probe the impact these major forces of historical change had on Ike's career. I consider how he attempted to respond to and influence these developments to the advantage of his own
career and that of the United States, its allies, and, to a considerable extent, the entire world.

You are probably thinking that some things don't change as we mature and encounter new challenges. You are right on target. And that
was as true of Eisenhower as it is in all of our lives. I will pull some of
those threads out of the fabric of his life story and try to understand
them as well as the dramatic changes that took place as a small-town
boy from tiny Abilene, Kansas, became a five-star general, a national
hero, a president of the most powerful nation in the world, and the premier international leader in the 1950s. While we are studying this
unusual career, I will try—with two significant exceptions—to avoid

looking forward to the Eisenhower presidency, that is, to the end game in the White House. All of that was still far in the future when we start this exploration of his leadership.

My own study of Eisenhower's career began in earnest in the 1970s when I became a co-editor and then editor of *The Papers of Dwight David Eisenhower* at Johns Hopkins University. Professor Alfred D. Chandler Jr. had edited the first five volumes of the *Papers* before leaving Hopkins to take an appointment at Harvard Business School. Chandler and I overlapped on volumes 6 and 7, and then I took over the leadership of this formidable editorial project.[5] In the course of tracing Ike's career through military service, his presidency of a great institution of higher education, his leadership of the military forces of the North Atlantic Treaty Organization, and his eight years as president of the United States, I became fascinated by his leadership style and the manner in which his distinctive personality shaped his interactions with other foreign and domestic elites and with the American people. Before we finished the *Papers* in 2001, I decided that I would try someday to capture in print the development over a long career of his identity, his reputation, and his leadership.

Now we should get on with our story. We start by turning back to 1920, a troubled year for the United States Army and a troubling time for Ike.

Part I

Getting a Grip on Ike

One

Eisenhower standing with a tank at Camp Meade, Maryland, in 1919.

Trouble

Major Eisenhower was in trouble. It was not the first time he had challenged his superior officers and the authority of the US Army. But this was a career-threatening incident. It was a challenge that could not be laughed off as a spirited cadet's kick at the merciless discipline of West Point or even a young officer's failure to stay in uniform and maintain precise army decorum. Eisenhower was thirty years old in 1920. Married, with a young son, the major had recently been the commanding officer of more than 10,000 soldiers getting ready for battle in Europe. But the world war was over now. The army's leadership was frantically trying to hold its own as Congress chopped the military budgets. Eisenhower's criticism of the army's leadership and tactics was not welcomed.

As Ike quickly discovered, it is risky for a professional soldier to challenge higher authority.[1] It is risky in any organization, large or small, public or private, if you wish to have a successful career. Any senior officer, corporate executive, or university president inclined to be honest can explain just when and how it is possible to swim against the current of established organizational dogma and doctrine. If that person happens to be insightful and exceptionally open, he or she will also tell you how dangerous it is to short-circuit the hierarchy or criticize an organization's values and established ideas—especially in print.

In the years immediately following the Great War, it was particularly dangerous to ignore the US Army's hierarchy and promote heretical ideas. The nation's military was shrinking. Congress in the early 1920s did not cheer the American contribution to victory in Europe. The majority in Congress was unwilling to honor the army's achievement by spending more tax dollars on national defense. While American veterans had good cause for pride in what they had accomplished "over there," most Americans were in a big hurry to get the experience behind them. They placidly accepted the US Senate's rejection of the peace treaty, the Versailles settlement in which President Woodrow Wilson had invested so much of his reputation.[2] Republican Warren G. Harding's campaign slogan in 1920 was "Normalcy," and voters found that brand of politics appealing.

After the United States opted out of the League of Nations and President Harding took office, there seemed to be little need for an expensive military force. To most Americans there appeared to be no obvious threats to US security on the horizon. A surly Congress cut the army's proposed strength from half a million to 300,000, and chopped it again the following year to 12,000 officers and 125,000 enlisted men—a skeletal force at best.[3]

The shrinking army was an especially unpleasant organization for professionals, whether they were enlisted men or officers. Squeezed down in rank following the war, officers—even the most promising individuals— had little to look forward to in their military careers. That was true above all for those men who had new ideas about their service. Shrinking organizations encourage everyone on the inside to defend their turf and avoid risk.[4] That is precisely what the Chief of Infantry did when he read Eisenhower's article in the *Infantry Journal* calling for changes in accepted tactics—the same tactics that had just won the war in Europe.[5] Major General Charles S. Farnsworth had commanded an infantry division in France, and he was understandably unhappy to read an essay that was critical of the army's tactics and the attitudes of its officers.[6]

The article proposed a different kind of infantry division, one in which a relatively new weapon, the tank, would play a decisive role in combat. The author, who had not been to France and had never experienced war firsthand, challenged the wisdom of his superiors in the chain of command. "A great many officers," he wrote, "are prone to denounce the tank as a freak development of trench warfare which has already outlived its usefulness." Other officers, the article said, had never been in action with the tanks and apparently based their views "on hearsay." Having little experience with tank warfare, "they simply ignore it in their calculations and mental pictures of future battles." As a result, Eisenhower said, many officers fell "into a grievous error" and needed to be rescued by "facts" and "by sane and sound reasoning."[7]

The article had a sharp edge. It cut with particular force his superior officers, the ones who apparently needed to be instructed in proper infantry tactics. We will probably never know if Major General Farnsworth placed himself among those who based their decisions on "hearsay" or those who were given to "grievous error" by grounding their professional judgments on a slim or nonexistent base of information. What we do know is that the Chief of Infantry took hold of the issue at once. He called in the audacious major and told him his ideas were wrong, even "dangerous." Calling for changes in the organization of the infantry at that time, in that tenuous political and budgetary environment, was a mistake, and he told Major Eisenhower to keep his ideas to himself. If he persisted, he would be court-martialed. The Chief of Infantry harshly stifled this critique of the existing structure and established tactics of his forces. The army was circling its wagons.[8]

Ike had been encouraged to write on tank warfare by his good friend and fellow officer at Fort Meade, Maryland, George S. Patton, who wrote and published his own article on the great potential of the tank. Patton's article, which was even more aggressive than Ike's, called for radical changes in army strategy and tactics.[9] Patton had returned from the war in Europe as a confirmed devotee of tank warfare. Never given to understatement, he recommended making the tanks into an entirely separate force that would be freed from the slow-moving infantry and allowed to operate as a relatively autonomous battle force.

Patton, too, was admonished for his critique of the infantry, but his courageous service in France, his powerful friends in the army, and his image as an officer uniquely dedicated to combat shielded him from the worst effects of the incident.[10] It did not hurt at that phase of his career to have a Distinguished Service Cross and a Distinguished Service Medal from the Great War. He, too, was vulnerable to attacks by the top echelons of the military bureaucracy, but he was tolerated as a unique variation on the traditional American officer: a man from the West (in his case) or the South and from one of those "better families" that provided backing for many a military career. Major Eisenhower lacked Patton's background, his polo ponies, and his panache.[11] Patton could get away with his article because he was Patton, and besides, he shortly returned to the cavalry.

Eisenhower, by contrast, was vulnerable to Major General Farnsworth's threat. Ike understood that the Chief of Infantry was not bluffing and decided to keep his mouth shut about tanks.[12] He had been promoted to lieutenant colonel during the war (at the age of twenty-eight), reduced following the armistice of 1918 to his regular rank of captain, and then promoted to major. It was not at all clear in the early 1920s that he would ever make it beyond that rank.

He was happy at Camp Meade, where he temporarily commanded a tank brigade. But he had barely cleared the crisis over his article in the *Infantry Journal* when he found himself threatened by another superior officer with a court-martial over a different matter. He had applied for a housing allowance that he was specifically not entitled to receive.[13] He later said he made a mistake because he had not done his homework and did not understand the army's intricate manual of regulations. He had never even bothered to read it, he said. That was a flimsy excuse that the army's Inspector General was not about to accept. When the facts in the case became known to Brigadier General Charles G. Helmick, Eisenhower was caught in an embarrassing and threatening situation. Helmick was not inclined to brush aside an illegal payment of $250.67. Hard times made dollars and even pennies matter. Helmick wanted a court-martial that certainly would have ended the major's military career. While Eisenhower managed to wiggle through this second career crisis, his army ratings in "tact" and "judgment" slid down.[14]

These experiences leave us struggling to understand how and why Ike was having so much trouble with superior authority. Why did this young officer—at the time of this last incident Eisenhower was still only thirty—get into situations that pushed him to the brink of failure? These were not isolated incidents. There were others.[15] The general pattern suggests that his efforts to become an effective military leader were seriously threatened by his failure to acquire a good sense of how his senior officers would respond to what he did, what the particular situation of the US Army was during the early 1920s, and what he needed to do to make a success of his career as a professional soldier.

To that date, he had not displayed the kind of hard-driving ambition we usually see in young professionals tagged for successful careers. He did not have the tightly focused sense of purpose that puts a professional in any organization on the fast track. He seemed, in fact, to have on blinders that obscured much of the setting that would control his career and the development of the entire US military—all services—for the foreseeable future.

To Major Eisenhower, of course, it looked different. From his perspective, it seemed as if the army was determined to thwart his career. Otherwise, he would have been sent to France during the war to lead men into combat. He had almost made it on one occasion, only to be stopped virtually at the dock. As a result, he acquired a great deal of experience in organizing and implementing training regimes during the war. The army tagged him as an officer with a special talent for training raw recruits and militias, and that tag locked him out of the combat command he coveted.

Football also kept leading his career astray. He loved the game and had played it fairly well before a crippling injury knocked him off West Point's team. He then became a talented coach and found that his reward was a series of assignments that somehow always involved coaching. Coaching was not likely to lead him to high command. In the early 1920s, Ike explained his troubled career by looking outside himself for the source of his problems. But that is what most of us do when things are not going too well.

To some extent, he was right. He was being pigeonholed by the army bureaucracy, tucked into a category that suggested his career could be interesting and useful to the service and his country—even though it would certainly not lead to the top level of command, either battlefield command (his clear choice) or command in shaping strategy or the army's all-important political context. The army bureaucrats had locked Ike in a dead-end organizational role. It was not at all clear in the early 1920s what he could do to break away from the path being charted for him.[16] But it was very clear that he had the primary responsibility for finding a new path if he was going to get ahead. It was also clear that if he kept causing trouble for senior army officers, that would not happen.

He had to change because the US Army's hierarchy was digging in for peacetime service and years, maybe decades, of shrinking budgets and slow promotions. Ultimately Ike would need to understand that hierarchy better and learn to control his tendency to be an abrasive subordinate if he was going to be a successful leader. During the war, he had demonstrated what he was capable of doing. With limited resources, he had built up an exemplary training camp. He had done this under the pressure of a wartime schedule that left no room for mistakes, no room for delays. But in 1920 and 1921, it appeared that his good works might not save his career. He might have only two choices: either he would leave the army, junking a decade of military experience, or he would learn how to deal with superior authority in new ways and with new results.

In order to understand the choices he made, the way they played out in his career, and his distinctive style of leadership, we need to look more closely at his personality, his identity, and the society that had shaped it. We need to start by looking further back, before the Great War, to his life in the small town of Abilene, Kansas, and to his interesting, rather unusual family.

Two

*Young Ike (at front) camping with his
Abilene buddies around 1904.*

Abilene

Abilene, Kansas, was a small town with a big reputation. Although it was just a tiny speck in the vast plains of Middle America, it had earned a role in the nation's history as the drop-off point for the western cattle drives. For a time that was where the horse gave way to the railroad, the crucial link to eastern markets. Saloons kept some of the cowboy money in Abilene, and prostitutes got some of what was left. The cowboy years were wild and lucrative, but the railroads pushed on and the cattle drives quickly dwindled. Then Abilene settled into a more sedate life as one of the thousands of tiny commercial centers that served local farmers out west.[1]

For the first three centuries of American settlement and expansion, these little towns and their countryside played a leading role in the nation's economy, social relations, politics, and culture. In many of these towns, you could walk a block or two and see fields full of corn, wheat, cotton, hay, cattle, or pigs. Relationships in that setting were very personal. When someone looked you in the eye, you said "Hello" or "Howdy." Political campaigns turned on individuals, their agreements, and their reputations, and often on their willingness to negotiate and compromise. There was a sense of community, and cooperative values conditioned the individualism that was well grounded in rural and small-town capitalism.

Of course, the flip side of community was insularity, a lack of interest in much that happened beyond the local setting. Although social classes were loosely defined, there was seldom any doubt about who was in charge. The leaders were white men who had some local claim on status. It was assumed that these relationships and their underlying values had always existed, had always guided the communities toward material success, and would always provide individuals, old and young, with a pathway to the good life. Normally in these communities organized religion affirmed the small-town ethos, as did prosperity.

By the end of the nineteenth century, Kansas had plenty of experience with both good and bad times. Around Abilene, the soil was rich, and when there was enough rain, farmers could make a solid living, build up some savings, give their daughters a dowry, and maybe even send their sons to the state university at Lawrence. In the early 1900s, that kind of progress was taking place in farm country all over America.

The "Executioner"

Unfortunately, Kansas had a dry year in 1909, when Dwight Eisenhower was a senior in high school. So there were some hard times in Abilene and the rest of the state. The people grumbled about high taxes and wondered why the state government still could not pay all of its bills in cash.[2] The hard times reached down into the south side of Abilene, near the railroad tracks. The north side of town was the good side, the middle-class side, where families had parties that were reported in the local newspaper. The Eisenhowers never had one of those parties. They were living on the poor side of Abilene, on South Fourth Street, right beside the railroad tracks. Six brothers, their parents, and a girl who helped with the housework were crammed into a small frame house. Fortunately for the Eisenhower family, the father, David, had steady work at the Belle Springs Creamery, a local cooperative. Since his brother-in-law, a foreman at the creamery, had given him the job, David's position was safe.[3]

Job security notwithstanding, David Eisenhower's life was a study in serial disappointments. He was school-smart and had started with some advantages. His father was one of those successful farmers—the kind who had farmed well, invested wisely, and accumulated some capital. He cared about his family and was able to send David to Lane University, in Lecompton, Kansas. At Lane, a small school organized by the United Brethren in Christ, David took a hodgepodge of courses, including ancient Greek. He began to look forward to a career as an engineer. A cocky young fellow, he irritated some of his classmates but found at least one loyal admirer: a bright, determined young lady named Ida Elizabeth Stover. She quickly supplanted engineering in David's heart and head. They were married in 1885.[4]

Leaving school and engineering behind, David quickly found a new enthusiasm for business. He started fast. His father, well grounded in the middle class, was able to give David and Ida $2,000 and 160 acres of rich Kansas land as a wedding present. David, however, had no interest in working the land. He had already had a good taste of farm work as an extra hand during the harvest season, and he wanted no more of it. Spurning the hard life of a farmer, he used his stake to start a store in the nearby town of Hope, Kansas. That venture quickly failed. He had neither the personality nor the experience to run a business. Apparently David never caught on to the fact that people generally do business with people they like. He and his partner also seemed oblivious to the fact that farmers are unable to pay their debts in a bad year.

David's failure in business sent his family into a downward social and economic spiral. He and his wife had started their marriage from a firm position in the middle class of Middle America. They were relatively well educated. They owned some books, as well as a piano. They were part of an extended family that owned property and held responsible positions in the community. But David never recovered from the collapse of his venture into business. Bankruptcy was not a mortal sin in nineteenth-century America, but David, who was more concerned about the appearance than the reality of his failure, molded a fictional cover story. He created an appealing family myth about the evil partner who had done in the trusting David and the business. The family seemed to buy into this story. But one can assume that the small-town gossips ferreted out the truth.[5]

Now the young man was left without a job or money or a skill, without a future, and with a growing family.[6] At this crucial point in his life, he was limited to unskilled jobs that a college-educated man would not really want to hold. His search for a way out took him first to Denison, Texas, where he hired on as a lowly "engine wiper." He brought Ida and the boys to Texas, where they lived in a shack by the railroad tracks. They were dirt poor, and the family was growing. Dwight was born in October 1890, into a household that was barely keeping its head above water. The Eisenhowers would not easily surrender their middle-class pretensions, but David's failures had dumped them into the working class along with the millions of other Americans who worked with their hands and were paid by the hour.

Ida was sustained through this grinding life by her deep religious faith and the kind of American optimism that seems to have no limits. David, however, soured on life. He had a mean streak that got broader and deeper as his dreams collapsed, forcing him to turn again and again to his family for support.

David's father visited them in Denison and was stunned to see how they were living. He persuaded them to return to Abilene, and David's brother-in-law got him a job tending the machinery in the creamery. They still had a hardscrabble life, with David at first earning only $25 a month. Still dependent and grumpy, David was able to move the family into the house on South Fourth only because his brother Abraham left town and sold him the property on good terms.[7]

David dealt with his disappointments and dependency by presenting an impeccably middle-class appearance to Abilene. Anxious for status, he made much of the fact that he could read ancient Greek and thus could read the Greek version of the Bible. One wonders how deep his knowledge of ancient Greek was and how often the language was useful in that farming community. But I imagine it was "useful" to David every waking moment.[8] He dressed the part. When he was not working at the creamery, he wore the clothing associated with the middle class. He was clearly white-collar, not blue-collar, in his mind.[9]

This was not an easy fit for a man who seemed frequently to be on the edge of a rage. David was withdrawn and distant most of the time when he was at home, but he was too involved when he was angry. He was quick to point out the moral failings of those around him, including his own family members and neighbors. On at least one occasion, he went too far. He gave a serious spanking to a neighbor's child and was arrested after the parents filed a complaint. Jailed, he had to pay a fine to get released.[10] The town gossips must have loved that story. More important to the family were the spankings and whippings David doled out to his own sons, using a leather belt when the boys misbehaved or when he felt his authority was challenged.[11] Young Dwight had a temper, and he earned his share of these beatings. His father was a source of authority but certainly not of the balancing affection the boys needed when they were growing up.

Disappointed in the material world that was of great importance in Abilene and the rest of America, David sought refuge outside of that world. He was a seeker. Raised in the intense culture of the United Brethren in Christ, a Mennonite sect, he and his wife, Ida, made Bible reading an everyday part of their family life. For David, however, neither the Brethren nor the Bible-reading sect that attracted Ida satisfied his longing for otherworldly explanations of life. Searching for meaning, he flirted with a thoroughly materialist philosophy and ran for the school board as a Socialist in 1903. Although the Socialist ticket got some votes, capitalism was solidly in the saddle in Abilene. The Republicans won the election and enabled Abilene smugly to "continue its progressive, yet conservative policy."[12] This was David's last venture into politics, and apparently he quickly jettisoned the Socialists and bobbed to another philosophical extreme, dabbling in the occult. Concerned that he had not finished his education, he also took correspondence courses from a school that sold him a diploma in engineering in 1904.[13] The degree did not get him a new job or raise his pay at the creamery, but it must have helped satisfy his longing to get a foothold on the bottom edge of Abilene's middle class.

As a symbol of authority or a role model for a youngster, Dwight's father fell substantially short of what his sons needed. Young Ike had problems with authority, and the father he later labeled the family's "Lord High Executioner" clearly had a great deal to do with that outcome.[14] It was not easy to have a father who was distant and irritable, a man who took out his anger on others. David's insecurity and his search for status in Abilene put pressure on everyone around him. This included Dwight, who already had as much pressure as he could handle from his older brother Ed.

Big Ike

Ed was a little less than two years older than Dwight, but that was an enormous gulf when they were in their teens. Ed was bigger, stronger, and certainly more mature than the brother on whom he and their classmates laid the diminutive "Little Ike." The brothers fought all the time, and "Big Ike" always won. This would not have been such a problem if the Eisenhowers had lived in one of the spacious houses on the north side of Abilene. But they were stuck on South Fourth Street. The two boys had to share a tiny bedroom and a single bed. When they cooperated—as they did occasionally—Ed always took the lead.

Early on they worked together selling the family's surplus vegetables. On South Fourth Street, they had enough land to plant gardens and to harvest a good bit of the food they ate. They had a barn and could raise chickens and pigs. They had some fruit trees. All of this helped to make David's meager pay doable for a family that included six hungry boys. In the summer and fall months, they also had some extra food that could be sold.

This introduced Ed and his brother Dwight to marketing, country style. It also introduced Ed to some of the negative aspects of a small-town class system that obtained despite popular belief that it did not exist. The two Ikes trundled their produce in a wagon up from the south side of town to the north side, where there were people with cash. They went door-to-door showing their produce. Some of their customers grumbled, picked over the produce, and made remarks that hurt Ed's feelings. He later said, "In a boylike way I resented that. I developed then a feeling that the railroad tracks separated the classes in Abilene—those who lived north of the tracks thought that they were just better than those who lived south of the tracks. Being older than Dwight, I was probably more sensitive about this. I talked to him about it years later. He said he never had any such feeling."[15] Given Little Ike's age, that may have been the case.

But it was also true that the Eisenhower family was not headed to the north side of Abilene when David was still only earning $65 a month.[16] Money was so tight that Ed had to drop out of school for a time to work at the creamery with his father. Little Ike was also unable to finish his freshman year in high school, but this was because of a serious leg injury. Unfortunately, that meant he had to repeat the first year and was thrown into the same class with his older brother Ed.[17] In high school, the unequal competition continued.[18] Ed quickly found his way into the one dimension of small-town life in which money, hand-me-down clothing, and social class did not matter: sports. He made the football team that year as a fullback and stayed on the team through the next three years. When he was a senior, the yearbook proudly proclaimed that Ed was "the greatest football player of the class."[19]

This was tough competition for Little Ike, who did not go out for football until his junior year. As one of his classmates noted, Dwight "was too awkward for the backfield so we put him in the line."[20] Those who have had experience with small-town football will recognize that both Ikes were caught up in an athletic status system. The linemen worked hard to make heroes of the backfield players who scored the points for their team. Since the football players were of course not paid, the boys in the backfield had to be satisfied with other rewards—local attention, honor, and, for some of them, the prettiest girlfriends in the school. Little Ike did better in baseball. Ed held down first base, while Dwight played center field. But when the team elected a captain in 1908, it was of course Big Ike.[21] Sports continued to be extremely important to both Ed and Dwight, and the older brother's dominance continued through four years of high school and beyond.

An early life in the shadow of his older, more accomplished brother did nothing to improve Dwight's already skewed relationship to authority.[22] If anything, it reinforced the attitudes stemming from his daily dealings with the family's ultimate power, David. In both cases, Dwight had ample reason to resent authority, to look for ways to get out from under it, sometimes to scorn authority, and to anticipate eventually besting those who were making his young life difficult. In a few years, he would be in a position to challenge Ed, but for the immediate future, that would have to wait.

When they both graduated from high school, Ed raced off to the University of Michigan, where he would graduate a few years later with a law degree. Dwight stayed in Abilene, working for two years to help pay for Ed's college expenses and ending up where all of the Eisenhower males seemed fated to work: the creamery. By the spring of 1910, he was already earning $55 a month, not too short of David's pay of $76.[23] At that point, though, Little Ike's future looked rather bleak. He had a high school diploma, but he was doing the same kind of low-skilled, manual labor that his father had done as an engine wiper in Texas. Meanwhile, Big Ike was headed toward a professional career and the income and respect that all of the Eisenhower boys craved.

Saint Ida

This was a family that deserved a savior. Unlike most such families, the Eisenhowers got one. What they got was certainly what young Dwight needed. Ida Stover Eisenhower was a mirror image of her husband. Where the father was almost always gruff and grumpy, Ida was indefatigably cheerful and patient. Despite having six boys in the house, Ida was calm, fair-minded about their fights, and decisive about the important things in life. She was tolerant of their shortcomings (and those of her husband), supportive, and above all dedicated to her religion. She seems never to have complained about their hardships, even when they were living in poverty in Texas. Marrying Ida took David out of college, but it was the single best decision he ever made.

Ida was like David in one important regard: they both were restless seekers in search of a true faith. In Ida's case this took her away from the River Brethren and brought her to the Bible Students. This sect suited her emphasis throughout her life on direct knowledge of the Bible without the intervention of a formal church or pastor. In the centuries since the Reformation, the Protestant religion had continued to fracture into sects, many of which emphasized either individual revelations or direct knowledge of the Bible. The Bible Students did not stress a decisive religious experience. Instead, they sought through knowledge to deepen and broaden their faith in an incremental, rational fashion. This suited Ida's personality, and it provided her with an emotional anchor through the difficult years when she was running a large family on a meager income.[24]

She organized their household like a talented master sergeant training a company of raw recruits. Her recruits were the boys, and she mustered them almost every day, assigning each one his chores. The boys took care of the family's animals, weeded the garden, helped can fruits at harvest time, assisted with dinner, and cleaned up afterward. The worst chore was starting the fire on a cold morning. One of the boys had to get out of a warm bed and build the fire. The house had to be heated, and they needed the fire for cooking.

When the boys misbehaved and chores did not get done, Ida reasoned with them instead of exploding. In brief, she taught Dwight and his brothers how to exercise authority without beating them with a leather strap. She was always there for them when they needed help or reminders about their responsibilities. One of the most important of those responsibilities was education.

Ida's dedication to learning was interwoven with her approach to religion and her own family background. After her mother died, her father was unable to work and cope with his large family, so Ida was sent to live with one of her grandfathers. Undeterred, she pushed forward with her education. At a time when most Americans did not attend high school and when many of those who did were unable to finish before starting to work or getting married, Ida completed her high school education.[25]

Determined then to attend college, she followed her brothers, who had moved halfway across the country to Kansas, and enrolled at Lane University. She used the small inheritance she had received and finished her second year at school before she and David were married. This, too, was unusual in a nation in which very few men and even fewer women had any form of college or university education.[26]

Ida oversaw the boys' education with the same quiet, positive determination she demonstrated every day in dealing with their chores. Her voice was the voice of wholesome reason, stressing application, looking always to personal progress toward a better life. She worked patiently to help young Dwight learn to control his temper. He did not get rid of the anger that had apparently been planted in his genes and nurtured by his father and brother. But with Ida's help, he learned to bottle it up most of the time.[27]

Ida's involved, consistent guidance explains why six boys from a poor Kansas family were able to finish high school. This was a significant accomplishment in those years. The dropout rate was high in Abilene's schools, starting in the seventh and eighth grades and continuing through the high school years.[28] The farm called for young men and housework called for young women, especially those who lived on the south side of town or in the countryside.

For Little Ike, Ida's support for education became particularly important because he was enamored of sports and seldom enthusiastic about his schoolwork. Fortunately, he was smart and had a penchant for mathematics. His grades had sagged badly in his first year of high school, when he had to withdraw because of a serious injury.[29] But when he started over, most of his grades were in the 90s. He did well in Latin, German, English, algebra, and rhetoricals.[30] He kept his grades high through the next three years, and in his senior year he received an A+ in American history. This was a commendable accomplishment for a young man who was at that time far more dedicated to playing football and baseball than he was to compiling a sterling academic record. Neither he nor Big Ike was elected to leadership positions in their class—those plums went to north-side kids such as Herbert Sommers. But in his senior year, Dwight was elected president of the Athletic Association. The yearbook said he was also the "best historian and mathematician" in the class.[31] Ida had good cause to be proud of what she had accomplished by keeping Dwight focused and pointed in the right direction—toward a useful career.

Little Ike's Assets

While he had not displayed any great penchant for leadership by the time he graduated from Abilene High School in 1909, Dwight had logged some important experiences and developed some significant capabilities. Like all of his brothers, he was inured to hard physical work—and was relatively pleased to be doing it.[32] He had worked during the summers at the creamery, pulling around big blocks of ice. He had sprouted up a couple of inches. Although he was still only around five-eight, he was strong and ready to put in a "normal" eighty-four-hour week at the creamery.

He ended up there after graduating, working alongside his father and earning that extra $55 a month the family needed.[33] The money was necessary in part to support Ed, who was taking his first big step toward a professional life in one of the leading law programs in the Midwest. Dwight contributed with the understanding that Ed would return the favor after he had launched his legal career. True to his dominant role, Ed never bothered to pay "Little Ike" back.

At the creamery, Dwight did everything from firing the boilers to pulling the blocks of ice around and working for a time as a night operator, seven days a week, twelve hours a day. When he was on the night shift, he was in charge of two other employees. Dwight was responsible, bright, and as yet uncertain about his future beyond a vague expectation that he would follow Ed's path into some kind of higher education. He had no idea of what that might involve or where it might take place. The University of Michigan looked interesting in a vague sort of way, but Dwight had no desire to follow Big Ike into a legal career. Arthur, the oldest brother, had gone off to a job as a bank messenger in the big city—in this case Kansas City, about 150 miles to the east—where he was serving an apprenticeship that would gradually take him up to positions with more and more responsibility. Ida's influence could be seen woven into his career as well as Ed's. Arthur liked his work, the bank, and Kansas City, but the business world did not appeal to Dwight. Perhaps because he lived on the south side of town, he did not have any direct experience with commerce or finance other than the cooperative creamery, and that work was far too close to what his father, David, was doing twelve hours a day, six days a week, for very little pay.[34]

Education seemed to be the best way to do better than David had done and to move up, away from a life near the railroad tracks. Lacking the money he needed, Dwight decided to take the advice of a young friend, Edward E. "Swede" Hazlett. While Dwight was working nights at the creamery, they managed to spend a good bit of time together, and Swede convinced him that they should both try to get into the US Naval Academy at Annapolis, Maryland. Dwight knew nothing about ships, the ocean, the US Navy, or the Naval Academy, but a free education was appealing.[35] The history he had read had given him a bent toward the romantic aspects of military leadership, and he had already learned from a neighbor how to shoot a pistol, a weapon that really was useful only for hunting human animals. This probably helped him veer sharply away from his mother's dedication to pacifism.

He also drifted away from the family's attachment to fundamentalism. He was not a seeker after some fundamental truth, either in this world or outside of it. Even David's opposition to drinking, smoking, and card-playing was thrown overboard by young Dwight. In cards, he was guided instead by a local hunter and fisherman, Bob Davis, who taught him all of the intricacies of winning at poker.[36]

Dwight absorbed these lessons like a dry sponge picking up water. Poker appealed to his facility with mathematical reasoning and his willingness to work within the logic circumscribed by the fifty-two-card deck. Poker also tapped into his growing knowledge of other men and why they behaved as they did. He understood men much better than he understood women, but in those years, poker was a securely masculine hobby, entertainment, or occupation. Seven-card stud poker rewarded shrewdness as well as skill in understanding the odds. It also rewarded awareness of personal weaknesses and strengths. As Dwight mastered this game, he was moving forward with what would be a lifelong effort to master himself and shape his personality. Like Ida's lessons in self-control, poker gave him an edge in life as he began to think about what he might do when he left the creamery, the family, and Abilene.

Little Ike's Liabilities

As that new part of his life started to open before him, he had some personal baggage that would make it difficult for him to follow the paths toward a better life that Arthur and Ed were marking. He had problems dealing with formal authority, problems that stemmed from his difficult life with his father and his seemingly endless, losing competition with Ed. Wherever he went and whatever he did, this would follow him. He would not be able to leave it behind, shucking it off as he did the River Brethren, his mother's pacifism, and his father's bitter opposition to smoking tobacco. But like most young men, Dwight was less mindful of that weakness than he was of his strengths.

That aspect of his personality threatened, however, to become ever more important as he explored the possibilities of getting an appointment at the Naval Academy. The political process for appointment was—and still is—closely controlled by Congress. Candidates had to pass a written examination and a physical exam and then be appointed by a congressman or senator from their home state.[37] Obviously, young men from the south side of Abilene were far less likely to have the political influence that might be required to get that appointment. So Dwight initially had more to worry about than did Swede Hazlett, whose well-to-do family could swing some political weight.

Crucial at this point was the examination, a test that Hazlett had failed the first time around. He crammed with Dwight, and both took and passed the test. Little Ike did quite well, finishing second among the Kansas applicants. Having passed the exam, Swede headed off to Annapolis and a career as a naval officer. But it turned out that in one regard at least, they had not done their homework: Dwight was too old to matriculate at the Naval Academy. Quickly flipping to a new page in the application process, Dwight targeted West Point. Since he knew as little about the US Army as he did about the navy, he found it easy to change course. After the leading candidate for the West Point position failed his physical examination, Dwight scored. Senator Joseph L. Bristow gave him what he wanted: a pass for a free education at the United States Military Academy.

That education would not be entirely free, of course. West Point would throw Dwight into a setting that would impose a type of discipline that he had never experienced. It would bring to the surface the anti-authoritarian streak that his father and older brother had nurtured in Little Ike. The temper his mother had taught him to suppress would not always remain beneath the surface, hidden from others. For the next four years, the military academy would impinge on his life, day after day, in a manner alien to Abilene's small-town culture and challenging to a young man who remained uncertain about who he was and what he wanted to become.

Had he been able to go to a state university in 1911 instead of West Point, he would have found a setting that created less social pressure and offered more intellectual opportunities. This was the path three of his brothers—Ed, Earl, and Milton—took when they left Abilene.[38] Most of the state schools also had remedial programs for those who either had not attended or finished high school or had gone to one of the many weak high schools. The state universities had the advantage of offering a variety of career lines for a young person undecided about the future, as certainly was the case with Dwight. Instead, he was locked in financially to a program designed to produce a single type of graduate for a single type of professional career. He did not have four years to decide on which professional career he wanted to follow. Trained from the first day to be a soldier, he would find occasions to question that profession, its authority figures, and values.

He was on a course dictated primarily by negatives—that is, by the things he did not want to do. Above all, he did not want to remain in the creamery in Abilene, Kansas.[39] He wanted to get a jump start that would take him away from his parents' hardscrabble life and intense religion. Like Ed, he saw education as the path away from the life he wanted to leave, even though Dwight had no real idea of where that path led. He simply put that question on hold when he boarded the train that took him to another world along the Hudson River in New York.

If you had met him on the long train ride in 1911 and asked him in a friendly way to tell you about himself, Ike probably would have dwelled on the things he did well. Some of them were physical accomplishments: center field on the baseball team, a tough linesman in football, and a hard, serious worker—a night boss—at the creamery. He could have mentioned that he was honest and trustworthy and that he had plenty of friends, including various girlfriends from time to time. Then he might have mentioned the academic part of his life, the intellectual accomplishments that were manifestly less important to Abilene and Ike than being manly and well liked. There would have been no references to the tug-of-war going on between his anti-authoritarianism and the conciliatory approach to life that his mother, Ida, had encouraged him to embrace. Pressed to look to his future, he would have been intensely optimistic. He would have made it clear that he was looking forward to success, even though he would not have been able to tell you exactly how that part of his story would unfold.

Three

First Lieutenant Dwight D. Eisenhower and Mary Geneva "Mamie" Doud were married in Denver on July 1, 1916.

Locked In

Ike's path in 1911 was full of promise. He had assimilated his mother's confidence that education was the best route for a young man from Abilene to follow. That optimistic idea had become part of his identity.[1] But he knew how poor his family was and he understood that in 1911 there were three other Eisenhower brothers approaching that crucial turning point in their lives. They would need any extra money the family might be able to scrape together. So he headed to West Point even though he had yet to discover any specific career or intellectual byway that was more deserving of his enthusiasm than sports.

While he leaned toward history and was good at math, neither was more important to him than football, baseball, and the vague but compelling American challenge to get ahead in life. He was certain he would become something better than he was and better than his father was. He sought certification as a college graduate more than education.[2] That desire had a specific family content provided by his father's failure to graduate from college and achieve the social standing his intelligence warranted. So Dwight went off to West Point to build his future, just as Ed had gone off to seek his fortune in Michigan.

Ed's pull on Little Ike's personality was still powerful. During Dwight's trip to New York, he made two stops: one to see Ruby Norman, an Abilene

girlfriend living in Chicago, and then a jaunt over to Ann Arbor to see
Ed. Ruby bolstered his rather thin layer of confidence. He felt he could
be open with her, and he later confided in a wonderfully guileless way that
one of the advantages of West Point, New York, was that it "looks awfully
nice as an address on an envelope."[3] With Ed, the visit was entertaining
and friendly—they didn't renew their wrestling matches. But it unfortunately brought to the surface the kind of anxiety that had been nurtured
by years of putting up with a brother who excelled in sports. Now Ed was
excelling in education, romance, and the kind of sophistication that was
admired from afar by kids growing up on the south side of Abilene. Little
Ike was still contending with Ed as he headed toward New York.

West Point

Arriving at West Point, Ike and his fellow members of the class of 1915
were quickly immersed in a program that demanded more obedience to
senseless authority than he had ever experienced. West Point hazing
seemed immature to Dwight, who was a few years older than his peers.
He bristled at authority in an institution in which obedience trumped
brilliance.[4] He had by this time become addicted to smoking cigarettes,
and that too created problems for him. Because he needed a smoke when
he was not supposed to have one, he simply broke the rules—and got
caught. There were other infractions as well. Dwight piled up demerits
and bobbed about in rank. On one telling occasion, he challenged with
juvenile humor an instructor in military engineering—a man known as
a martinet, with an inflexible approach to every aspect of the course he
was teaching. Dwight survived that episode, but he kept pushing at the
edges of what West Point would tolerate.[5]

The classwork was demanding and the schedule rigorous. The academic element of West Point played to Dwight's weakness in part
because it was time-consuming and in part because it involved rote
learning—the program was heavily weighted toward memorization instead of the kind of analysis that appealed to him. Even the history
courses bored him, and he was a relatively indifferent student who constantly flirted with academic problems. It was a tribute to his native in-

telligence and to his long experience with Ida's rigor about homework that he was able to finish sixty-first in a class of 164.[6]

While he was troubled by the discipline and emphasis on memorization, young Dwight was successful in two regards at West Point. He was well liked, even admired, by his fellow cadets. Groaning under a system of discipline that often seemed totally irrational, they found Dwight's disrespect for authority appealing. He had other things working in his favor, too. Having come to manhood in Abilene, he had the advantage of having learned important lessons about work—hard physical work. Long before he finished high school he knew that relentless work was the norm for adults. He was strong enough and disciplined enough to pull his own weight on any job, inside or outside, whether it was digging a ditch, mowing, or helping with the canning in harvest season. He had a sense for the rhythm of farm work, as did almost anyone who lived on the south side of Abilene, only a few yards from the fields.

He was not a city boy. He was a country boy. So the physical aspects of soldiering and training at West Point played to his strengths. All of his brothers had acquired the same lessons and had also learned in the family something special about sharing, teamwork, and human nature. While Ike's instructors at West Point frequently had good cause to ignore these aspects of his personality, his peers appreciated and respected them.

Having played sports during and after high school, he should have encountered no difficulties with the physical requirements at West Point. But, alas, he was still relatively clumsy and was placed on the "Awkward Squad" with the other plebes who had difficulty learning to march.[7] Despite this embarrassing start, he continued to pursue his intense interest in football. He was small and had to start out on the scrub team. On entrance he was slightly over five feet eight inches tall and weighed only 150 pounds.[8] This was long before the current age of football behemoths, but Ike was small even for his time. He was, however, very determined. No longer having Big Ike to contend with, he finally made it into the backfield. Bulking up and training hard, he started to blossom as a running and blocking back under coach Ernest Graves. On defense, he tackled hard and impressed the coach.

He made the varsity team in 1912 and began to attract some attention from sportswriters, even though he was still second string to the regular halfback. In a game that depended more on grit than on finesse, he was a fierce linebacker and the type of halfback who moved the pile forward. Football at that time was a brutal cousin of rugby. The players were relatively unprotected and the sport regularly produced a full array of injuries. Ike's dream of becoming West Point's football hero ended abruptly when he injured his knee and then reinjured it in a horse-riding exercise.[9]

The injury left him off the football team and depressed.[10] "When I was broken up," he later said, "I was not able to play actively in athletics again at West Point, so I started to resign a couple of times, but my classmates talked me out of it. Once I put in my papers and my classmates held them up. They got the company captain to hold them up while they talked me out of it. I stayed."[11]

Ike worked very hard to get his knee back in shape, but he had to accept alternatives to playing football. Instead of sulking, he focused on supporting the team and was elected cheerleader. Then he became a cadet coach. He began to guide the junior varsity football team and very quickly became a first-class instructor.[12] He understood the game, and he was able to get the most out of players who loved football but were not big enough or good enough to make the varsity. Word got around that the junior varsity was playing well against the teams from secondary schools in the area, and Ike established a reputation as a talented coach.

His label as an excellent football coach would follow him after he graduated from West Point in 1915. The US Army, like any bureaucracy, handled the infinite variety of its individuals—officers as well as enlisted men—by categorizing them in terms of their usefulness and potential for further advancement. In the years since the nation's war against Spain, the army had experienced a phase of "modernization," which consisted largely of centralization under the authority of a general staff headed by the chief of staff.[13] In the new army that emerged from this process, an officer's profile in the general staff's bureaucracy exerted a powerful influence on his opportunities to advance his career. In Ike's case, the capability that distinguished him from his peers as he left West Point was his ability

to coach football. Soon he would also exhibit an equal skill at training recruits, an activity closely related to coaching. For better and worse, this
would become his profile, his pigeonhole in the new army system. Getting
into that pigeonhole was natural and easy. Getting out of it would be painfully difficult and would, in fact, be impossible without some serious, sustained assistance. When his class graduated in 1915, however, Ike was not
nervous about being typecast in the army. There were far more important
things to occupy the mind of a freshly minted second lieutenant.

For the first time there was reason for Eisenhower to begin looking
somewhat differently at a military career and even to become enthusiastic about it. A war had started in Europe, with the Central Powers arrayed
against the British, Russians, and French. In France, the conflict had settled into a slow-moving, brutal campaign of trench warfare, with heavy
losses on both sides. New weapons, including poison gas, the airplane, and
the tank, failed to break the stalemate. As Dwight graduated and accepted his commission, the possibility that America would be involved
in the war began to be considered on both sides of the Atlantic.

If the nation honored tradition and the guidance of its first president,
George Washington, it would remain neutral and leave the fighting to the
European belligerents. But America had already turned outward as it became the world's leading industrial power in the late nineteenth century.
After defeating Spain in 1898, the country had acquired an expanded
overseas empire. As it pushed further into the Caribbean and into Asia,
America and its powerful fleet of battleships and cruisers seemed to be
preparing the nation for another giant step toward full involvement in the
international struggles of the great powers.

This momentous transition helped Second Lieutenant Eisenhower
shelve many of his doubts about his career. He reacted positively to the
immediate challenge of becoming a leader of infantrymen should the nation enter the war. In the previous year he had qualified as a sharpshooter
on the rifle range, and at this point he acquired some enthusiasm and
maybe even a touch of romanticism about his military service.[14] The enthusiasm was tightly interwoven with threads of careful calculation—
as was always the case with Ike—but he had yet to display the kind of

determination or instinct for networking so important to professional success. He had acquired the certification he wanted from an educational institution familiar, at least in name, to most Americans. Now he owed the army two years of service for this "free" education. He was not drawn to any other profession and had no contacts outside of his family that would give him entry to a business career. As a junior officer, he would have all of the status and eventually some of the income that had long eluded his father. Add a sliver of patriotism, and you have an explanation of his new dedication to the US Army. His story about himself, his identity, was now shifting decisively toward the profession that he had joined while he was still diffident about military life and especially military discipline.

His football injury almost blocked his appointment. But a lenient colonel let him be commissioned so long as he agreed never to seek duty in the cavalry, where his bad knee would be an impediment. That sent him into the infantry, one of the less desirable parts of the army, generally reserved at that time for officers graduating in the lower two-thirds of the class. But Ike was happy to accept his new role and assignment in September 1915 to Fort Sam Houston in San Antonio, Texas.

The Lone Star State was a diplomatic and military hot spot for America in 1915. While there was growing concern in Washington, DC, over Germany's submarine warfare, there was also tension over the border with Mexico. The Mexican Revolution had been in full swing since 1910, and President Wilson was concerned to prevent armed attacks on American cities along the border. In 1914, US forces had occupied Veracruz, Mexico, for several months, and there was reason to believe that armed revolutionaries under Pancho Villa might mount attacks across the US-Mexico border.

Close to what might soon become a war zone, Eisenhower got his first opportunity in command with Company F of the 19th Infantry Regiment. It quickly became apparent to his superiors that he had substantial ability both to train and to lead infantrymen. He could be firm, but in a way that commanded respect rather than anger. By army standards, his proficiency was being demonstrated only with small units. But this was still a significant accomplishment for a junior officer who had been sent into the field with a caveat to the effect that he would need strong guidance in his army career. The commandant of cadets at West Point had noted that his judgment, originality, energy, efficiency, and character were all "very good." But, taking note of Ike's frequent abrasive encounters with authority, the commandant added that Ike would need a "strict commanding officer."[15]

That soon became evident in Texas when his commanding officer caught Eisenhower out of uniform on the base. Ike was attempting to win a bet with his colleagues by climbing a cable holding the flagpole. This was the same sort of boyish behavior that had piled up demerits for him at West Point. But now he was twenty-five and an officer in the division. He was thoroughly reamed out, and apparently that sufficed to prevent any similar incidents in the rest of his time at Fort Sam Houston.[16]

Major Conklin and Captain Helms, commanding Company F in 1915, were concerned about Eisenhower's lack of attention to detail and noted his need for further experience. Nevertheless, Helms said that Ike had already established his ability to shape up a company of enlisted men. His "attention to duty and professional zeal" were excellent, and in war, Helms said, Ike would be "best suited for duty . . . with troops." He was still a bit short of being "an excellent officer," and more experience might improve his performance. After hedging his evaluation, Helms added some light praise: Eisenhower was, he said, an "energetic" officer who "takes an interest in his work."[17]

His work as a second lieutenant continued to mold Ike's new identity. Threatening war clouds were gathering to the east and south, and Ike concentrated on the challenge of being an effective leader in a venture far more demanding and dangerous than football. The fighting in Europe had to be on the mind of every military officer in America. So, too, with developments next door in Mexico, where General John J. Pershing was leading an American force in pursuit of Pancho Villa. Mexico's revolutionary renegade had recently attacked across the border and killed eighteen Americans in Columbus, New Mexico.

With deadly combat looming and Ike more intense about his military career, he had another reason to become more serious about his professional and personal life: he had acquired a new status and a partner who would now share his life in the US Army.[18] Mamie Doud and Ike were married in July 1916, shortly after he was promoted to first lieutenant. The bride was young, attractive, and accustomed to more luxury than a lieutenant's pay could provide.[19] Support from her well-to-do father would help. But the marriage frequently left Lieutenant Eisenhower struggling with cash flow problems—a situation many professionals encounter early in their careers. In Ike's case, as we saw in Chapter One, it would at one point get him into serious trouble over an apparently trivial housing allowance.

While married life doubtless pumped up Ike's dedication to his career, the promise and challenges of impending war appear to have been the most significant factors reshaping his approach to his professional life. The martial spirit, I believe, trumped matrimony, just as football had trumped military science at West Point. Following his promotion, Ike had every reason to be optimistic about his immediate future. He had established his ability to lead infantrymen, a basic job in the US Army. In 1917, Lieutenant Eisenhower was even more certain than Captain Helms that in the event of war, he was "best suited for duty with troops."

As with any profession, however, there are two central aspects of getting ahead. One involves the development of the capabilities called for by the profession. This was what Eisenhower was doing very well in this early phase of his army service. Once he accepted the fact that he was for the immediate future likely to continue his service, his talent as a leader began to emerge. As yet, however, it was not at all clear that he would do particularly well in coping with the second major challenge all aspiring leaders face: getting chosen to lead. Here Eisenhower still had a serious problem. Both his sense of identity as a military officer and his reputation among his superiors were changing, sliding toward closer agreement. Helms's evaluation reflected that change. But without any formal recognition of that fact, the army bureaucracy in Washington had locked Ike in as a talented trainer and coach. To their mind, he was a good candidate for only secondary positions in the service.

High command seemed out of sight for an officer with Ike's personality and experience. His reputation as a football coach had spread, and while he was in Texas his superior officer had pressured him into leading the team of a local military academy. Then he was recruited to coach the football team of a Catholic college in San Antonio.[20] Each success made it less likely that he would ever manage to escape being typecast as an officer who had a special knack for coaching but had not established that he could provide the kind of leadership demanded at the army's upper levels.

Whether he was coaching players or training troops, Ike's personality gave him an advantage. He was comfortable with his men and treated them firmly and fairly. His package of small-town values and his instincts about leadership served him well. It was no coincidence that he exercised authority much the way his mother, Ida, had run their household in Abilene.

But there was a second lesson embodied in Ida's life, a lesson that Lieutenant Ike was still having some trouble learning. Ida knew how to bend to authority without sacrificing her values and individuality. This proved a hard lesson for Ike to learn. He seemed still to be rebelling unconsciously against a father and older brother who had saddled him with a deep streak of discontent about authority. As war clouds drifted closer to the United States, Eisenhower found it especially difficult to accept the authority of the army bureaucrats who were deciding his future.[21]

An Army at War

When America entered the war in April 1917, Ike was ready to go. As he saw it, he had every reason to believe that he would soon be traveling to Europe to lead a company or maybe even a battalion of infantry into battle. He was undeterred by the news about trench warfare and the bloody mass attacks that had already killed or wounded hundreds of thousands of Europe's young men. The losses on both sides, which were horrific, had made the Great War the most destructive of human life in history. As yet, neither the Allies nor the Central Powers had been able to produce a breakthrough that would bring the war to an end. The American forces would, their leaders assumed, do that job, quickly shifting the war in France into a new phase and gaining victory for the Allies.

Understandably, Eisenhower, now twenty-seven years old, looked forward to his first opportunity to lead American soldiers in battle. He was not the only American army officer who had dreams of heroism and glory. He was probably neither more nor less optimistic about that challenge than his superior officers, none of whom had yet to go to battle against a powerful, well-led army using modern weapons.

What the army needed first, however, was training for raw recruits and militia of the sort Eisenhower had been working with at Fort Sam Houston. In 1917, the army was not prepared for war. It was not even prepared to train and arm new soldiers. The immediate needs of the service thus deepened and confirmed the army bureaucracy's concept of Eisenhower's capabilities and potential. His army evaluations all pointed toward Ike's strengths in getting recruits and poorly trained militia detachments into shape for service. Now, suddenly, there were far more soldiers who needed training than there were experienced officers to train them. Ike and others with his talents were in great demand. Major Conklin had made it clear that Lieutenant Eisenhower had a "peculiar fitness for detail on militia duty," commenting that "he has shown good judgment and tact on duty as Inspector-instructor with militia." Conklin's praise—"well qualified by temperament for this duty"—suggested that the combat duty Eisenhower now sought might not be what was dictated by his "temperament" and by the needs of the service.

One can understand then, why the army first transferred Ike to the 57th Infantry Regiment, which needed men, supplies, and as much training as could be squeezed into a short schedule. While serving as supply officer for the regiment, Eisenhower experienced one of the nation's great military transformations when suddenly promotions went into high gear. There was a caveat—all of the promotions were temporary. Still, it was encouraging to become Captain Eisenhower as of May 1917. That fall he was also encouraged by the birth of his son Doud Dwight Eisenhower, who of course had a nickname: "Ikky." Soon the new father had another appointment and was back to the training grind at Fort Ogle-thorpe, Georgia. From there he went on to Fort Leavenworth, Kansas, and the Army Service School for more responsibilities in training. Through-out these duties, his superior officers judged him to be "capable and in-dustrious," "average" in most regards, but a "good instructor."[22]

As his repeated requests for active duty in combat were denied, he began to turn against his superiors. He pushed too hard and was admon-ished. His desire to serve his country on the gory battlefields of France was laudable, but he could not break the tight grip the army bureaucracy had on his official reputation. The consolation prize was another promo-tion in 1918 to lieutenant colonel, after he had been sent to Camp Meade, Maryland, for service with the tank corps. The tank was a new weapon that promised to be one means of ending the stalemate in France. Gen-eral Pershing, commander of the US Expeditionary Force, was impressed with the potential of the tank, as was Captain (and then Lieutenant Col-onel) George S. Patton. Eisenhower thought he would be able to join them in France when his 301st Tank Battalion was ordered overseas. At the last moment, however, he was pulled back and sent to Gettysburg, Pennsyl-vania, for yet another training mission at Camp Colt.[23]

To his credit, Ike controlled his explosive temper when this last as-signment came down the army pipeline. Nor did he let his extreme frustration prevent him from doing another superb job of organization, supply, and training at Camp Colt. With thousands of newly enlisted men under his command and little equipment to work with, Eisenhower nevertheless built up a successful tank-training organization. We all have upper limits on our capabilities, and Ike probably pushed very close to his in this assignment. He had never been in charge of this many en-listed men, never been in command of this many officers, never been under this much pressure to train his troops for immediate service in combat.

As a lieutenant colonel, he continued to exercise authority much as he had with smaller units in his previous posts.[24] His men respected his style of leadership and his personality. His growing responsibilities and the frustrations they produced occasionally sparked flashes of temper from him. But during his progression of assignments, from a platoon to a company to a camp the size of a typical army division, Eisenhower's ability as a leader had grown while his style of leadership had remained relatively consistent. He treated those in his command with respect and gave careful attention to their needs. He demanded discipline without being petty.[25]

By the fall of 1918, his command had experienced a tremendous expansion and sent many officers and enlisted men to Europe. They were there to add the manpower and firepower that would enable the Allies to break the German defenses. They achieved their objective, forcing Germany to accept an armistice on November 11, 1918. The sudden end of the war was a bittersweet occasion for Lieutenant Colonel Eisenhower. He was pleased that the killing had stopped but still frustrated by his inability to convince the bureaucrats in Washington, DC, that he should join the American Expeditionary Force in France.

The Backwash of War

While the end of a brutal war was a joyous event for millions, Eisenhower and the other US Army officers who had not made it to France had every reason to be disappointed. They had been unable to contribute in combat to the military victory. For Ike, who had now commanded a force larger than a brigade, the immediate postwar years were a tremendous letdown, a low point in his life. Reduced in rank to captain and unable to escape the reputation that had kept him out of service overseas, he faced a bleak future.

His disappointment is understandable. He had by 1918 become an accomplished leader at Camp Colt. He had created an effective organization, fine-tuned it, and kept it running until the war ended. He had provided the leadership that normally would have been left in the hands of a brigadier general. Then he handled the demobilization of Camp Colt without incident. He impressed his commanding officer, Colonel Ira C. Welborn, who said Ike was "one of the most efficient young officers I have known" and lauded his "capacity for command."[26] Welborn recommended Ike for a Distinguished Service Medal "for especially meritorious and conspicuous service in connection with the organization of the

Tank Corps, in establishing a Tank Corps camp, organizing an officers' training camp, and successfully administering same, and organizing and training units to meet the demands for Tank Corps units overseas."[27] Welborn wrote, "The services of . . . Eisenhower were invaluable to the Tank Corps, and indispensable so much so that he was not allowed to go overseas as he desired. As a captain he started with nothing and organized the Tank Corps camp and training center at Gettysburg; received untrained recruits, established schools, started an officers' training camp for selected enlisted men, and organized and trained Tank Corps units." But the army turned down the recommendation, explaining that "the services performed by this officer, while efficient, are not exceptionally meritorious."[28] There he was again, left in the "good but not great" category.

He got some relief when he was able to take part in a cross-country motor convoy in 1919. Despite the problems the convoy had with poor equipment and terrible roads, it provided Ike with the kind of adventure he loved. The convoy crept sloth-like out of Washington, DC, through Maryland, and across the Midwest. The farther they moved from the coast, the worse the roads became and the more frequently they had to struggle with broken-down equipment. Eisenhower recalled much later that the venture "had been difficult, tiring, and fun."[29]

With no challenging commands forthcoming when he returned from the convoy, however, he again began to wonder whether he should stay in the army. His brothers all appeared to be doing better than he was. Arthur was succeeding in banking. Edgar was building a reputation as a corporate and tax attorney. Roy seemed happy and independent in his pharmacy. Earl was well situated as an electrical engineer. Even Milton, the baby of the family, seemed to be making more progress than Ike.

He clearly had acquired new capabilities and a new identity to go with them. But he had not yet learned how to navigate the army's Washington-centered bureaucracy. Doing an outstanding job was not enough, apparently, to get him ahead in the service. Unless he could develop the political skills and personal support needed to reorient his career, he seemed likely to top out before he got well into middle age. That was a bitter lesson to learn, and Ike began to sour on the army. There was no sign of closure in the gap between his demonstrated leadership capabilities and his potential for promotion. He had bought into the army, but the army had yet to buy into Ike.

In that dismal context, Dwight and Mamie suffered what Ike later said was "the greatest disappointment and disaster in my life."[30] Their son, a happy, thriving child, suddenly became ill in 1920 with what turned out to be scarlet fever, a strep infection. Today we can knock out the infection with antibiotics in a day or two. In 1920, however, there were no quick cures, and Ikky died just after the New Year in 1921. He left behind a distraught mother and a father who had every reason to believe that the gods had turned against him in all aspects of his life.[31] Twice threatened with courts-martial, he seemed to have little to look forward to in the army.[32] Even when he was recommended for the general staff and his leadership praised, he continued to be sent to posts where he was charged with training—and from time to time, of course, coaching football.[33] By 1922, Major Eisenhower's military career seemed to be careening toward an unfortunate ending. It appeared that he would soon be headed back to Abilene and perhaps to a job in the creamery.

Patton and Contingency

But not everything in the postwar era had turned sour for Eisenhower. At Camp Meade he had developed a deep, lasting friendship with George Patton, an officer who had had even more trouble than Ike getting through West Point—Patton had to repeat his first year.[34] Like Eisenhower, he had been injured in football, but unlike Ike, Patton had excelled in all activities associated with military discipline. He was intensely dedicated to the profession. When he graduated in 1909, he was already starred for command in a service that admired men who were enthusiastic about horses, swords, and the physical aspects of combat.[35]

Patton had made it to France, where he served for the second time under General Pershing. It would be hard to imagine two officers less alike than Pershing and Patton. "Blackjack" Pershing, who headed the Allied Expeditionary Force, was austere, introverted, and precise almost

to a fault. Patton was outgoing, inclined toward exaggeration, and ready—
even eager—to take risks in unusual acts of heroism. He had previously
served under Pershing in Mexico, where they unsuccessfully pursued Pancho Villa. In France, Patton was a leader in the army's new tank forces
and was seriously wounded in battle. For his leadership at the front, he
was honored with a Distinguished Service Medal and a Distinguished
Service Cross.[36]

Patton had been encouraged to seek out the tank service by Pershing's
chief of staff, General Fox Conner. Conner was an unusual army officer,
something of an intellectual in a profession that valued action and ac-
countability far more than original ideas, however good they were.[37]
Conner had a unique talent for recognizing the potential of those around
him long before it was evident to others. He saw in Patton a man who
could be of great service to his nation and the US Army, and he guided
him toward an activity that would make best use of his unusual capabilities in war. Conner was also convinced that innovations such as the tank
would have an important impact on the ability of the United States to defend its national security in the future. Following the armistice in Europe and the Versailles peace settlement, Conner was certain that there
would be another world war and that America would need officers such
as Patton to fight that war.

Patton had quickly confirmed Conner's faith in his potential by his
performance on the battlefield, and he continued to pursue the promise of
the tank following 1918. That service brought him to Camp Meade,
where he assumed a new position in command of the tanks of the
304th Brigade. It was here that he and Ike became close personal friends
and professional colleagues. They agreed about the need for innovation
in infantry tactics and about the central role improved versions of the
tanks used in the Great War could play in future conflicts. They also had
a solid basis of agreement in their opposition to the stodgy leadership in
the peacetime US Army, an organization in which seniority constrained
careers and encouraged passive behavior on the part of young officers.

Determined to chip away from below at the infantry authority structure, Eisenhower and Patton wrote the articles on tanks and tactics that

earned both of them sharp reprimands from their superiors. Since Patton was heading back to the cavalry shortly, he would be able to continue his army career without a serious setback. Ike, however, had no way out—unless, of course, he wanted to resign his commission and start a new career in his early thirties. But he had no fixed idea about what his goals would be if he made that leap or what kind of civilian work he might want to do. He was stymied, disconsolate, and uncertain whether his path would now take him to new opportunities in the US Army or back to Abilene—maybe even to the creamery.

Then by chance he met Fox Conner, who was visiting the Pattons.

Four

General Fox Conner was Eisenhower's mentor and sponsor in the 1920s and 1930s.

Epiphany

Eisenhower did not know it, but his time of troubles started to ease the afternoon he met Brigadier General Fox Conner. The occasion was provided by one of the Patton family's formal lunches. Conner spent the afternoon touring Camp Meade and discussing the interesting ideas Patton and Eisenhower had about the potential for new patterns of tank warfare.[1] Unlike many of his fellow officers, Conner was open to new ideas—to changes in military organizations, weapons, and tactics. Instead of threatening young officers such as Patton and Eisenhower with a court-martial for considering innovations, Conner encouraged them to continue thinking about ways to improve the US Army.

One way for Conner to achieve that goal and to get the army ready for the next, inevitable war was to mentor young officers such as Eisenhower and Patton. Conner and Patton had first met when they were both on their way to Fort Riley, Kansas, in 1913, and they had quickly become friends.[2] They had met again in 1916, later in Washington, DC, and then at greater length in France during the world war. At that time, Conner was becoming a vital player—the operational wizard—on General Pershing's staff, and he strongly advised Patton to make his future with one of the army's newest weapons, the tank. Patton's aggressive personality meshed very well with the tank's potential for aggressive, mobile tactics.

Conner believed in getting out of headquarters and into the field, and he and Patton shared these experiences. He was pleased when Patton took his advice and moved into a position running the new American tank school in France.[3] The army actually had a school before the United States could manufacture tanks, so the American Expeditionary Force had to borrow them from France. In combat, Patton made good use of the primitive tanks he had, and following the Armistice of 1918, he continued to be a vigorous tank advocate.[4]

Brigadier General Conner and Major Eisenhower had some common experiences. Both men had small-town backgrounds: Conner was from Mississippi, and like Ike, he had not distinguished himself at West Point. In 1898 he graduated seventeenth in a class of fifty-nine. Both men had accumulated an impressive number of demerits, many of them for smoking.[5] Both were now looking for ways to change an army that was firmly and dangerously locked down—dangerously because, as Conner recognized, the Treaty of Versailles had planted the seeds of another great war, a war that would inevitably involve the United States. Conner convinced Patton and Ike that American national security would again be threatened, probably in the course of their careers. At this autumn meeting, their discussion was more intense and more focused than one might expect of casual conversation at a weekend luncheon. All three officers were left contemplating a dangerous global context in which the United States would, willingly or not, play a major role.

Conner also had an impressive understanding of the army and military careers. Unlike Ike, Conner had developed capabilities that the army understood and appreciated, capabilities that accelerated his advancement. He had, in short, created an important reputation for himself: through self-study and experience he made himself a leading authority on artillery and artillery doctrine. While senior infantry officers could be (and normally were) skeptical about new weapons such as the tank, they were enthusiastic and positive about artillery. Conner had served as the first American exchange officer to a French artillery unit at a time when the French were acknowledged leaders in this area of military science.[6]

He had been able to apply his knowledge during the Great War, adding combat authenticity and a combat wound to his academic knowledge of warfare.

Conner had become an organizational innovator at a time when the army was vulnerable to change. As chief of staff for General Pershing, who headed the American Expeditionary Force, Conner had in effect created the position of Chief of Operations. This slot became the model for army staff organization, an innovation that stuck after the war and was written into law in the Defense Reorganization Act of 1920.[7] In his new position in France, Conner had reached down and promoted Patton and another young officer whose potential he recognized.[8] As a result, George C. Marshall acquired the wartime experience he needed to keep his army career advancing.[9]

By the time Eisenhower met him, General Conner had become the army's "Grey Eminence"—"grey" because he operated behind the postwar army's public face, "eminence" because his close links to the army's top leaders and his exquisite sense of how to manipulate the service's organization gave him power that exceeded his position.[10] He was the master Machiavellian whose continuing support could accelerate a career and, as it turned out, even foster in others a powerful sense of professional ambition.

Ike's Mentor

Conner was thus not new to mentoring officers whose potential he recognized, and he was inclined to emphasize the younger man's capabilities rather than the problems Ike encountered in 1920 and 1921. The fact that Eisenhower had published an article that upset a stodgy Chief of Infantry did not faze Conner, who had been pushing tank warfare for several years. More serious was the threat of a court-martial over the illegal $250.67 housing payment. But to Conner that was a mere bump in the road that deserved nothing more than some smoothing out: the repayment Eisenhower made and the reprimand he received from his commanding officer should do it. With Conner's support, they sufficed.

Agreeing with Patton's positive evaluation of Ike, Conner set out to give Major Eisenhower a new attitude about his army career—that is, a new identity that would enable him to make full use of his potential for top-level military leadership. Conner could be satisfied that he had already had a positive influence on the careers of Patton and Marshall, so he had some reason to be confident he could guide Major Eisenhower's career out of the hole Ike was digging for himself in the postwar army. In reality, however, neither Patton nor Marshall had needed any serious mentoring to cultivate their military identities. While they had sharply different backgrounds and personalities, they were both intense and determined about their professional careers. They had, as well, established their reputations in wartime service. All they needed were nudges. Ike, by contrast, was a thirty-two-year-old officer in need of substantial guidance and support.

The odds did not favor Conner and Eisenhower. The US Army in 1922 was not a friendly organization for anyone who was—as Ike was—contemptuous of regulations, at odds with the army's hierarchy, and uneasy with the infantry's status quo. Conner and Eisenhower would be fighting uphill against a military bureaucracy that was clearly determined to keep this major in the lower levels of service as a coach and trainer of recruits.

At first the odds seemed to be confirmed. Conner launched his new mentoring venture by asking Ike to join him as his executive officer in Panama. There was, however, no football team in Central America, and Major Eisenhower's institutional image was so well planted that even a request from the Grey Eminence could be turned down. It was. The army's first response to Conner's request was a harsh no. Ike's commanding officer at Camp Meade needed him to remain in his current position, where, among other things, he could continue coaching the post's football team. Ike's temper rose at this latest rebuff, but there was nothing he could do about the situation.

It was not easy to thwart Conner, however, and he continued to press for Ike's appointment. Challenged, Conner used his friendship with the army's new Chief of Staff, General Pershing, to get the man he wanted as his executive officer in Panama. Shortly thereafter Ike received orders to report for duty under Conner. This episode offered a startling lesson in how the upper reaches of the United States Army actually operated. Bureaucratic authority was dominant from the middle of the institution down to the lowly recruit. Personal authority, reputation, and friendships were potent forces at the top. Eisenhower would not forget this lesson. Happy to be relieved of duty as a coach, Ike, with Mamie, quickly got ready for a voyage to Central America and for their first experience with military duty outside of the continental United States.

Reeducation in Practice

Soon after Ike arrived at Panama's Camp Gaillard in 1922, Conner started his campaign to reorient his new executive officer. Ike's new boss was a determined, smart, and very well-organized teacher. For the first time in Ike's life, he had a male authority figure he respected, understood, and liked. It was no small task to wipe out the anti-authoritarianism rooted in Ike's Abilene years, and the job would never be 100 percent finished. But Eisenhower, in his thirties, started the process under Conner's tutelage and soon began to acquire a new and intense focus on the intellectual and organizational aspects of his career as a professional officer. If he and Conner succeeded, they might also succeed in transforming the army's image and evaluation of Ike. That would be an entirely different task, but first they had to get Major Eisenhower thinking in a different way.

While Camp Gaillard was a wonderful post for Ike, it was a wretched place for Mamie, who was pregnant. A marriage that had taken a stiff blow when their son Ikky died began to fray even more. Ike burrowed deeper and deeper into his career, leaving Mamie further and further behind. Unable to cope with conditions in Panama, she returned to Colorado and the protective shelter of her family.[11] When their son John was born in August 1922, there was an opening—an opportunity for the mother and father to draw back together. But they never really recovered the emotional bond that had been at the heart of their marriage.

Meanwhile, Conner devoted his full attention to the task of reconstructing Eisenhower's military career. How exactly did this happen? We know a good bit about what Conner asked Eisenhower to do, and maybe we can mesh that with what we already know about Ike's identity to this point in his life. For one thing, Conner guided his new student deeply into military history and taught it using a Socratic method of analysis: What, in brief, did the text mean? What were the alternatives to what the leaders did? What, then, likely would have been the outcome? Early in his life in Abilene, Eisenhower had been interested in the great battles and careers of the past, especially in ancient history. He had developed a romantic fascination with heroic accomplishments, but not with the type of counterfactual analysis Conner emphasized.[12] This type of history enabled Ike to build on his bent toward mathematical reasoning. Conner's method was the antithesis of the rote learning found in history courses at West Point, and it enabled Eisenhower to see the relevance of history to a successful military career.

Conner was teaching Eisenhower two other things. One would have an almost immediate and extremely important payout. By requiring Ike to write a field order for the Canal Zone every day, Conner made this type of systematic procedure a habit instead of an imposition. Looking ahead, Conner insisted that his pupil use the language and categories of the army's Command and General Staff School. This was a drill, and as such, it was repeated over and over. Conner thus taught Eisenhower how to deal effectively with the army's brand of bureaucracy—something that Ike had been resisting and resenting. Conner wanted him to be completely socialized into army routine so he could move up with ease and encounter more sophisticated problems of strategy and organization.

The other lesson was more subtle: Conner was instilling in Ike the confidence that he could actually achieve great success when he focused his mind completely on an army career. This is one of the most important aspects of mentoring, but it is hard to nail down and almost impossible to analyze in any systematic way. When Ike left Abilene, years before, he lacked the kind of driving ambition that would take him to the top in any profession, including a career as a professional soldier. Conner understood that aspect of Ike because he too had left West Point with a similar attitude toward his military career. Now he convinced Ike that by concentrating his considerable mental resources on professional accomplishments, he could advance far beyond the limited horizons of Abilene or Fort Meade. He could break out of the army's typecasting, the deeply planted image of a talented trainer and football coach who perhaps had the capacity to lead a regiment or brigade, but nothing more.[13] Confidence was the ingredient that had to be added to the special skills and the capabilities for military leadership that Conner was assiduously grooming.

Many accomplished leaders cannot mentor their subordinates. Why? Not because they cannot teach technique and improve their subordinates' capabilities. The limit to their mentoring is their inability to instill confidence in another person. The drive and concentration that got them into a leadership position make it difficult for them to foster confidence. Conner did not struggle with this problem and was thus the perfect mentor. His own ego did not get in the way, much to Ike's advantage. The long hours engaged in intense discussions about history, leadership, and the lessons to be learned from Carl von Clausewitz's *On War* gave Eisenhower the knowledge base he needed to become a senior officer. The experience writing field orders prepared him for advanced training (and testing). The confidence he began to acquire in Panama in his own intelligence, goals, and education would be the essential stepping-stone to success as a professional officer. Conner calculated that Ike was the kind of person who would make full use of the lessons he was learning—to the advantage of his career, the US Army, and ultimately the United States.

Conner was an inspirational teacher, and he quickly began to bring out the best in his new trainee. For Eisenhower, this was the first authority figure in his life since leaving Abilene who had a sustained, forceful, and positive impact on him. It helped that Ike had once been interested in history and was not contemptuous of past leaders and their military campaigns. He had lost his interest in history at West Point, but he quickly regained it in Panama and was able with tutoring to begin thinking historically and analytically about the rich, deep military lore of the past. He was not so oriented to action that he could not engage in extended reflection on both military principles and tactics.

His two-year stint in Panama was essentially a practical graduate program in how to be an effective leader in the upper reaches of the US Army. Not an ideal army. No, Conner and Eisenhower were thinking about the army that existed in the 1920s and would probably be needed in the future, if Conner's calculations were correct. By the time Ike left Panama, he was eager to get ahead with his career. He had every reason to believe that his army reputation would quickly change and would become congruent with his new identity. He would then no longer be labeled as an adequate but less than exemplary officer with an unusual knack for training recruits and coaching amateur football players.

Ike's Sponsor

The long months of intense education with Fox Conner built up Ike's expectations as well as his confidence. While in Panama, he received General Pershing's Order 43 (October 23, 1922), which awarded Ike the Distinguished Service Medal for his efforts in training troops at Camp Colt in 1918. This was the recognition that had been denied earlier. But that was before Major Eisenhower had friends in high places. Looking forward to an opportunity to build on what he had learned, he applied for the Command and General Staff School at Fort Leavenworth, Kansas. Years earlier, Conner had aced the school, which was then in an intensely "competitive period." Some of its student-officers were reported to have committed suicide or to have suffered nervous breakdowns.[14] The program had since become less cutthroat, but the school was still a demanding and crucial step on the way to a senior position in the army.[15]

Alas, the army's image of Ike was not changing as quickly as he was. The only service school he had been to was the infantry's tank school, a program that was neither demanding nor prestigious enough for an officer looking to give his career a kick start. That worked to his disadvantage, as did the army's skepticism about Conner's high evaluation of

Eisenhower.[16] Conner said Ike was "one of the most capable, efficient and loyal officers I have ever met. On account of his natural and professional abilities he is exceptionally fitted for General Staff Training."[17] This, however, was the first such ecstatic evaluation the thirty-three-year-old Eisenhower had received. That prompted suspicion in Washington.

The army was quick to point out that his organizational profile—established with a variety of superior officers between 1915 and 1924—had not, in fact, changed. As a result, he was sent back to Fort Meade, where he could help his friend Vernon Pritchard coach the post's football team. This was another crushing blow to Eisenhower. Then the Chief of Infantry compounded the disappointment by turning down Ike's application to the Infantry School at Fort Benning, Georgia. It was beginning to appear that his second-rate reputation was not going to change and would continue to define his military career—Fox Conner's support notwithstanding. No longer satisfied to be considered second-rate, Major Eisenhower fought back. He requested and received an interview with the Chief of Infantry and asked point-blank to go to the Infantry School. The answer once again was no. Instead, he was sent to Fort Benning to command a light tank battalion—a command he had already held briefly in 1917 before he was denied an opportunity to serve in Europe.[18]

By the fall of 1924, Eisenhower's career appeared to be set in the same bureaucratic cement that was holding together the army's organizational culture. Chief of Staff Pershing retired that year, and apparently Conner's efforts had been in vain. The best that Ike could expect was to stay in the army, advance in rank slowly—very slowly—and perhaps retire as a lieutenant colonel to Abilene or a town with an army post. This was not an unusual career for an officer in America's army in the 1920s and 1930s.

But this time his erstwhile mentor became his sponsor and cleverly broke the army bureaucracy's lock on Ike's career.[19] Fox Conner was in Washington, serving as deputy chief of staff of the army, and he had not lost his confidence in Eisenhower's ability as an officer. Whether because of Conner's influence or a sudden, unpredictable stroke of intelligence on the part of the Chief of Infantry, Eisenhower was suddenly rescued from coaching and from career stasis. He learned that he had indeed been appointed to attend the Command and General Staff School as part of the 1925–1926 class. Here at last he would get an opportunity to make full use of his ability to focus on a problem, develop an appropriate policy solution, and explain how it could be put into effect.[20] Here at last he would get a chance to create a new image of Major Dwight David Eisenhower.

Right at that crucial point in his career, however, Ike's confidence wavered. It was still thin despite Conner's guiding influence and months of intense, informal postgraduate instruction in Panama. After all, Eisenhower had been reminded over and over again, directly and indirectly, that the army officers sitting in judgment on his career were—Conner excepted—convinced he did not have the ability to become a general officer. He had been told repeatedly that he was an excellent football coach and a good trainer of infantry at the regimental level. It would have been hard not to have self-doubts at this point. The doubts that were pushing forward in his mind were reinforced by a message he apparently received from an aide to the Chief of Infantry, who said that Eisenhower would probably fail the tough course at the Command and General Staff School. Conner tried to pump up Ike's confidence. But the outlook was not at all favorable as the Eisenhowers headed to Fort Leavenworth and this new challenge.

Luckily for Ike, the school was now using a one-year curriculum that stressed strong offensive actions designed to avoid the trench warfare of the world war and the horrific losses associated with "concentrated brute force." Here, built into the program, was a direct critique of the British approach to infantry in the Great War, an approach to strategy and tactics that had emphasized neither air nor mobile tank warfare.[21] This was the type of critique that Ike and Patton had been working toward with the articles they published in the *Infantry Journal* in 1920.[22] The challenge for Eisenhower was to follow the logic of that analysis without drifting out of the boundaries set by the school's concepts of correct answers to each of the problems presented to the officers. Fortunately, that was what Conner had trained him to do, day after day after day.

Opening the Door

The intellectual exercises that Eisenhower performed in Panama embodied an important element of wisdom about getting ahead in any modern institution. Every participant in a bureaucratic organization who plans to move up the hierarchy and get greater authority faces the same problem Ike encountered. In business, in government, in nonprofit organizations, the rewards go to those who achieve a high degree of efficiency within a paradigm set by the top leadership. Those who show the leadership how to make the organization and the existing paradigm more successful are likely to move ahead. Those who question the entire paradigm are seldom successful—except in fictional accounts. On those rare occasions when challengers are successful, they later get opportunities to set or recast the paradigm. Then the process starts over again. In this regard, the US Army and its Command and General Staff School were just a particular military variant on the common model of the modern organization.

Problem-solving in the military was thus rank-appropriate. And the one-year program that Ike entered was designed to be appropriate for ranks above his, that is, above major. Later, the school's two-year program would deal more effectively with the differences in capabilities required for successful leadership at different ranks. But the program Eisenhower was taking was focused on only three main aspects of the performance of a general officer: tactics and technique, tactical principles, and command staff and logistics.[23]

As the intensive program got under way, Ike at first had some problems accommodating to the rigid curriculum. But rather quickly Conner's training and Ike's determination, analytical ability, and self-discipline paid off. In the early running he ranked fourteenth in the class of 248. After the first month, he pushed up into the top ten. And stayed there. Partnering with his friend Leonard T. Gerow, Ike sprinted as the class approached the finish line: fourth in the class in March, he was third in April and May. He won a tight race at the end and finished in first place.[24] His efficiency report rated him superior in "attention to duty, initiative, intelligence, energy and resolution, judgment and common sense, and leadership."[25] Conner's ecstatic evaluation had been confirmed. In the most challenging test the peacetime army could impose, Eisenhower had demonstrated that he clearly had the intellectual ability and professional skill needed for high command. The officers at the War Department in Washington, DC, could not possibly ignore these results.

Or could they? When his orders came through, it seemed that nothing had changed. The War Department still had him in the same old category: he was sent once more to Fort Benning, Georgia, as executive officer of the 24th Infantry Regiment—and coach of the post's football team. If he felt like he was trying to march in knee-deep molasses, well, that would be understandable. Even when the Chief of Infantry opened the way for him to attend the War College, in Washington, DC, there was a caveat: he was told he probably did not have enough command experience to join the general staff. How could Eisenhower not be discouraged?

But the Grey Eminence was still on his side, refusing to be thwarted. Conner was again able to intervene, providing Ike with an opportunity to acquire a new advocate, a powerful friend. He managed to get Ike an appointment in Washington, DC, to the American Battle Monuments Commission. This might at first glance appear to be a dead-end job. But it gave Eisenhower an opportunity to work directly with General Pershing on a book—a guide and historical account—about the American Expeditionary Force's battles in France. Eisenhower had not been allowed to take part in those battles, but now he would be able to study them in detail and in close cooperation with the general who was America's leading hero in the world war.

Conner's strategic move pushed Eisenhower into a new position in the army. At last his official military reputation started to change, though more slowly than one might expect. At least his reputation was now edging closer to the capabilities he had and the identity he had molded in Panama and Fort Leavenworth. He was for the first time offered a job with the general staff. But he wisely stayed on the course that Conner charted: he attended the Army War College in 1927 and once again demonstrated a very high level of ability in understanding the materials and problems presented to him and his fellow officers. Then he followed Pershing to Europe to work on the guide to what American forces had accomplished in the Great War.[26]

A Dangerous French Interlude

While his service in France was designed to build on the foundation Conner had helped him create, the duty seemed like a vacation for Ike and for Mamie, who had pressed hard for something more romantic than Kansas or Texas or Panama could offer. For the first time since 1915, Ike had a relatively high degree of independence. He still had a commanding officer, but it was apparent that he had only to satisfy General Pershing in order to make this venture successful.

That twist in his command structure helps explain why Ike regressed a bit. Forgetting what he had learned about the personal dimensions of higher command, he drifted back into the type of anti-authoritarian behavior that had characterized his years at West Point. He let his personal feelings about Major Xenophen H. Price, his immediate superior, show, marring what should have been another quick step forward in his career. Eisenhower was impatient with Price's "impossible ideas and methods of operating." Price, he said, was "old maidish," and Ike was not interested in flattering a boss he did not respect.[27]

When Eisenhower's contempt bubbled to the surface in France, one of the consequences was the worst efficiency report that he had received in his army career. Major Price summed up Ike's performance in Europe in primarily negative terms. In certain aspects he was still "excellent," but in others only "satisfactory." While he had "great natural ability," he allowed "family worries" to affect his performance and "had difficulty adjusting to changed conditions existing in France." He was, Price said, "not especially versatile in adjusting to changed conditions."[28]

Fortunately for Ike, Pershing's high regard for him and his work trumped the comments of Major Price, so the negative evaluation did not hold Ike back. Pershing, whom Ike admired, was not an easy person with whom to collaborate, but Eisenhower took a strong interest in the commission. Ike mastered the details of the campaigns and the topography. He took a particular delight in walking through the battle sites and understanding on the ground the bloody struggles that had taken place there. His interest showed in the work he produced and Pershing's favorable response to his report.[29]

During the entire time he was with Pershing, Ike only made one serious mistake. It has some significance because it provides a measure of how much he still needed to learn about getting ahead in the US Army. Pershing had produced a draft of his memoir, in the form of a narrative history of the American Expeditionary Force, and asked Eisenhower to read it and offer his advice. Eisenhower promptly went through the manuscript and was shocked to discover that Pershing had written the account in strict chronological order: it was, as a result, unintelligible to any reader except perhaps the author or George Marshall, who had served with Pershing. Eisenhower—who failed to see that he had a political problem, not an intellectual one—tried to reorganize and redraft the history so that it made some sense. This was a serious error.

Pershing was not happy with the redraft. Disappointed with Ike's version, he called on George Marshall for help. Marshall immediately recognized what had to be done. He helped Pershing polish his draft and publish it in its gross, unintelligible form. That was what the boss wanted. That was what the boss got from Marshall. Most of those who tried to read Pershing's publication probably agreed with Ike's critique, but that was beside the point.[30]

Eisenhower had learned a great deal from General Conner. But as the foolishness with Price and the editorial episode with Pershing indicated, he still needed to master the task of understanding when exactly to press a point and when simply to yield because there was no chance to do what he thought was best. In the 1920s, George Marshall was already better at doing this than Ike was. If Ike did not soon learn how to emulate Marshall, it was almost certain to curb his career.

New Opportunities, New Threats

In the next few years he would face additional challenges after he returned to the United States. He went from France to a new and special task working with the Office of the Secretary of War and with the deputy chief of staff, Major General George Van Horn Moseley. He was placed in charge of a study of American plans for the wartime mobilization of industry. The nation's economic performance in 1917 and 1918 had been far from satisfactory. The United States had not been prepared to fight a major war, and it showed. On the industrial front, the government had quickly discovered that it lacked the information it needed to control and redirect the economy. After some misguided attempts to introduce centralized controls, the government turned to a Wall Street investor, Bernard Baruch, who implemented a plan based on the compromises he could persuade the nation's leading businessmen to make.[31]

Ike's job was to develop plans for a more effective means of controlling the largest industrial economy in the world. He studied the problem systematically, interviewed leaders in industry and government and the military, and developed a plan that was promising enough to gain for Ike a new level of support among some of the nation's top political and military leaders. Colonel Irving J. Carr, who worked in the Office of the Assistant Secretary of War, found Eisenhower to be "an ideal soldier. Especially conscientious and painstaking, frank and open to his superior and wholly loyal in carrying out his missions." He was, Carr said, "particularly suited for civilian contact in any capacity."[32] Lieutenant Colonel Earl McFarland commented on Ike's "real literary ability" and noted that he had "greater skill in written expression of thoughts than any other officer of my acquaintance."[33] Major General Moseley added an enthusiastic letter to his file. Moseley pointed out that Eisenhower was "personally commended by the Chief of Staff" and was "qualified to occupy positions of the highest importance in the military service."[34] Ike's standing in the army was now closely correlated with his promise as a leader.

His service with the mobilization study, like his service with Pershing in Europe, was moving Eisenhower along the path that Fox Conner had charted. Many of Ike's evaluations now surpassed the one Conner had given him when he left Panama. The *boy* from Abilene had become a professional soldier and was maturing into a military officer with a new capacity for top-level leadership. His new identity was as *the perfect staff officer*. He had made a decisive transition. Within the army's highly centralized system, he was positioned to be worthy of the rewards that Conner had urged him to seek and which his success at the Command and General Staff School had led him to expect.

Then the army dropped another bomb in his lap. In 1932, he received two offers for his next assignment, and once again they involved training and a job teaching and directing army athletics at West Point. If consistency is a virtue, the military bureaucrats making decisions about Eisenhower's career were preparing themselves to win an international award for their ability to ignore contradictory evidence and hew to an outdated line of reasoning. These repeated rebuffs were creating mounting tension in Eisenhower's life, a tension that began to create problems with his health. He had experienced a short bout of gastrointestinal distress when he was a cadet, but his Panama epiphany was followed by a series of more serious episodes that proved difficult to diagnose and treat. Were they stress-related? Was he paying a personal price for his charged-up professional ambitions? We cannot be certain (any more than he or his doctors could be), but the correlation is convincing. As is the manner in which the outbreaks continued.[35]

Fortunately for Ike, by the time he had to make a decision about his next post, he had a third choice. He had recently gained the enthusiastic support of the most powerful man in the American army, Chief of Staff Douglas MacArthur. In his current office since November 1930, MacArthur was still molding his team. He saw in Eisenhower an officer who was a team player, who produced on demand, who had substantial literary ability, and who clearly would strengthen the Chief of Staff's organization. It was a significant accomplishment in 1931 to have General MacArthur acknowledge Ike's "outstanding talents" in performing "highly important missions."[36] Now the Chief of Staff asked Eisenhower to serve as his assistant—an offer that was impossible for Ike to refuse.

As Ike already knew, this new job could be dangerous. He would be under the thumb of an officer far more demanding, difficult, and powerful than Major Xenophon H. Price or even General Pershing. Although it was obvious that one slip might send him back to coaching football at some distant, dusty army post, Ike accepted MacArthur's offer. Eisenhower would soon have new reasons to wonder whether he had made the right choice.

Five

General Douglas MacArthur and Eisenhower confronting the Bonus Army in Washington in 1932. Printed with permission of Getty Images.

Tested

Now forty years old and an experienced, well-traveled major, Eisenhower should have been fully prepared to understand and work with any superior officer. But hardly anyone was fully prepared to deal with General Douglas MacArthur, an officer whose personality and accomplishments produced complex mixtures of astonishment, envy, awe, and some fear on the part of those with whom he served. Chief of Staff MacArthur was a combination of Ike's successful older brother, his fiercely demanding father, and a brilliant war hero, all rolled together in the person of the US Army's most flamboyant four-star general.[1] MacArthur was as likely as any officer in the entire US Army to spark Ike's pent-up anger and hostility—especially authority that he could not always respect. It would take patience worthy of Job if Eisenhower was going to avoid a blow-up with MacArthur.

The two officers were mirror images: "Ike asked to be liked, and he was; MacArthur demanded that he be revered, and he wasn't. He had no diminutive. Even his wife addressed him as 'General.'"[2] MacArthur's family was upper-class just as surely as Ike's was working-class.[3] While Eisenhower's family was profoundly pacifist, MacArthur's was US Army to the bone. His father, General Arthur MacArthur II, won a Medal of Honor for his bravery in battle during the Civil War. In the years that followed, he served in a long list of dreary stations in the western United States, forts that young Douglas loved almost as much as his mother detested them. Throughout these trying years, the outspoken Arthur made some enemies, but he also made some powerful friends, including two men who had served under him and would later become Army Chief of Staff: General Peyton C. March and General John J. Pershing.[4]

Their influence would come into play after Douglas did his part by graduating first in the class of 1903 at West Point. Like Ike, Douglas had a taste for analysis and hated the military academy's dull style of rote learning. Unlike Ike, MacArthur "bent with the system, aware that a lowly cadet could not change it."[5]

He was not perfect. Early on in his career as an officer, he did not always remember how to yield to authority and had some troubling, Ike-like encounters with his superior officers.[6] He was given to special pleading, but he learned how to suppress that trait and turned his career around while serving at Fort Leavenworth, Kansas. Good fortune and a touch of influence later placed him in Washington, DC, in 1912, serving as an assistant to the Chief of Staff, Major General Leonard Wood.

Promoted to major in 1915, MacArthur remained with the General Staff until the United States entered the world war. Then he became chief of staff of the "Rainbow Division," so nicknamed because the 42nd Division was stitched together from various National Guard units. Advancing quickly to colonel, MacArthur went to France with the American Expeditionary Force in 1917. Given the opportunity that had been repeatedly denied to Eisenhower, MacArthur served with distinction and experienced the kind of success in combat that most officers dream about but seldom achieve.[7] He soon had a chest adorned with medals that attested to his heroism in action. Contemptuous of danger, he frequently led his troops into battle from the front, not from the rear lines. Wounded in action, MacArthur recovered in time to take part in the defeat of the German forces that had earlier pushed almost to Paris. In the critical St. Mihiel and Meuse-Argonne offenses, MacArthur's troops pushed deeply into the enemy lines and played an important role in tipping the balance of the war in favor of the Allied armies.[8]

Despite the postwar sag in the army, MacArthur continued his relentless ascent. He served as superintendent at West Point, where he did his best to reform an institution that had long been mired in an educational style more suited to America's Civil War than to the nation's prominent role in the world politics of the twentieth century. Later, in the Philippines, MacArthur attempted with some success to break down barriers between Americans and Filipinos and to encourage respect in Washington, DC, for Filipino soldiers.[9] In 1930, at the age of fifty, he became a four-star general and Chief of Staff of the US Army.

Like any talented, successful leader, General MacArthur built a team that would serve his interests as well as those of the US Army and the nation. Eisenhower, who was then an assistant to General Moseley, came to his attention, and MacArthur gradually came to use more and more of Ike's time and energy.[10] Upon officially becoming MacArthur's military assistant, Ike already had a full book of knowledge on the Chief of Staff.

Fortunately, we can still read that book today. In the middle of June 1932, Ike used his diary to compile sketches of many of those with whom he worked, including his new boss. The evaluations that accompanied each sketch were just what you would expect from a middle-aged officer who was a good poker player. His observations were shrewd and insightful. They provide a window on the weaknesses and strengths of some of the men most important to American military policy in those depression years. They also provide a window on Ike's personality. Sitting on the bottom ledge of Ike's evaluations were the assistant secretary of war for air ("A nice little boy") and a boot-licking colonel who was "slow, if not stupid." The secretary of war, Patrick J. Hurley, was "jealous and unstable": "He is not big enough to go higher," Ike wrote. Up near the top of Eisenhower's personal grade sheet were three officers. It is no surprise to find that Major General Fox Conner was "a wonderful officer and leader with a splendid analytical mind." Eisenhower was also a fan of General

Moseley, who was "honest," "straightforward," and possessed of "great moral courage."

Ike had a bit more trouble with General MacArthur. He characterized his new boss as "essentially a romantic figure." The Chief of Staff was "a genius at giving concise and clear instructions." He was also "impulsive—able, even brilliant—quick—tenacious of his views and extremely self-confident." There was clearly some danger here. But Eisenhower noted with pride that the top officer in the service had assured him "that as long as he stays in the Army I am one of the people earmarked for his 'gang.'"[11] As it turned out, that would be almost true.

The Bonus Army Threatens America

A few weeks later, Ike was probably having some second thoughts about being in MacArthur's "gang." The first serious strain in their relations came in July 1932, in the final days of the Bonus Army. In some of the worst months of the Great Depression, ex-servicemen from World War I had marched on Washington, DC, to demand early payment of the bonuses Congress had promised them. But like the rest of the nation, the government was short of money, and so Congress refused. The veterans—many thousands of them—hunkered down in empty government buildings and on the mudflats of the Anacostia River. Seeking to turn a battle into a war of attrition, the vets built a shantytown that protected them from the worst of the winter weather but not, eventually, from General MacArthur and the US Army in which they had served.[12]

In July 1932, MacArthur personally led a military force sent by President Hoover to help the local police preserve order in the capital. MacArthur, thirsting for a fight, decided to expand his mission and push the Bonus Army off the mudflats and out of Washington. Accompanied by Major Eisenhower, who hated what was happening, MacArthur escalated a conflict that caused several deaths and in which the veterans' shanties were burned down. MacArthur had convinced himself that communists were somehow controlling the Bonus Army. If they were not subdued and driven out of the nation's capital, he thought, they would bring down the American government.[13] MacArthur clearly delighted in this embarrassing exercise of power against the bedraggled remnants of the Allied Expeditionary Force.[14]

The affair of the Bonus Army gave Ike some things to worry about as he settled into his new position. No longer could he look to his mentor Fox Conner for support if he got into trouble with the mercurial MacArthur. Conner had been ill and his influence in the army was gradually dwindling. Pershing had retired in 1924, and the clique of officers who had served together in the AEF was no longer a dominant force in the service. In 1930, when Conner was a contender to be appointed Chief of Staff, the Grey Eminence lost out to MacArthur. The implications for Ike's career were clear: he was now flying solo, and he might well be flying straight into a hurricane. In dealing with the Bonus Army, MacArthur had ignored Eisenhower's advice to stay in his office and let others handle the problem. Instead, MacArthur reveled in the assault and was surprisingly comfortable with his warped view that he was saving the country from a radical revolution. What would it be like to work closely every day with an officer whose powerhouse ego enabled him to see the world in such a distorted fashion?

One of Ike's painful jobs was to draft the Chief of Staff's report on the "Bonus Incident of July 28." Eisenhower said his paper was "as accurate as I could make it."[15] The report to the secretary of war was, in fact, a standard white paper that served a short-term purpose. The veterans had "defied police authority and were then engaged in riotous activity." Without loss of life or serious casualties, the army had quickly restored order. After stopping the rioting near Pennsylvania Avenue and 4½ Street, MacArthur turned "then to the encampment, alleged to be occupied by Communists, at 13th and C Streets." This was followed by the move against the shantytown at Anacostia Flats. As the report concluded: "Thus a most disagreeable task was performed in such a way as to leave behind it a minimum of unpleasant aftermath and legitimate resentment."[16] The press, of course, disagreed with this rosy conclusion. The "Incident of July 28" left a deep, public scar on MacArthur's reputation—a scar that would cause the Chief of Staff some concern after the Roosevelt administration took office in 1933.[17]

Swallowing any nervous reservations he had about his new boss, Major Eisenhower went back to work in a tiny cubbyhole (he called it a closet) adjacent to MacArthur's office.[18] The general's senior aide was on a short leash and was kept very busy.[19] A depressed economy was crimping every government and private institution in the United States, and the army was taking its share of hits. MacArthur mounted a rearguard political campaign in an effort to minimize the budget cuts, and Ike provided backup for the general.

Following Roosevelt's election in November 1932, Ike was pleased to see Congress and the White House controlled by one party. His perspective on the nation's leadership was broadening and becoming somewhat deeper. In the worst years of the economic collapse, he remained hopeful. Power, he thought, had to be centralized if the nation was going to get out of the depression. "Only in that way," he wrote, "will confidence be inspired; will it be possible to do some of the obvious things for speeding recovery, and will we be freed from the pernicious influence of noisy and selfish minorities."[20] From Ike's perspective, the army was not one of those "selfish minorities." He was concerned when it suffered painful budget cuts despite his and MacArthur's efforts.

Other than commenting on the need for centralization during the Great Depression, Eisenhower had little to say about the details of reform politics. He was not inclined to muse on the changing nature of the administrative state or on the surges of liberal reform that predated and had considerable influence on the New Deal. Neither nineteenth-century Populism nor twentieth-century Progressivism popped into mind when he was surrounded and practically suffocated by the nation's most formidable reform movement since the abolition of slavery. His brother Milton, who was now an important executive in the Department of Agriculture, had a much better knowledge of the political transformation taking place in Washington during the New Deal.[21]

Ike's interest in politics was instrumental and relatively narrow. He and his boss were focused on the fact that the army was shrinking while its responsibilities were increasing. In the summer of 1933, the army became responsible for transporting and housing the millions of young men who were being taken into the Civilian Conservation Corps (CCC). As Ike noted in his diary, the New Deal first tried to launch the program entirely under the CCC, but the new organization was slow to get under way. To make a dent in the high unemployment rate, the administration needed quick action using existing organizations. The army was called in, and it rapidly got the program moving. This success probably helped the Chief of Staff fend off more drastic budget cuts, but the CCC program strained the resources of a slimmed-down military.[22] Pay cuts followed, and Eisenhower found himself playing a growing role in a shrinking, dispirited army that was under attack from Congress and the press.[23] Overworked, underpaid, and suffering renewed bouts of ill health, Eisenhower came to resent "the years spent as a slave in the War Department."[24]

Despite this "slave's" resentment, his master found little to criticize in Eisenhower's performance. Ike had learned how to function within the parameters set by his boss and the US Army, and he produced in clear, forceful English the orders, reports, and plans that General MacArthur needed on a daily basis. Fox Conner had been a great teacher, and his student was now able to pound out, on schedule, day after day, exactly what the army's top officer demanded.

By this time, Ike had become a more polished, urbane person. He had lived in France, in Panama, and now in Washington, DC, and those experiences were smoothing out some of the burrs and sharp corners of his small-town personality. He had not sacrificed to the city culture his basic optimism, his small-town friendliness, or his tendency to trust those with whom he worked. But he had changed as he became accustomed to dealing on a daily basis with experienced, powerful leaders. No longer in serious doubt about his professional career, he had reason to be optimistic about his future role in the army. As staff to MacArthur, he had compiled a record that any officer in the US Army would have been pleased to have.

Dangerous Duty on the Philippine Frontier

Eisenhower was so successful in this role that MacArthur decided to keep him on his team when the general left the Office of the Chief of Staff for his next tour of duty. That would be in the Philippines, where MacArthur had served before. Now he would be the military advisor to the newly created commonwealth government of the Philippines.[25] MacArthur would need an effective team if he was going to succeed in organizing a new fighting force capable of defending the commonwealth. In 1935, he built his team around Eisenhower, who was offered an appointment as assistant military advisor. MacArthur cleverly sweetened the offer by allowing Ike to choose a regular army officer to assist him.

This was a hard decision for Ike. He wanted to command troops instead of serving another tour as a staff officer. He was also nervous about spending more time under MacArthur's thumb. For the previous two years he had not disappointed his boss or challenged MacArthur's authority. When there were differences, Ike bit his tongue, suppressed his anger, and did everything he could to advance the work of the Chief of Staff and the US Army. That was a hard life for Major Eisenhower even though he had made considerable progress in developing a conciliatory, compromising approach to military authority and his career.[26] Convinced that he could always master his anger, he was tempted and ultimately persuaded by the honor of being chosen by the top officer in the US Army.[27] Even though he knew that duty in the Philippines would mean more years of living on the edge of professional disaster, he accepted MacArthur's offer and selected his friend Major James B. Ord to accompany them. He and Ord shortly got a memorable display of the general's capacity for anger.

Leaving Mamie and his young son John in the United States, Eisenhower and Major Ord accompanied MacArthur and his entourage on the long, slow journey to the Philippines. The trip started on a low point. The general erupted in rage when he learned that he had immediately been demoted to his permanent rank as a two-star general. He had hoped to arrive in his new post as the army's only four-star. But President Franklin D. Roosevelt either forgot his agreement with the general or, more likely, embraced an opportunity to cut into the prestige of the former Chief of Staff.[28] Fortunately for Ike, he had done nothing to inspire the outburst. All he had to do was listen and nod. He was already good at that and was going to get even better. But the episode stuck in his mind and gave him an unforgettable sense of MacArthur's potential for explosive anger when he was thwarted.[29]

Living on the Edge

After a comfortable sea voyage, General MacArthur and his military mission landed in the Philippines in October 1935. Ike started his diary record of the mission in December. "The group," he wrote, "is so organized that the detailed work connected with the development of the Philippine Defense Plan falls principally upon Major James B. Ord (in this narrative referred to as 'Jimmie') and myself. Captain T. J. Davis serves as General MacArthur's aide, is the administrative officer for the whole group and is in charge of such matters as motor transportation, clerical assistance, normal administrative contacts with the Philippine Department and so on. Major Howard J. Hutter, Medical Corps, is specifically charged with the development of a sanitary plan for the Philippine Army and in addition serves as personal physician for the group. General MacArthur is the head of the Mission and is officially designated as the military advisor to the Philippine government. He directs policy and, except in matters of detail, does all the contact work with the President of the Commonwealth."[30]

While perfectly logical, this plan for the organization of the mission would quickly begin to change as personalities and the daily demands of practice trumped the standard army style of organization. Some of the changes eventually clouded Ike's relationships with his volatile boss. But initially Eisenhower and MacArthur worked together in an effort to develop a force that could defend the Philippines. Neither man was pleased by the situation they found in their new outpost. Both were severely limited in what they could accomplish in the Philippines, on the far eastern edge of an overextended American empire. Japan's military and industrial power had been growing for many decades, but neither MacArthur nor Eisenhower—nor, for that matter, the US War Department—seemed fully aware of how serious that threat was to the status quo in the Pacific. A great gulf had opened between American interests and American power.

When the Roosevelt administration hesitated about shipping some obsolete rifles to the Philippines, Ike got an early warning that the defense of the new commonwealth was not a major priority in Washington. For most Americans the top priority seemed to be staying out of another war. Even those who were charged with charting strategy in the event of war were doubtful that the Philippines could be defended. Eisenhower thought the administration's policy was "short-sighted," but all he could do was to keep pushing.[31]

That forced MacArthur, Eisenhower, and Ord to turn to the new Philippine government for the resources they needed to conduct their American military mission. But as the first president of the Commonwealth of the Philippines, Manuel Quezon, repeatedly made clear, his country could not afford a major rearmament with modern weapons. True to their personalities and leadership styles, MacArthur and Eisenhower reacted differently to that constraint. The general chose largely to ignore the lack of Philippine resources. He simply adopted unrealistic plans, exuded optimism, and left Eisenhower and Ord to scrape around the bottom of the barrel for the men, arms, and munitions they needed. This was a second showing for Ike, who during the world war had trained a tank battalion without any tanks. He had organized Camp Colt in the bitter cold without stoves for the tents. So he swallowed his concerns and tried to get as much as he could from the Philippine and American governments.

Not much was available. The United States—which by Filipino standards was a rich nation even in the depressed 1930s—had begun paying a price for the deep cuts Congress and presidents had made in military budgets since 1920. "Our budget," Ike noted, "had been based on the assumption that every material assistance in the armament question would be forthcoming from the United States and if this support should be denied, we are going to be very badly handicapped."[32] They were. Neither the Roosevelt administration nor the services could decide whether the Philippines could or should be defended.[33] Ord's trip back to Washington in 1937 to beg for support yielded only some antiquated arms, and too few of them.[34] Eisenhower, who had an excellent grasp of the problems of mobilization, did not do much better when he, too, went to Washington the following year seeking support.

The Team Starts to Fracture

While straining to get a defense organized, MacArthur's team started to come apart. The first break came quickly, when the general was appointed a field marshal in a Philippine army that existed only in planning documents. Ike thought it was absurd. He told MacArthur that it was a serious mistake to accept the new commission and to receive the handsome salary he was provided.[35] Eisenhower turned down a similar appointment for himself, as did Ord. MacArthur exploded. "The General is," Ike noted, "more and more indulging in a habit of damning everybody, who disagrees with him over any detail, in extravagant, sometimes almost hysterical fashion. I've seen him do this, second hand, in the past, but now he seems to consider that the combined use of his rank, a stream of generalizations that are studded with malapropos, and a refusal to permit the presentation of opposing opinion will, by silencing his subordinates, establish also the validity of his contentions."[36] MacArthur's outbursts drove Ike, Ord, and T. J. Davis together as increasingly nervous and concerned partners in an enterprise that was stumbling.[37]

At times the spats between Ike and his boss had an almost comic aspect, especially when they involved issues that had nothing to do with their mission. The US presidential election in 1936 provoked MacArthur, who remained fiercely bitter about the way FDR had treated him as he left for the Philippines. The bitterness warped his political judgment and left him looking forward with hope to a victory by Alf Landon, the Republican candidate from Kansas. Although deep in his heart Ike was still a Kansan, he had a more realistic view of the election. He and T. J. Davis urged caution, but the general exploded again: "We couldn't understand the reason for his almost hysterical condemnation of our STUPIDITY until he suddenly let drop that he had gone out and urged Q[uezon] to shape his plans for going to U.S. on the theory that Landon will be elected. . . . WHY should he get sore just because we say 'Don't be so d—— certain, and go out on a limb unnecessarily'??? Both of us are 'fearful and small minded people who are afraid to express judgments that are obvious from the evidence at hand.' Oh hell."[38]

A far more ominous development took place gradually, without any explosions—at first. The initial plan was for the general to handle ongoing relations with President Quezon. They had known each other for years, and MacArthur's reputation in the islands was strong and positive. Ike encouraged the general to see Quezon once a week, but MacArthur refused. Ord and Eisenhower tried, Ike wrote, "time and again, to get the general to stay in closer contact with Q. Things happen, and we know nothing of them. We're constantly wondering whether the President will approve or disapprove. We ought to *know*! We could if the general would take the trouble to see Q weekly—but he apparently thinks it would not be in keeping with his rank and position for him to do so!!!!!"[39]

With no apparent plan in mind, Ike slowly began to fill this vacuum. He had an office in the presidential residence, the Malacañan. He and Quezon began to spend more time together, first discussing the military organization and then eventually covering other political issues and even personal matters. Eisenhower drafted a speech for the president.[40] In brief, they became friends and colleagues in a common enterprise.[41] Unfortunately, this left the general feeling pushed aside, off the playing field. That was a situation MacArthur would not long abide. The relationships became especially dangerous after Ike had some secret meetings with the president to discuss the military options they were facing.[42]

The central issue of most of the discussions and the work that Eisenhower and Ord were doing on a daily basis involved getting a reasonable force organized despite the unreasonable financial restraints that none of them could change. Numbers loomed large. MacArthur started out planning for a thirty-division force. By training 20,000 to 25,000 men a year, MacArthur estimated, they would soon have a strong reserve and the core of the divisions he contemplated. Ike (forcefully) and Ord (more pleasantly) contended these plans were unrealistic. "After days of wrangling and arguing on the subject," Ike said, "he gave J[immie Ord] and me a ridiculous lecture on 'sufficiency in strength' of armies. . . . He makes nasty cracks about 'technicians' and 'small-minded people' when we try to show that we are simply arguing from the standpoint of the amount of money available."[43] Eisenhower dutifully wrote a report along lines prescribed by the general. He had learned how to swallow hard and write a white paper on the Bonus Army affair, and he did the same thing in Manila. But as Eisenhower had already concluded, the plan left a deficit of more than 30 million Philippine pesos.[44]

Ike was worried. He and Ord thought there was too much emphasis on numbers and not enough on efficiency. "When the blow-up comes," Eisenhower asked himself, "I wonder how he [MacArthur] is to convince anyone that the present plan can be executed for a total ten year cost" of 160 million pesos.[45] The issue was temporarily left smoldering while the general and Ord were in Washington arguing the case for support to the Philippines. But the financial bind became worse, not better. Like any intelligent politicians facing a similar crunch, MacArthur and his team had begun to mortgage the future by taking 1937 expenditures from the 1938 budget.[46] Now, however, President Quezon was upset by the size of the budget. The reckoning seemed to be coming sooner than Ike had expected.

When the general returned, he did not want to consider the "hard facts" that Eisenhower was presenting. Ike said, "We're like a bunch of skaters on thin ice, going faster and faster to keep from falling through, and always desperately looking for some lucky break that will carry us to firm footing."[47] Deeply distressed, Ike lamented his decision to join MacArthur's Philippines team. He felt isolated. While Mamie and his son John had joined him, he only had one close friend, Jimmie, upon whom he could always depend. He and Jimmie, he wrote, had "concerned ourselves with trying to develop for this gov't and country the best possible army with the means at hand. We have been beset on all sides by difficulties arising from personal ambition, personal glorification, personal selfishness of the hot shot (66,000 pesos a year and a penthouse), etc., etc. When we have objected strenuously to measures which we believe unwise such as the Field Marshal-ship; the 1937 calling of 20,000 trainees; the 1938 boosting of the budget; we've been finally told to shut up."[48]

In the next month, a bad time grew much worse, and Eisenhower found it impossible to remain silent. He protested when the general announced his plans for an expensive military parade that would bring 20,000 soldiers to Manila. They were already operating on a bare-bones budget, Ike pointed out, and were forced to rob from the next year to keep their training mission going. After President Quezon heard about the plan, he agreed that they couldn't afford it. That outraged MacArthur, who was convinced that Eisenhower and Ord had gone behind his back to President Quezon and undercut his authority. The general decided to strike back. As he knew full well, he could have promptly ended both Ike's and Jimmie's careers over this issue.[49] Instead, he decided to let Machiavelli guide his hand.

Ike now found the endless squabbles tiring, the beratings childish, and the dishonesty reprehensible. He was frustrated and again uncertain about his future in the army. When his gastrointestinal problems flared up, he retreated to the hospital in agony. He escaped without surgery, but then he suffered another severe blow. Jimmie Ord, his closest colleague and personal friend, died in an airplane crash in the Philippines in January 1938. Ord's tragic accident left Eisenhower alone between the general and President Quezon, alone to deal with his tempestuous boss, and alone to create a fighting force that could somehow defend a commonwealth of 2,000 islands.[50] Ord's replacement, Major Richard K. Sutherland, was a brittle, harsh man who clearly was not going to be the close partner that Ord had been since 1935. Ike was isolated now and vulnerable, with his career hanging in a balance that was entirely in the control of a moody General MacArthur.

By this time, conciliation and forbearance were out of season with Ike. For months his relationship with his boss had been spiraling downward. Now Ike's anti-authoritarian streak came to the surface. His bitterness prompted thoughts that were unbecoming at best and far beneath what even a "hot-shot" boss with a "penthouse" apartment deserved. Particularly undeserved were Ike's nasty remarks about MacArthur's service in the world war: "The popular notion of his great ability as a soldier and leader, is, of course, not difficult to explain to those that know how war time citations were often secured. These, plus direct intervention of Sec. Baker to give him his first star (Regular) have been parlayed, with the help of a magnificent front both vocal and in appearances to a reputation of wisdom, brilliance and magnificent leadership."[51] Angry, Ike ignored the fact that he had no firsthand knowledge of the general's wartime service. He ignored all that Fox Conner had done, above and below board, to push Ike's career ahead.

MacArthur also did little to distinguish himself in these difficult months. He, too, had reasons to be grumpy. He had been forced in December 1937 to retire from the US Army. While he was still a Philippine field marshal, he was no longer the senior officer in the military mission. That was now Lieutenant Colonel Eisenhower.[52] But of course MacArthur was still the de facto head of the organization, and he refused to give up on his unrealistic budget. He tried to tailor a fair-seeming plan that would fit the original figures on which he had based his optimistic projections. Having assured President Quezon that he could defend the islands on an annual budget of 16 million pesos, he blended realistic cuts with fantasy changes to get the bottom line he wanted. Recognizing that Ike was able to shoot holes in his fraudulent accounting, MacArthur tried to break the friendly relationship between Eisenhower and the commonwealth's president.[53] Instead of exploiting the friendship in order to achieve America's strategic mission, the general behaved like a spoiled middle-school boy unable to get his way with the teacher. Neither the general nor Lieutenant Colonel Eisenhower should have been in this position as war edged ever closer to America and its empire.

The General's Gambit

Then, rather suddenly, in the early summer of 1938, General MacArthur became the sort of friendly senior officer that Fox Conner had been. This should have made Ike suspicious. But he was so pleased to have a rational environment again that he reveled in the tolerance of the new Mac-Arthur. "The General," he wrote in June, "has been extraordinarily sympathetic, increasingly so, with my views, opinions, and personal situation. At one time it seemed almost impossible to discuss with him any point in which there was the slightest difference of opinion, but for the past few months this has not been so. He is willing to talk over things—and his answer is more often than not, 'as to that I'll accept your judgment.'" So startling was the transformation that Ike was left fishing for an explanation of what had changed. Still something of the boy from Abilene, he opted for the most charitable explanation: "It is difficult to believe that Jimmy's loss should have occasioned this change, but the fact is, that ever since then he has progressively grown more mellow, less arbitrary and less ready to allege sinister motive for every mere difference of opinion."[54]

The new MacArthur quickly approved Eisenhower's plans for a trip to the United States. It was to be a combination of leave and renewed effort to get support for the Philippine defense forces. At that point the general almost revealed his hand. "Nothing that occurs around here with respect to *you* is to be considered a precedent," MacArthur said. "In all respects you represent a special case, and it is my hope to keep you here a long time." That might have aroused some questions about what, exactly, was likely to change, but Ike was bowled over by the general's friendly overtures. "The atmosphere has cleared to such an extent," he said, "that this job, at long last, has become personally agreeable as well as professionally interesting."[55] Pleased by his boss's transformation, Ike forgot his experiences with poker.

A happy lieutenant colonel and his wife and son sailed from the Philippines on June 26, 1938. Their trip took them to Hong Kong, Kobe, Yokohama, and Honolulu before they landed in San Francisco.[56] There was time to visit with Mamie's family and make one side trip to Yellowstone Park. But then Mamie had to have surgery, and for a time it appeared that John might also need an operation. Fortunately, their son's condition improved without a surgical procedure, and Mamie recovered in time to join her husband on his second trip to Washington. There, Ike continued to grind away at the army's leadership in an effort to get support for the Philippine forces. This was micro-management at its best: deciding whether to get 60 mm or 81 mm mortars and trying to ensure that they would have ammunition for whatever they bought; negotiating directly with the arms manufacturers, the companies making light planes, and a series of army officers who were in no hurry to satisfy Ike or his boss. A successful meeting with Army Chief of Staff Malin Craig helped accelerate the process, but it was still excruciatingly complex and slow—a peacetime army at its worst. Still, Ike was satisfied that he had made some progress before he and his family left on October 14, 1938, on the *Empress of Japan* for their return trip.[57]

Arriving in Manila in early November, Eisenhower was shocked to discover that he had been sandbagged.[58] MacArthur had stripped him of his responsibilities and given them to Dick Sutherland. Searching for an explanation, Ike focused on the tight links he and Jimmie Ord had established with the Philippine leaders: "So, while I was gone, he reorganized the office, so as to remove me completely in official affairs from Malacañan. Not content with this he re-arranged the office force so that I'm no longer his C. of S. [chief of staff], but only another staff officer—he is theoretically the coordinator of the whole group. My section is plans, training, mobilization education, etc.—the purpose being to keep me absorbed in academic work at my desk, and to rob me of any influence in the Army or at Malacañan."[59]

Feeling robbed, Ike contemplated revenge: "The only thing he forgets is that all of us are attached to Department Headquarters and whether he likes it or not the Senior Officer of the U.S. Army on duty with this group [that is, Eisenhower] is compelled to make efficiency reports on the others." He labored to explain to himself what MacArthur had done: "Why the man should so patently exhibit a jealousy of a subordinate is beyond me. I guess it's because he is afraid a conviction will grow in the minds of local people that he personally is not so important to the Army and to the P.I." He went on, "Administratively, the new scheme is so clumsy as to require no comment. . . . I will not give him the satisfaction of showing any resentment. But my usefulness is so curtailed as to rob the job of much of its interest, so I'm going at the earliest possible moment. If the d—— fool had only sent his plan to me while I was in the States I would not have returned." But of course that was part of MacArthur's cunning plan: to change his team with a minimum amount of disturbance either in the Philippines or in Washington, DC.[60]

This was Ike's first Machiavellian moment, the first time that he had been deceived and boxed out of a major leadership position by shrewd administrative maneuvering. It is not clear that he reflected initially on his own role in what had happened. He was too mad to do that. "My fury," he wrote, "is academic rather than practical and actual." He released that fury by enumerating MacArthur's vulnerabilities, including his hush-hush affair with a Filipina who had become his mistress in Washington and his wild blasts at President Roosevelt when the general was demoted from four-star to two-star rank. "Oh hell—what's the use. The point is he *knows* we won't tell these things. Now that I've jotted all this down I hope that it never again comes, even momentarily, to my mind."[61]

While that would not be true, Eisenhower had certainly learned a great deal about how he would have to deal with superiors—rational or irrational—if he wanted to get ahead. He already knew how he should handle those who worked for him. That was never a problem for this forty-eight-year-old lieutenant colonel. With his superiors, however, he would have to control his natural tendency to be completely open and honest about their proposals—no matter how much he disagreed with them. He needed to learn from what Fox Conner had done—on the positive side of Machiavellianism—to promote Dwight's career. He needed to reflect on the fact that his repeated efforts to constrain MacArthur's exuberant plans for the Philippine forces had poisoned their relationship and left him in limbo, grumbling to his diary. He would not have to be what he described with disdain as a "boot-licker."[62] But he would have to be more cunning if he was going to be successful.

Caught between the Philippine president Quezon, who was friendly and relatively open with Ike, and General MacArthur, who was formal, precise, and distant, Eisenhower played out the string in his final months in Manila. He received orders to join the 15th Infantry at Fort Lewis (Tacoma, Washington), and quickly began to negotiate the date when he would leave for his new post. The Fort Lewis posting was not an accident. He had clearly learned something from Fox Conner about how to maneuver successfully in the top reaches of the army. On the tail end of his 1938 trip to the United States, Ike had visited with his old friend Mark

Clark, who was serving at Fort Lewis. Later he wrote to Clark and asked for his help in getting command of a battalion of infantry. Clark and his friends—including George C. Marshall—helped "arrange" Eisenhower's assignment. At last, he was about to be in the position he had sought since the 1920s.[63] No longer a coach, no longer assigned to training, no longer a staff officer, he would at last serve in direct command of troops.

When the war began in Europe in 1939, it accelerated Ike's effort to get back to the United States. Impatient, he wrote to Clark: "I'm ready for anything! Field, garrison, wilderness, let them send the outfit wherever they please. I'll be happy as long as I can go with a regular unit."[64] By this time, he was counting down the days to his departure like a student looking forward to summer vacation.

Ike and his family finally left on December 13, 1939, on the SS *President Cleveland*.[65] A wave of luncheons, reviews, dinners, and speeches preceded the departure. General MacArthur added a finishing touch to their service together by attending the farewell parties and seeing them off at the dock.[66]

The general was careful to close out their relationship in a formal manner that suited his interests as well as those of the US Army. In 1936, his evaluation of Eisenhower had been extremely positive. The general said Ike had "no superior of his time either in Command or General Staff capacity in the Army." These were powerful words coming from a former Chief of Staff. MacArthur recommended Eisenhower "for immediate appointment to General Officer rank in time of war."[67] Now in 1939, with war on the horizon for America, he gave the War Department and the army bureaucracy no reason to believe that he had changed his judgment. Although he had recently demoted Ike from his position as chief of staff of the military mission, MacArthur simply ignored that unpleasant subject. The general's performance in the last months of Eisenhower's Philippine duty was a tribute to his self-discipline, deep knowledge of the army bureaucracy, administrative skill and aptitude for duplicity.

In 1939, Lieutenant Colonel Eisenhower was unable to match the talented MacArthur in any of those regards. Despite Ike's ability as a poker player, he was in his professional career still relatively open in the Abilene style, still more oriented to performance than to power, still expecting others to follow the rules. But he was learning. He would be sandbagged only one more time in his career, and he was from this point on somewhat more willing to be cunning and maybe even deceptive in order to achieve his objectives.

The Philippine experience clearly helped to develop Eisenhower's distinctive leadership style. He had passed this test and a more forceful leader emerged from his years with MacArthur. That experience strengthened Ike's natural proclivity to pay heed to what his subordinates had to say—that is, to take seriously their advice and thus make full use of their capabilities. He had learned as well how to deal with political leaders in an unstable setting that imposed severe constraints on American policy. He was now even more attuned than he had been to the personal aspects of power relations in the army, and he had begun to think more seriously about the geopolitical relationships of nations in peace and war. He still had much to learn in that regard. But with Europe exploding and Japan's power growing, he would soon have new opportunities to deepen his knowledge of strategy and to remember the lessons he had learned from reading Clausewitz's *On War*.

Part II

Becoming Supreme

Six

Newly promoted in 1941 to brigadier general, Eisenhower sent this photograph to his family.

Combat

The whirlwind of war in Europe and Asia in 1939 had begun to transform Eisenhower's career even before he and his family landed in San Francisco. Germany had quickly conquered Poland and divided the country with an opportunistic Soviet Union. France and Britain braced for an anticipated German invasion, one that they hoped would be stalled by the seemingly impenetrable fortifications of France's Maginot Line. In Asia, Japan was pressing forward with its invasion of China after skirmishing unsuccessfully with Soviet troops on the Manchurian border. Alert to this tumultuous world, Ike was paying increasing attention to questions of strategy. As late as August 1940, he still thought Japan would not launch a full-scale invasion of the Philippines, but by that time he knew that Fox Conner's predictions about another world war were devastatingly accurate. Although the United States was legally and politically locked into neutrality, Eisenhower and many other US military officers had little doubt that America would soon be drawn into the war in Europe. When that happened, Ike realized, the nation would need to "achieve unity of purpose and effort."[1] Unity would shortly become central to his career as a military leader.

As war in Europe and Asia shoved national security back up near the top of the nation's political agenda, President Roosevelt cautiously began edging America toward a decision that he knew was inevitable. Lieutenant Colonel Eisenhower was no less certain that he and his country would get involved in the war, but he predicted that it would not happen until America's national security was clearly threatened or it was directly attacked. After listening to a broadcast of Britain's declaration of war against Germany, Ike reflected: "If the war . . . is as long drawn out and disastrous, as bloody and as costly as was the so-called World War, then I believe that the remnants of nations emerging from it will be scarcely recognizable as the ones that entered it. Communism and anarchy are apt to spread rapidly, while crime and disorder, loss of personal liberties, and abject poverty will curse the areas that witness any amount of fighting. . . . Hundreds of millions will suffer privations and starvation, millions will be killed and wounded because one man so wills it." Hitler, Eisenhower said, was "criminally insane": "Hitler's record with the Jews, his rape of Austria, of the Czechs, the Slovaks and now the Poles is as black as that of any barbarian of the Dark Ages."[2] Motivated by an apocalyptic vision of the past and the future, Eisenhower became a crusader against fascism.[3]

Determined not to spend more time serving as a staff officer or training militias in the United States, he repeatedly looked for support from his network of army friends. Major Mark Clark was already helping.[4] Eisenhower was also in contact with his close friend Leonard Gerow and with Brigadier General Thomas A. Terry as well as Colonel George Patton, Lieutenant Colonel Omar Bradley, and others.[5] He made it well known that he was available and interested in commanding a regiment. While trying to play the appointments game as Fox Conner had, Ike got a scare when he and his family were on the boat back to San Francisco. He received word that he had been given a staff assignment at Fourth Army Headquarters in San Francisco. The job turned out to be temporary, and he was soon able to take over as executive officer with the 15th Infantry Regiment at Fort Lewis, Washington. He could see, however, that the threat of a staff appointment was not likely to disappear. Regardless of what he did.

As his career to date clearly indicated, the United States Army was not quick to change its mind. He was relentlessly pulled back toward the staff.[6] After begging Patton for command of an armored regiment, Ike was assigned as chief of staff with the 3rd Division at Fort Lewis. As he settled into his new job, he was promoted to colonel. His career was accelerating at an astonishing rate for an officer who had spent two decades locked in a stodgy bureaucracy in which seniority was the guiding principle. Shortly after this promotion, he was given another staff appointment with the IX Corps, and then in 1941 he was assigned as chief of staff to Lieutenant General Walter Krueger's Third Army. Krueger—like his boss George Marshall—was in search of young talent. He saw in Eisenhower an officer who "possessed broad vision, progressive ideas, a thorough grasp of the magnitude of the problems involved in handling an Army, and lots of initiative and resourcefulness."[7] This was high praise from one of the army's top officers. But it was praise coming from a general in ardent search of a new staff officer. No longer typecast as a football coach, Ike in his fifties was still left squirming—unsuccessfully—to get out of his new role as one of the army's ideal staff men.[8]

One can sympathize with Krueger and the other officers who kept pushing Eisenhower into the staff and away from a field command. Ike's mastery of the staff function was reflected in the memorandum he wrote for his successor when he left for his new job with the Third Army. The memorandum also highlighted the lessons Ike had learned being mentored by Conner and then working with MacArthur in the Philippines. Efficient implementation of the commanding officer's policies was the primary task. It could be achieved only by carefully communicating both up and down the command and by drawing upon the skills of all of the personnel in the team. Attention to detail was crucial: "In the field as well as in garrison a brief blotter should be kept which will serve you as an aide memoire, in assuring that you overlook no item." Coordination in the field required daily staff meetings. Orders had to be written in "straightforward, direct English." When reports from subordinates were not well written, they had to be edited into a "usable form." The chief of staff should reach out in a cooperative mode to "cultivate" close "relationships." Cooperation required "constant attention" and *constant training of all subordinates.*" With "real discipline" and a "smooth staff operation," the organization could achieve "teamwork throughout the . . . Corps."[9] Unity of purpose and action were Ike's central concerns as he looked backward to MacArthur's mission for a negative model of leadership and forward to the positive model he would employ in his new post with Krueger's Third Army.[10] Once again he would be a staff officer, but there was solace in his promotion in October 1941 to brigadier general.

The chance for a breakout appointment commanding a regiment increased as the thunder and lightning of war crashed on America's eastern and western horizons and the army rushed to repair the damage left by two decades of budget cutting. There was much to fear by the summer of 1941. Hitler's forces seemed omnipotent on land and in the air. Having conquered Norway and Denmark, the German army drove forward in North Africa and then launched a sudden, startling invasion of the Soviet Union. Japan, which was now applying increased military and diplomatic pressure on Southeast Asia, was steadily becoming more of a threat to America's position in the Philippines.

One part of the US Army's response was the largest peacetime field maneuver in the nation's history, and Ike's new post in the Third Army put him at the center of this military exercise. His friend Mark Clark drafted the scenario for the 450,000 soldiers involved in the Louisiana operations, and Ike's buddy George Patton was there with his 2nd Armored Division. Eisenhower's role was to implement the plans that General Krueger had developed with input from his chief of staff. As the contest got under way, three conclusions soon became apparent to Eisenhower and to the army's top leadership. First, it was obvious that many of the service's older officers had to be replaced and a new generation of leaders brought to the top. Army Chief of Staff George C. Marshall had framed the maneuvers as "a great college of leadership of the higher officers."[11] Many of the corps commanders failed their courses in Marshall's "great college."[12] Second, it was also clear that the aggressive plans General Krueger employed and Ike implemented were more successful than their opponents' more conservative approaches to the exercise. The tank, as Conner, Patton, and Ike had predicted, was changing battlefield tactics in a major way, and the US Infantry could no longer ignore the potential of new weapons and new tactics.

Third, it was evident to all that Eisenhower had for the second time in his career emerged as a media star of sorts. His first experience with the press had been through football during his second year at West Point. His injury had abruptly cut short that interlude of fame.[13] But in 1941 nothing happened to cut short the newspaper adulation he received. And such encouraging stories were just what a nation nervous about war wanted to read. General Krueger, a less newsworthy figure, was not entirely pleased to see Eisenhower credited for the two victories his Third Army achieved. But General Marshall was less concerned about headlines than about performance. He had already decided that both Krueger and Ike were going to be important officers in the war for which America was at last preparing.[14]

Marshall's Decision

Marshall was not a man to avoid controversy. Recognizing that the seniority rule and the sluggish life of the peacetime army had left him with an aged, underqualified corps of senior officers, he had already set out with great vigor to attack that problem. President Roosevelt supported Marshall in this effort. FDR's backing was important because Marshall's initial efforts to transform the army were risky. He was ruffling some military feathers by changing the nature of the army's divisions in an effort to make them more mobile and effective. Then he went after the older leaders, some of whom had political allies and others of whom had friends in the War Department. But Marshall pushed ahead, determined to give the army a fighting chance when the war began.[15] The young officers he promoted over their seniors encountered resentment. But that was a small price to pay to have a younger, more combat-worthy officer corps.

In search of a unified military, Secretary of War Henry L. Stimson called a meeting on December 3 to evaluate the maneuvers in Louisiana and North Carolina. The theme of disunity rippled through the discussions. The air and ground forces had found it difficult to work together. Both the military officers and civilian executives agreed "that air-ground communication was poor," but they could not generate any specific ideas about what to do. Even coordination between the foot soldiers and the artillery and between various infantry units was a problem. Disagreement about mobile tank warfare still existed. Much, the participants concluded, remained to be done to get the army into fighting condition.[16]

But there was no time left. Four days later, Japan bombed the US fleet at Pearl Harbor. Suddenly a task that had been daunting grew ten-thousand-fold in a day and became at the same time a matter of national survival. It was apparent on December 7 that the United States was going to fight a war in Asia as well as in Europe with an army that was raw, poorly equipped, and troubled at every level. As Eisenhower had earlier predicted, the nation now needed a high degree of unity within the military and between the military and the rest of American society. Neither America's democratic tradition nor the nation's historical patterns of military development favored that outcome.

When the war started, Marshall was still building the command post he needed to revamp the army. His team included Ike's close friend Brigadier General Leonard Gerow, who was chief of staff in the War Plans Division, and another Eisenhower colleague, Wade Haislip, who was handling personnel at the War Department general staff.[17] At the army's General Headquarters, Lesley J. McNair was in charge, and his deputy, Mark Wayne Clark, had already pulled strings to get Eisenhower appointed at Fort Lewis. Clark had continued to beat the drum for Eisenhower during and after the Louisiana maneuvers.[18]

Prompted by Clark and Gerow, General Marshall summoned Eisenhower to Washington to a new post on the general staff. If he passed muster—and he quickly did—he would serve in the War Plans Division as deputy chief for the Pacific and Far East. When he disembarked from his flight to the nation's capital, Ike was in effect rejoining the group of officers who had served with Pershing in the world war—the so-called Chaumont clique[19]—and had dominated army policy intermittently since that time. He was pleased with his sudden ascent to the army's command-ing heights but disappointed to be assigned yet again to a staff job. All of his anguished messages to Gerow, Patton, and others seemed to have had no effect. Instead of being in the field with the infantry, he would be behind a desk writing reports. That began, in fact, at his first meeting with Marshall, on December 14, 1941. Marshall asked him bluntly, "What should be our general line of action?" Ike requested a few hours to pro-duce an answer and was able to hand his new superior a concise, thought-ful proposal that same day.[20]

With his actions having confirmed the strong recommendations the Chief of Staff had been receiving, Eisenhower was securely on board with his new boss.[21] The two men had some common ground that helped ce-ment their relationship. Both had established their careers as staff offi-cers. Both had been disappointed in their efforts to get command of troops in the field. Both Marshall, a graduate of Virginia Military Institute (VMI), and Eisenhower, a graduate of West Point, had suffered through many dreary years when they were frozen in rank in the peacetime army.[22] Unlike MacArthur and George Patton, neither man was a flashy showman of an officer, the kind of person who is often called a "natural leader" very early in his or her career. Instead, Marshall and Eisenhower leaned toward quiet accomplishment and away from parades. Both had explosive tempers that they struggled to keep under control, often with-out success.

They had their differences. Marshall had never been in doubt, as Ike once was, about being a career officer and never had problems with dis-cipline. If Marshall had an anti-authoritarian streak, he hid it very well from everyone who knew him. From the beginning of his education at VMI, he had been focused intently and solely on a military career. He was a grinder who finally pushed himself up to finish fifth in his graduating class.[23] Unlike Eisenhower, Marshall made it to France in World War I and distinguished himself in a central position planning the American role in the offensives that forced Germany to sign the Armistice in 1918. From that high point, he slid to near exile in the early 1930s, when he spent time as an instructor with the Illinois National Guard.[24]

As the world edged toward war in 1939, however, President Franklin D. Roosevelt rescued him. FDR jumped Marshall over thirty-three senior officers, gave him his fourth star, appointed him Chief of Staff, and soon anointed him as his most trusted military advisor.

Marshall, who had been watching Eisenhower's development for some years, knew of Ike's skills as a staff officer. That was why he brought him to Washington to the War Plans Division. Disappointed with his staff appointment, Eisenhower could at least see that he was not working on trivial matters. A few weeks later, he attended a British-American conference in Washington, DC, to map global strategy for the Allies.

He was on the sidelines at the Arcadia conference, watching as Marshall attempted to impose on the Allies his well-defined positions. From a military perspective, Marshall maintained, the United States and Britain needed to engage Germany on the Continent as soon as possible and relieve the pressure on the Soviet Union. The situation on the Eastern Front looked dire. Germany's twin drives toward Moscow on the north and Stalingrad on the south had produced tremendous Soviet losses of men and matériel.[25] In the months ahead, the campaigns in the Soviet Union would continue to have a controlling influence on the war against Germany, on the Allies' strategy, and, incidentally, on Eisenhower's career.

Eisenhower could see that the unity of the Allies was all-important and would be incredibly difficult to achieve and maintain. Different goals, different military and political traditions, different values, and different experiences in the war all tugged the leaders apart over strategy and tactics. Even such a straightforward matter as unity of command generated intense discussions and numerous position papers. While the Allies agreed on the need to defeat Germany first and then Japan, they disagreed respectfully but strongly on almost every other aspect of the means to achieve those goals.

Churchill and his chiefs of staff leaned against Marshall, countering the American strategy with a plan to attack in North Africa and mount a Mediterranean campaign that would provide the Allies with an opening toward what the British prime minister liked to call the "soft underbelly" of Europe.[26] Churchill seemed initially less concerned than were

Marshall and Eisenhower about the Soviet Union's ability to resist the Nazi invasion. He was naturally more concerned than any of the American leaders were about the future of the British Empire and on occasion appeared to worry about the long-term threat that Soviet communism posed to western Europe. Sensing that FDR would yield to Churchill, Marshall did everything short of resigning to bolster his position.[27] But the result of this first major battle over strategy was a convincing British victory.[28] Others would follow shortly. Eisenhower, who became head of the War Plans Division in February 1942, had to start planning for a joint British-American invasion of North Africa later that same year.[29]

Following the Arcadia conference (December 22, 1941–January 14, 1942), Eisenhower understood that he would be spending a good bit of his time countering powerful centripetal forces in the British-American alliance. Unity, if it could be maintained, would call for heavy personal nursing and an occasional touch of Machiavellian shrewdness. Marshall had won a partial victory on unity of command in the Far East. But the ensuing controversies and the work of drafting an elaborate agreement to implement the plan gave Eisenhower a realistic perspective on the difference between the rhetoric of the alliance and the internal tensions it produced.[30] Those tensions and the emotions they inspired were a constant challenge to the conciliatory approach to leadership that Ike had acquired from Fox Conner and refined in the years following his Panama experience.

Neither Marshall nor Eisenhower gave up on the proposed cross-Channel attack, but they were thwarted by crucial shortages, by Roosevelt's tendency to lean toward Churchill's position, and by adamant British military and political opposition.[31] When Marshall visited Britain to discuss strategy, the British seemed to agree to an emergency attack on France if it appeared the Soviets were about to be forced out of the war.[32] But that agreement soon collapsed, and the British succeeded in fixing President Roosevelt's attention on the North African campaign.[33]

In the spring of 1942, Eisenhower acquired a new role in these Allied strategic maneuvers. He was promoted to major general, and Marshall gave him a new opportunity to work directly with the British.[34]

Marshall sent Ike to London—accompanied by General Clark—to find out how well the American officers in Britain were doing in laying the foundation for an assault on the German forces in France.[35] The answer was depressing. According to Ike, the US detachment lacked a strong sense of urgency. It did not have the discipline that Marshall wanted and the task demanded. Clearly, the United States was not prepared for the bold attack on the Continent that Marshall was advocating. The commanding officer, Ike said, had to be replaced.[36] Marshall agreed with him, but he rejected the man Ike suggested for the position, General Joseph T. McNarney.[37]

Marshall's choice instead was Eisenhower, with Mark Clark as his deputy. This decision marked the second dramatic break in Eisenhower's career as a leader. The first had followed his service with Fox Conner, when a recharged, professionally intense Ike finally began the difficult task of escaping his label as a talented but limited coach and trainer of recruits. Now Marshall broke decisively with Ike's solidly established reputation as a staff officer. What accounts for Marshall's decision? Even Marshall's biographer writes that the choice "seems remarkably casual." Marshall later said, "I sent Eisenhower and some others over so the British could have a look at them, and then I asked Churchill what he thought of them. He was extravagant in his estimate of them, so then I went ahead with my decision on Eisenhower."[38]

Since Ike had not met with Churchill on the trip, had barely any experience in troop command, and had no experience in combat, Marshall's choice was stunning.[39] He had every reason to believe that Eisenhower would provide solid, well-informed support for the cross-Channel strategy that Marshall was promoting. The Chief of Staff knew firsthand that Eisenhower now had a good grasp of US global strategy. Marshall also believed that Eisenhower would have good personal relations with the British political and military leaders—some of whom could be extremely thorny with Yanks. The thorniest of all was General Alan Francis Brooke, Chief of the Imperial General Staff. Lieutenant General Bernard Law Montgomery, Army Commander in the Southeast, was a close second.[40]

Still, Marshall's choice seems unlikely. He, like Fox Conner, had divined in Eisenhower qualities, present and prospective, that were not in his military assessments and were not apparent to most of those with whom and for whom Ike had worked.[41] That insight persuaded both Conner and Marshall to take risks in pushing Eisenhower ahead, into a new test of his capabilities as a leader. Many lives would depend upon his ability to pass this newest and most important test in what Ike knew could be "the biggest American job of the war."[42] He would now be personally responsible for the unity and ultimately for the success in combat that the Allies badly needed in 1942.

In London, Eisenhower became deeply involved with Churchill and his plots to shape the strategy and, indeed, sometimes the tactics of their joint forces.[43] Ike's experience in dealing with President Quezon in the Philippines now served him well in adapting to the intricate, idiosyncratic British prime minister. Although they were as different as two men could be, they got along easily. That was important as the Americans and British worked out the sticky details of their military plans. To Eisenhower's and Marshall's chagrin, Churchill ran their flank and persuaded President Roosevelt to make a final decision in favor of the first phase of Britain's Mediterranean strategy.[44] Ike and Marshall bemoaned the British strategy and the tight deadline FDR gave them. But the president and Churchill ruled, and the Allies would soon start their assault on the Axis powers with an attack through North Africa.[45]

Grumpy but compliant, Eisenhower was of course pleased to learn in August 1942 that FDR had appointed him the top commander of the joint ground, naval, and air forces for the North African campaign.[46] He would now at last lead an American army into combat. He had the core American leadership team he needed: Mark Clark, Alfred Gruenther,[47] John Lee,[48] George Patton, and Walter Bedell Smith.[49] Later he would add Omar Bradley.[50] Under tremendous pressure from his commander in chief to plan and execute a complex invasion before the end of 1942, Eisenhower pounded out a command structure that stressed unity of the services and nationalities.[51] Differences between the British and American military leaders sprouted up quickly, often over scarce resources.[52] There

was not enough shipping, enough aircraft carriers, enough planes and pi-
lots, or enough time to mount a perfectly planned attack against North
Africa.

There were also never enough high-energy, well-organized officers—
men like Mark Clark and George Patton—to drive the effort ahead.[53] So
Ike began the unpleasant process of sifting out the incompetents, a process that he had begun when he first landed in Britain.[54] Eisenhower was
uneasy with this essential part of his role as a leader. His background in
a small town, his conciliatory, team-oriented approach to leadership, and
his experience in the peacetime army pushed him toward compromise
rather than abrupt dismissals. He knew he had to get rid of some officers.
But he was always happier handing out praise and promotions.

Even with good leadership, the expedition Ike was planning seemed
more dependent than he would like upon imponderables, the weather in
particular.[55] At every turn there were also threats to the unity he sought
and knew that he needed. There was a major fissure between the British
style of command by committee and the American style of centralized
command by a single superior officer. There were other crucial differences
that kept disturbing the new commander's digestion. The air, naval, and
land forces had different traditions and different concepts of what Eisenhower's role should actually involve on a day-to-day basis. Accustomed
to controlling their own operations and resources, the services of both nations had much to learn about cooperation.[56] While Ike struggled to
hold the services and the two nations together, he tried as well to bring a
new and disreputable partner into the alliance.[57]

The French Puzzle

As Eisenhower's first D-Day loomed, his time and attention increasingly
involved efforts to prevent the French military in North Africa from resisting the invasion. He also wanted to get French support in controlling
their provinces, and he hoped that the Allies could then enlist the French
in the fight against the Axis armies. When France had surrendered to
Germany in 1940, General Philippe Pétain was left in control of southern France and the colonies in North Africa. His Vichy military forces—

properly labeled collaborationists by the Allies and many French citizens—included a substantial naval contingent and the army units in French North Africa. With American and British forces set to land in Morocco and Algeria on November 8, the position that would be taken by the French military was of deadly import. The Allies hoped that the French would quickly recognize that US generals George Patton (at the Casablanca landing), Lloyd Fredendall (at Oran), and Charles Ryder (at Algiers) were coming to rescue them from their German oppressors. But that prognosis took too little heed of the extent to which Vichy's collaboration had deep roots in respect for German military prowess, in anti-Semitism, and in hatred of their former allies, the British, who had launched a deadly attack on the French fleet at Mers-el-Kébir in 1940.

Ike's first problem was to find a leader with whom he and his generals could do business. Eisenhower sent General Clark on a daring mission to Africa to negotiate with some French officers who thought they might be able to arrange a peaceful landing for the invasion force.[58] When that effort failed, Eisenhower and Clark turned to General Henri Honoré Giraud as their go-between. They struck out again when it became obvious that Giraud wanted too much for his assistance and probably would be unable to carry the day with the other French commanders.[59] Giraud remained on the scene, but he could not provide Eisenhower with the leadership the Allies badly needed.[60] As the effort at rapprochement dwindled, Patton attacked at Casablanca and met fierce resistance from Vichy land, sea, and air forces. Patton pushed ahead, but the French did not surrender until November 10. The other two landings encountered less resistance, but that still left Eisenhower concerned that he would not be able to use French manpower in governing the colonies.

In desperation, he turned to Admiral François Darlan, whose standing in the French military was secure enough to suggest he could bring off a formal armistice. While mindful that his task was as odious as it was perilous, Eisenhower pressed on with his effort to persuade this Nazi collaborator to switch sides again. He had support throughout from Robert Murphy, an experienced diplomat who was helping with the negotiations in Africa. With some anguish, Ike told his friend Walter Bedell Smith,

"I've promised Giraud to make him the big shot, while I've got to use every kind of cajolery, bribe, threat and all else to get Darlan's *active* cooperation. All of these Frogs have a single thought—'ME.'"[61]

This time chance favored Ike in his first venture into high-level diplomacy. Darlan was captured in Algeria, and Eisenhower and Clark persuaded him to call a cease-fire for all French forces. The price, however, was Darlan's appointment as military governor in North Africa. That ensured French support in governing the colonies, but it was painful to Ike to buy the allegiance of an officer who had just crawled out of bed with the Nazis.[62] Recognizing that his primary goal was to get started in the drive toward Tunisia, and needing the major French ports to support that campaign, Eisenhower grimaced and signed on. He was, he said, "making the best of a rather bad bargain."[63]

As Eisenhower knew, he had put his head on the block by appointing Darlan.[64] The "Darlan Deal" evoked a storm of press criticism in Britain and the United States. Charles de Gaulle, leader of the Free French forces in Britain, was furious that a Vichy collaborator would be allowed to remain in power in North Africa—or, for that matter, anyplace in the world. De Gaulle was not alone in attacking an agreement that seemed to have brought too little return for selling out the high moral ground the Allies held in fighting German and Italian fascism. The crusade was compromised.

Ike went into the deal with open eyes and a sure sense of the opposition it would engender. He had two objectives that he knew were more important than his position as Allied commander: he was attempting to save as many American and British lives as possible while achieving the Allies' immediate strategic objective of seizing North Africa. The well-armed tribes that populated the area needed to be controlled. He had neither the manpower nor the time required to perform that task. He wanted to move as fast as possible toward Tunisia, and Darlan appeared to him to be a reasonable price to pay if he could get his Allied force quickly into Bezerte.[65]

He of course reflected on what would happen if the Darlan business backfired. Roosevelt and Marshall could easily replace him as commander in chief of the joint forces moving into North Africa and send him back to yet another training mission. That would hang a disappointing ending on his military career. After twenty-seven years as an officer, he at last had his ideal command, but he had now gambled his position on an agreement with a French military officer for whom he had neither friendship nor respect. He knew he could be betrayed by Darlan. Or he might be undercut by FDR, who had every reason to be deeply concerned about the political and ideological fallout from the agreement.[66]

Eisenhower never wavered during the ensuing political eruption. But as he blew off steam with his staff, he revealed how little he understood French political and military life.[67] Although he had spent time in France in the 1920s, he had mastered neither the language nor the psychology of the nation. Darlan, Giraud, and de Gaulle were all as mysterious to Ike as MacArthur had been. Eisenhower instinctively understood the British even if he frequently disagreed with them. His sympathy with their society and culture was reciprocated by the British public. But the French would always be an enigma for Ike, who barely weathered the messy collaboration with Darlan.

Confrontation at Casablanca

By the time his forces had completed their landings, consolidated their positions, and begun the long march east toward Bizerte, Eisenhower had more to worry about than the French.[68] He had for the first time to confront Germany's experienced, well-equipped, well-led army. The Allies had hoped to close off the Tunisian ports before German reinforcements could move from Sicily and Italy to block the advance. But initial French resistance, difficult terrain, bad weather, and poor transportation all slowed the advance. As German troops, planes, and heavy equipment poured into Tunisia, they made it impossible for Ike to press forward against General Erwin Rommel's Afrika Korps. Instead of a quick thrust east, the Allied troops were bogged down, looking constantly to the sky as they awaited the next Luftwaffe bombing and strafing attack.[69] This was Ike's first major disappointment in combat. It was all the more discouraging because it fed the contempt many of the British officers felt toward the inexperienced American soldiers and their officers—including their commander.

In support of Allied unity, Eisenhower had given the British lieutenant general Kenneth Anderson command of the combined British, French, and American forces pushing east toward Bizerte. Anderson and the American major general Lloyd Fredendall had trouble working together, but for both of them most of the difficulty came from the well-coordinated German air and ground forces defending Tunisia.[70] With the rainy season setting in, the deep African mud became an Axis ally, and Eisenhower's Tunisian campaign floundered to a near halt by Christmas of 1942.

Ike's next challenge came from his friends, not his German enemies. For Eisenhower, it was his second Machiavellian moment. In their meeting at Casablanca in January 1943, FDR and Churchill planned the next phase in the Allies' global strategy. The conference could not have come at a worse time for Ike. The stench from the Darlan agreement had yet to blow away, and the campaign for Tunisia was stalemated. Meanwhile, the well-organized British staff contingent at Casablanca was led by General Alan Brooke, who was determined to convert his contempt for Eisenhower's military leadership into a new command structure.[71] Left unconstrained, Brooke probably would have dumped Ike and split the Allies apart. But Roosevelt and Marshall recognized that they needed to keep the American public in full support of the Allied effort. They insisted that Ike remain as commander, while compromising on two important issues: they accepted the British plans for an extended Mediterranean campaign through Sicily and Italy, and they agreed to appoint General Sir Harold R. L. G. Alexander as Eisenhower's deputy in charge of the Allied land forces.[72]

In effect, the British had extended Eisenhower's authority to include Montgomery's Eighth Army, which was moving west to Tunisia. But at the same time they pushed Ike upstairs, away from the leadership in the field, the position he had sought and now treasured.[73] He became the campaign's political leader, a role more akin to the staff work he had fled than to the combat role he wanted to keep. To exert any influence on the campaign, he would have to work through a solid layer of British air, sea, and land commanders.[74] For the second time in his career, he had been politely but forcefully sandbagged, demoted without changing his title.[75] The prime advocate of unity in the African campaign had been undone by the disunity of the Allied forces. The façade of cooperation was carefully preserved, but the reality of British control was obvious.

Kasserine Pass

Just as Alexander was taking over his new position and four days after Ike had received his fourth star, Rommel's Afrika Corps drove a threatening wedge between the British and American forces. The wedge this time was physical as well as cultural, military as well as political, and it had personal and social elements for the Axis as well as the Allies.[76] The attack came to the south of Anderson's forces, which were concentrated along the coast.[77] Rommel hit the II Corps under Major General Lloyd R. Fredendall, who was defending the right flank of Ike's army.

Fredendall, who had strong backing in his career from Generals McNair and Marshall, had performed well in the landings, but even before Rommel struck, Eisenhower had become concerned about Fredendall's leadership of the II Corps.[78] Ike was sufficiently worried to make his own visit to the southern front. His fears were quickly and forcefully confirmed.[79] The troops were deployed in vulnerable positions and were not dug in properly, and a reserve force had not been positioned to support the front line if the Germans attacked. This created for Ike the military variant on what a famous businessman called a "strategic inflection point."[80] It was a point where the nature of the combat was about to shift decisively and where Eisenhower, as top commander, badly needed the support of an aggressive leader such as Patton. Instead of touring the front and correcting the problems Eisenhower had seen, Fredendall was far behind the front lines in a command center carved deeply into rock. His post was resistant to all but a direct hit by a German bomb. More important, the command center was far behind the infantry and armor deployments that were causing Ike so much concern. The II Corps gave General Rommel an inviting target, and he did not miss it.[81]

Ike had been right about the positioning and preparation of the American infantry and armor, and the German attack came with devastating force precisely where Eisenhower had predicted it would start. In the US Army's first tank battle, the German battle groups rolled over the II Corps. The defeat at Kasserine Pass was as stunning to Americans at home as it was to Eisenhower, to his Algerian headquarters, and to General Marshall. For a time, Rommel threatened to outflank the entire Allied army in Tunisia and Algeria.

As the battle unfolded, however, Ike delayed what he knew had to be done. With Fredendall, he was still playing by the army's peacetime book, supporting an officer for whom Generals Marshall and McNair had great hopes.[82] Uneasy in his new role, Eisenhower talked about how tough he had to be. He talked about it a bit too much and did too little. Actually, he had just the officer he needed: eventually he got rid of Fredendall and brought Patton to the front for damage control.[83] He also relieved the intelligence officer who had erred in his estimation of where the Germans would attack. But Ike had been slow to move. In Tunisia, he learned that he could no longer let personal considerations override professional performance on the battlefield.[84] He could still not exercise direct control of either the British or the French top officers, but on the American side, he knew he had to move faster to improve his command team if he was going to engage successfully with the German army. In combat, he discovered, the mills of the gods grind fine and fast.[85]

The American defeat had severe implications for the unity Eisenhower had been pushing for more than a year.[86] Because Rommel did not have the full support of his commanders and the supplies he needed, he was forced to withdraw before he completed his grand plan.[87] But that did not erase the impact of the weak resistance the II Corps had provided at Kasserine. It took more than seven thousand American troops to get the Corps back up to strength.[88] Patton repaired the damage that Fredendall and the defeat had done to the US forces, but what could not be repaired quickly were the everyday working relations between the British and Americans in North Africa.

A lopsided coalition slumped even further toward the British in the weeks that followed. It was impossible to ignore the contrast between the panic of the retreating Americans at Kasserine Pass and the victory General Montgomery's forces achieved at Medenine in early March. In a well-planned, superbly executed battle, the Eighth Army defeated Rommel in the last encounter he would lead against the Allies in Africa. From the British field commanders down through the enlisted men, a culture of cooperation gave way to wisecracks about American incompetence and to cool indifference to the need for unity.[89] Lessons had been learned; it was clear to Ike, for instance, that communications and coordination between the Allied air and ground forces would have to be considerably better than they currently were in Africa.[90] But in the harsh present, Eisenhower was left struggling to make these kinds of changes while keeping the alliance together.

Up to this point, the British had been right about strategy. This suggested that they probably would be right the next time their leaders pressed for assaults on Europe's "soft underbelly." Marshall's power to influence FDR and Allied strategy in Europe was weakened—with important implications for what would happen when and if the British and American forces conquered Tunisia. From this point on, the British were in the driver's seat on high strategy and on battlefield tactics. Alexander, who quickly took a firm grip on his command, resolved to keep the Americans in a subordinate position through the rest of Churchill's Mediterranean campaign. As the American and British forces advanced, Alexander assigned Patton a secondary role: defending Montgomery's army from a flank attack.[91]

Victory

Reorganized and rearmed under Patton, however, the II Corps quickly became a more disciplined and aggressive force pressing toward the Tunisian coast with an eye on splitting the German armies. Montgomery's British Eighth Army advanced up the coast, and to the north, Anderson's combined British, American, and French troops and armor fought their way to the crucial port cities of Bizerte and Tunis. General Alexander

Eisenhower with General George C. Marshall in Africa in the summer of 1943. Army Chief of Staff Marshall was Ike's strongest supporter from 1941 through World War II.

ordered the II Corps to advance and then stop so as not to interfere with Montgomery's attack. But Patton objected and forced his corps ahead. After the fact, Alexander yielded to Patton's and Marshall's fierce objections and authorized the II Corps to do what it was already doing.[92] Moved next to the northern attack on Bizerte, II Corps—now under Bradley—played an important role in the final days of the Tunisian campaign.[93] Broken and trapped, the German and Italian forces surrendered in May 1943, ending the North African campaign.[94]

Eisenhower had leaned very far toward the British position. According to Generals Patton and Bradley, he had been too quick to support Alexander and too hesitant to buck the British tactical decisions.[95] They railed against war by committee. But Eisenhower, who had developed a "necessary veneer of callousness," continued to bend to British authority.[96] Knowing his American generals would grouse but not rebel, he applied some of his newfound cunning on the situation. His mantra was unity, not nationalism. What was important to him was the fact that Patton and Bradley had wrangled victory from a difficult situation and begun by their performance to undercut the deeply planted British prejudices.[97] It would take time to change the attitudes of the British officers and men. Some would never change their minds. In the meantime, Ike had to drive forward while holding the Allies together as a fighting force.[98]

Sicily

Ike's next challenge was to invade Sicily, but by the time his armies launched their new assault, he was no longer on the steep part of his learning curve. He now had the team of combat leaders he needed. He had gently and successfully worked to dislodge General Anderson, who had disappointed Eisenhower in the Tunisian campaign.[99] He had Bradley and Patton guiding the primary American forces, with General Montgomery—that is, "Monty"—responsible for the Eighth Army and the drive up the eastern side of the island. Montgomery's victories in North Africa had not mellowed his personality. Instead, he became ever more troublesome to Ike and to his ground commander, Alexander. Still, both officers recognized that Monty was an accomplished tactician, the most experienced officer in the force. He was methodical to a fault but dependable and resilient under fire. His great victory at El Alamein was still the centerpiece of his military reputation, and as the campaign in Sicily got under way, none of Ike's other commanders could match that accomplishment.

The amphibious and airborne landings on July 10, 1943, were flawed but successful. Poor coordination between the invading fleet and air forces resulted in tragic losses from friendly antiaircraft fire. Still, Ike's two armies made it ashore and were able to hold their beachheads. Monty led the major assault force on the southeast coast and started a steady, forceful drive toward the vital port city of Messina, the link between Sicily and the mainland. Alexander once again assigned Patton and Bradley secondary roles covering the flank of Monty's Eighth Army by advancing on the west of the island.[100]

German resistance to both attacks was fierce, and Montgomery's advance slowed to a walk and then stopped. In the middle of the island, however, Patton's tanks were able to drive deeply inland, and soon they captured Palermo.[101] He and Bradley then sent their infantry and tanks to fight their way east into Messina.[102] For Patton and the US media, the victories of his Seventh Army were a personal, professional, and national triumph that started to erase the painful memory of the American defeat at Kasserine Pass.

For Ike, the American accomplishments and the clear evidence that they still needed to improve coordination of their land, air, and sea forces shaped his vision of the immediate future. His confidence in Bradley had grown immensely, and he noted about Montgomery that "I have learned to know him very well, feel that I have his personal equation, and have no lack of confidence in my ability to handle him."[103] Convinced that "every commander is made, in the long run, by his subordinates," Eisenhower was satisfied with his team's performance in Sicily. He understood the flaws in their efforts and was especially concerned about Alexander's failure to provide decisive coordination once the action got under way. Neither Ike nor Marshall could be pleased that so many of the German defenders had been allowed to escape into Italy. But when it was understood as a rehearsal for the coming amphibious invasion of France, the attack on Sicily boded well for the Allied cause and for Eisenhower's future as a commander. He had systematically and successfully turned away every effort to bypass his authority.[104] When Patton's forces arrived triumphantly in Messina on August 17, 1943, it had been only six months since Ike's position had been seriously endangered at the Casablanca conference.

Eisenhower understood that he needed Patton's aggressive leadership in combat even though both Ike and Bradley were repeatedly angered by Patton's outrageous behavior.[105] Personal friendship aside, Eisenhower had every reason to fight to keep his swashbuckling general in action. Shortly thereafter Patton tested Ike's protective shell in the infamous slapping incident at an army hospital. Convinced that soldiers suffering mental collapse in combat were malingering, Patton accused them of cowardice and actually hit two of them—clearly court-martial offenses. Eisenhower rejected the screams for Patton's demotion and put his own leadership on the line, as he had in the flap over Darlan.[106] The commander was a much tougher leader than he had been in 1930 or even 1940. Once more he was able to hold his position with Marshall and Roosevelt.

Ike had endured, learned, and preserved the unity of an Allied force that frequently resembled a dysfunctional family.[107] His conciliatory style had been severely tested, and he had yet to earn the respect of Generals Montgomery and Brooke. After the Casablanca conference, Eisenhower certainly understood how fleeting his status could be, and that may have made him more tolerant of the shortcomings of his fellow officers, including Patton, than he had been. Throughout the campaign in Africa and Sicily, Eisenhower had deeply and repeatedly angered his own commanders. There was, indeed, a Machiavellian touch in the manner in which he handled Patton and Bradley. They frequently sputtered with anger over Eisenhower's support for the British positions on tactics and strategy. But the hard-fought victories in Tunisia and Sicily left them solidly aligned with their commander and ready for the next phase of the crusade. The victories in the Mediterranean also left his critics harping to one another and Ike securely in control of the most important American and British forces in the field.

Seven

Eisenhower speaking with paratroopers on June 5, 1944, just before the D-Day invasion of Normandy.

The Decision

While Eisenhower and his armies were completing the conquest of Sicily, the Soviet Union was winning the single most important battle in World War II. Lieutenant General P. A. Rotmistrov described what happened in July 1943 at Kursk near the western boundary between Russia and Ukraine: "The tanks were moving across the steppe in small packs, under cover of patches of woodland and hedges. The bursts of gunfire merged into one continuous mighty roar. The Soviet tanks thrust into the German advanced formation at full speed and penetrated the German tank screen. The [Soviet] T-34s were knocking out Tigers at extremely close range, since their powerful guns and massive armor no longer gave them an advantage in close combat. The tanks of both sides were in the closest possible contact. There was neither time nor room to disengage from the enemy and reform in battle order or operate in formation. The shells fired at close range pierced not only the side armor but also the frontal armor of the fighting vehicles. At such range there was no protection in armor, and the length of the gun barrels was no longer decisive. Frequently, when a tank was hit, its ammunition and fuel blew up, and torn-off turrets were flung through the air over dozens of yards. . . . Soon the whole sky was shrouded by the thick smoke of the burning wrecks. On the black, scorched earth the gutted tanks burnt like torches. It was difficult to establish which side was attacking and which defending."[1]

While most of the burning tanks were Soviet T-34s, the aggressive attack blunted the German offensive and left their army vulnerable to flanking attacks.[2] On August 23, 1943, the Soviet forces broke through the German lines and forced a withdrawal. From that point on, the Wehrmacht would be unable to mount a major offensive on the Eastern Front, where most of their armies were concentrated. The battle for Stalingrad had started to shift the balance of military power in the east, and Kursk finished that process decisively. In the battles that followed, the Soviet army would be the aggressor. Even more ominously for the Nazis, Germany could not replenish its massive loses in tanks and fighting men in all of the divisions that had been decimated at Kursk. Hitler was forced to decide whether to send new troops to Italy or to the Eastern Front. He could no longer do both. Germany was running short of manpower and would soon be sending raw teenagers such as Günter Grass into battle.[3] As the Soviets pushed forward on the road to Berlin, the future of both eastern and western Europe was being decided on the battlefield rather than in the conference room—FDR and Churchill notwithstanding.[4]

The Soviet military accomplishments would continue long after Germany was defeated and would provide Eisenhower with the primary challenge of his postwar career. The communist nation's ability to produce in abundance the weapons of modern warfare and to deploy them with skill threatened the global balance of power. Soviet military and economic strength and communist aggression would leave Eisenhower struggling to protect America's national security. He would work for the rest of his life to create and maintain a new balance of power in a world experiencing a series of cataclysmic political, technological, and economic changes.[5]

Italy

In the summer of 1943, however, Ike had too much to worry about in the Mediterranean to pay much attention to what was happening at Kursk.[6] Eisenhower was entangled in the politics of the Italian attempts to surrender.[7] His position throughout was consistent with his approach to the

Darlan Deal: he would do almost anything possible to save the lives of Allied soldiers. In this case that forced him to try to maneuver around the doctrine of "unconditional surrender" that had been announced by President Roosevelt and Prime Minister Churchill at the Casablanca conference.[8] Ultimately successful, the negotiations dragged on long enough to allow the Germans to rush troops into Italy and mount a fierce defense against the Allied invasion.[9] The German commander in Italy was Albert Kesselring, a master of defensive warfare, and the skill and discipline of the German soldiers made every yard of Italian soil costly for Eisenhower's forces.

The Allied landings at Salerno, Calabria, and Taranto had been initially successful. But the attempt to jump-start the campaign with an end run up the coast to Salerno was a tactical success and a strategic failure.[10] Fierce German opposition at Salerno—a landing that was saved by powerful naval and air support—gave a clear forecast of what Ike and his Allied armies could expect in this next phase of the Mediterranean strategy.[11] As the German army had already demonstrated in Sicily, it could make masterful use of mountainous terrain, and the rocky landscape of southern and central Italy was as inhospitable to an invading force as it was to farming. The Allies paid a dreadful price in lives for their slow advance toward Rome.

It soon was evident that Churchill and his commanders had thrown the Allies into a campaign that closely resembled the deadly trench warfare of 1914–1918. The fighting took place "in desolate mountains, creased by narrow valleys and deep gorges; on brush-covered heights, bald slopes, and high tablelands; along unpaved roads and mule tracks hugging mountain ledges. Late autumn weather would add fog, rain, and mud to the difficulties of the terrain."[12] Paradoxically, British military thought had long been dominated by an intense desire to avoid the incredible casualties of the First World War.[13] General Montgomery's methodical tactics were thus not peculiar to the man.[14] Now, however, the British and their American allies were forced to fight mountain range by mountain range as they struggled to dig the German infantry and artillery out of their protected positions.

Instead of the mobile warfare Patton had conducted in Sicily and the Soviets had mounted after Kursk, the Italian campaign was a slow, deadly, grinding advance that favored the defenders and repeatedly bogged down the Allied forces.[15] As Ike commented in his diary in November, "Our only recourse was to keep pounding away at the enemy's rear-guards, seeking out weak spots and pushing forward. . . . This process is still going on," he wrote, "but it is exceedingly slow."[16]

As the Italian campaign inched forward, the incremental power shift between the British and Americans continued. A war of attrition was gradually recasting the alliance as well as its German opponents.[17] While the ideas, personalities, and relationships of the two nations' leaders seemed always to be the dominant factors shaping the alliance's military and political policies, power was primarily a function of their ability to supply the men and equipment to carry the war forward.[18] This would have an impact as the British approached the limits of their replacement manpower.[19]

This new setting encouraged Ike to be more forceful in expressing his opposition to Churchill's latest proposal for another campaign in the Mediterranean.[20] An additional reflection of that underlying shift was Eisenhower's critique of the command structure implemented at Casablanca. He focused on the anomalous role of General Alexander, who was in command of the 15th Army Group but also deputy commander in chief. "Actually," Ike said, "Alexander cannot possibly function as a Deputy. . . . The result is that I am the over-all *ground Commander-in-Chief*." He wanted to get rid of "waste and . . . duplication." The British command structure and process of committee decision-making, he said, "cannot work where sizeable U.S. and British forces are placed together in one theater to achieve a common objective."[21] By the end of 1943, Eisenhower had almost completed his "learning by doing" in command of a joint force in combat.

Meanwhile, subtle changes were taking place in the close relationships between Marshall and Eisenhower. Marshall had promoted Ike when he had yet to prove himself in command. As Chief of Staff, Marshall had found it necessary to defend Eisenhower through the troubled

North African campaign. Now Marshall became more critical and slightly less supportive of his protégé.[22] Meanwhile, Ike became more assertive and slightly less subordinate to the man who had given him the leading role in the Allied campaign. Ike's experiences in that role had given him a sure grip on leadership and strong convictions as to how the Allies should move forward against Germany.

Less subtle changes were also starting to take place in the relationships between Stalin and the Allies. After Kursk, Stalin set out to exploit to the full his new position of strength. From his perspective, the Allies had delayed too long their much-discussed attack across the Channel. They had bogged down in an Italian campaign that occupied too few German divisions and promised little advantage after Italy was conquered.[23] Poland and Germany were the countries that interested Stalin, and in the Teheran Conference (November 28–December 1, 1943) he let FDR and Churchill know that he was already thinking very seriously about what, exactly, the postwar settlements would be. He wanted to know how much of Poland would be chopped off and added to the USSR. How would Germany be dismembered and the threat of a third world war averted? In the months ahead the Allies would hear more about these demands and would glimpse Stalin's plans to expand a victorious Soviet empire. They would have new opportunities to reflect on Marxist ideology and the role it would play in the postwar order of Europe.

First, of course, they had to win the war against fascism. Soon after the Teheran meeting, Eisenhower got a new command that placed him in a central position to determine how quickly the Nazis would be defeated and how much of Europe would end up in Stalin's control. Once again, FDR favored Churchill and unity by appointing Ike to command Overlord, the cross-Channel invasion of France.[24] As with most such top appointments—in business, politics, and the military—the choices narrowed down to a few alternatives. This time it was three. Eisenhower had been chosen over Alan Brooke, his most ardent critic, and George Marshall, his most enthusiastic and reliable advocate.[25] Marshall was an obvious choice for the post.[26] But his dealings with Churchill had struck sparks and sometimes flash fires. The British leaned toward Ike.[27] As a result, Marshall, Ike's boss, was denied what likely would have been the crowning achievement of his military career.

Now Eisenhower would lead the Allied part of the great crusade against Hitler and the Nazi regime. For a third time, he and the Allied forces would have to defeat a well-trained German army that would be fiercely defending the doorway to its homeland.[28] Ike was not cocky, but he was confident in his ability to lead this complex campaign. He had honed his capabilities as a leader in North Africa, Sicily, and Italy.[29] He knew the commanders he needed and how to get the most out of his forces.[30] He understood the enemy and respected the ability of the Wehrmacht's generals and the discipline of their enlisted men. Having debated the cross-Channel attack since 1942, he was ready to go.

Before Ike could get to London and his new command, however, he was forced by General Marshall to return to Washington, to meet with President Roosevelt, and to spend some time with his wife.[31] Mamie was an unhappy woman. She and her husband had been separated for a long time and there had been all too much attention paid in the gossip network to Kay Summersby, Eisenhower's beautiful Irish driver. Kathleen McCarthy-Morrogh Summersby had been with Ike since his first tour in London, and since then, the general had spent far more time with her than he had with Mamie or any other woman.[32] While Eisenhower tried on his visit to patch things up with his wife, the effort flopped—as those efforts often do—and he left for London with his marriage intact but less secure than his appointment as Supreme Commander. He took off on January 13, 1944, with plenty to worry about on both fronts.

Being Supreme

In London, the new Supreme Commander had a full helping of challenges. While soon he would be launching the largest amphibious operation in military history, the landings in France would have a narrow margin favoring success.[33] Even if the Allies could crack the formidable German defenses and create the projected beachheads, failure was a real possibility.[34]

As he told the Joint Chiefs of Staff in March 1944, "It would be fatal to underestimate the difficulties of the assault."[35] The operation would test the Allied ability to establish lodgments in the first wave and then with reinforcements expand them quickly enough to withstand the anticipated German onslaught. General von Rundstedt had substantial forces to deploy in that counterattack. His problem would the rapid movement and effective concentration of his divisions in the face of overwhelming Allied air superiority.

Nervous about the landings, Ike tried to squeeze as many divisions as possible into the grand plan.[36] He anticipated "stern fighting" on the ground. "The fact is that against a German defense" he needed "solid tactical power and overwhelming strength. Recently," he added, "a Russian general casually remarked that when they wanted to make a real drive they preferred to get a superiority at the critical spot of about four to one."[37] He would not have that advantage in Normandy. General Marshall and Secretary of War Stimson, too, were worried about whether Eisenhower had the forces he needed for the invasion.[38]

From 1942 through 1944, the bind on landing crafts had imposed severe limits on each of the Allies' amphibious operations. Now the Combined Chiefs of Staff had to decide if they had enough ships to attack through southern France as well as across the Channel.[39] Like each of the major debates over strategy, this one divided the Allies. The British wanted to abandon the southern assault and concentrate on the Mediterranean and Normandy.[40] The Americans had long favored an amphibious attack in southern France that would make full use of the forces already in Italy. At stake were the landing crafts that both campaigns would need.[41] The British-American split continued through seemingly endless debates that were, Ike said, "getting a bit wearing."[42]

Eisenhower finally resolved the issue by exercising his newfound authority. He persuaded the Chiefs of Staff to compromise by delaying— instead of cancelling—the attack in the south of France to enable Overlord to have a reasonable chance for success.[43] Even then, the margin on landing ships was thin. This was still true as late as April 1944, when nine German torpedo boats attacked a convoy of Allied landing craft practicing for the invasion at Slapton Sands on the coast of Devon. The E-boats sank two LSTs (landing ship tanks) and damaged a third, killing 700 of the soldiers taking part in the exercise. Eisenhower lamented the losses and pointed out to the Chiefs of Staff that his reserve of LSTs was now zero.[44] There were no more ships to be found.

There was nothing Ike could do to eliminate that constraint on his forces, but he thought he had a reasonable chance to improve his odds in Normandy by bringing the Allies' air forces into full support of the invasion. While it seems astonishing that the air commanders vigorously resisted Eisenhower's demands to devote 100 percent of their effort to the cross-Channel attack, this was indeed the case.[45] Nor was it a new problem. From the beginning to the end of the North African campaign, Ike had experienced trouble getting the results he wanted from his air force. National differences about military command blended with a distinctive air force culture to make thoroughgoing coordination almost impossible to achieve. Eisenhower had been seeking unity since the beginning of the war, but all too often he felt like a man on a merry-go-round grabbing at a ring that always slipped from his grasp.

Still, it was worth the effort and the emotions it aroused. He leaned hard on this issue and refused to back off.[46] Ike had learned from the struggle at Salerno how important airpower could be to an amphibious assault. It could, he knew, swing the battle in a tight situation. Anticipating that D-Day would be a close play, he was not going to leave any doubt about what he needed. In his mind, this would also determine whether he was now Supreme Commander of a thoroughly integrated force or, in essence, merely "Supreme Coordinator" of services that would make their separate plans and guide strategy as well as tactics.

The problem was complicated by the distinctive air force ideology that was in normal circumstances an important asset. While the British and Americans airmen disagreed about tactics (the United States favored precision daytime bombing and the British nighttime area bombing), all believed that airpower alone could significantly reduce Germany's ability to carry on the war, and perhaps even force a German surrender. The American approach was based on the assumption that there would be a decline in German air defenses, and the British assumed that their raids would destroy German morale as well as industrial capacity. Neither of these things happened, at least not initially, but this was not well documented in early 1944, and the leaders of the air campaign remained extremely optimistic about the impact of their bombing.[47] If you believed, as General Henry "Hap" Arnold did, that "the issue hangs now on which side first falters, weakens, and loses its punishing power," you were prepared to fight hard for the existing bombing operations.[48]

The debates over authority and strategy dragged on after Lieutenant General Carl Spaatz took command of the US Strategic Air Forces in Europe in January 1944. Amid some new signs that the German air defense was weakening, Spaatz put forward a proposal to concentrate on the enemy's oil supplies.[49] Eisenhower had no trouble understanding the importance of a modern army's supply of gasoline. He had struggled throughout the North African campaign to keep his forces resupplied with fuel as well as ammunition. But from his perspective, the priority of Overlord had to be acknowledged, as did the authority of the Supreme Commander.

Although the Combined Chiefs created the Ninth Air Force specifically to support the landings, the debates continued.[50] National and service identities were remarkably durable. The air commanders dug in and resisted being subordinated to a new international, hierarchical system under a single, powerful commander. Eisenhower wanted to settle the issue quickly and forcefully before the action started. Unfortunately, his directive from the Combined Chiefs did not specifically confirm his authority over the air forces of the two nations. So he went above the Chiefs of Staff and pressed Churchill on the issue. He stamped very hard, telling Churchill that he would give up his command if his authority was not affirmed. This was apparently the only time Eisenhower used that threat. It worked. The prime minister folded.[51]

But then, of course, the new directive had to be expressed in new language. Given the stakes in Europe, the discussion edged past embarrassing and became ludicrous. Would Ike have "command"? Or would he provide "supervision"? Men were dying and more would die very soon while their leaders, all intelligent, experienced military professionals, were nit-picking. They finally compromised on "direction."[52]

Semantics notwithstanding, Ike quickly solidified his position by providing "direction" to the air forces—in effect, transforming "direction" into "command."[53] The major bombing campaigns continued, and they had the side effect of wearing down the Luftwaffe fighter fleet. But Eisenhower got the planes and missions he needed to prepare the way for Overlord.

The first priority became destruction of the French infrastructure that otherwise would allow the Wehrmacht to continue to strengthen the Atlantic Wall and prepare to mount a counterattack against the landings. Even if all the landings were entirely successful—which seemed unlikely—the Allied forces would still be vulnerable until they could bring ashore additional divisions, tanks, and artillery. The air campaign was designed to provide insurance that the divisions that landed in Normandy would not be driven back into the sea before their reinforcements arrived.[54]

As soon as Eisenhower had that crucial issue settled and his command properly structured, he quickly took steps to keep his team united and working toward the same goal.[55] He compromised with Spaatz and his "oil strategy." Meanwhile, he had appointed a British air marshal, Arthur Tedder, as his deputy supreme commander to supervise air operations.[56] Tedder's appointment did not stop the niggling about strategy, but Eisenhower and his new deputy were able to combine forces and override the opposition.[57]

From Ike's perspective, this was the most important single form of disunity with which he had to deal in early 1944. There were others. But his struggle with the air command was the most taxing and the most important to the outcome of his mission. The results of the pre-invasion bombings in April and May 1944 justified the energy Ike had put into shaping this part of his command.[58] The Allied planes destroyed rail lines, bridges, and rail yards. They established such air superiority over France that they forced German commanders Rundstedt and Rommel to alter their plans for the counterattacks vital to their defensive strategy.[59]

Invading

By early June, Eisenhower's armies, navies, and air forces were primed for the grand assault on Normandy.[60] The size of the operation was staggering. On June 3 all of the 130,000 ground troops were aboard their ships and the twelve convoys were prepared to sail. The Allied battleships, cruisers, and destroyers were ready to escort them and provide the naval firepower they hoped would destroy German artillery and neutralize significant fortifications in the Atlantic Wall. For Eisenhower, relations with the Allied naval services had gone smoothly in North Africa, Sicily, and Italy—and once again in Overlord. Ike knew that he would need those naval guns to keep his ground forces from being stalemated on the beaches by German artillery fire.[61] Everything that could be planned had been planned, many times over.

Still, a great uncertainty loomed over the invasion and kept the Supreme Commander opening new packs of cigarettes, eating poorly, and sleeping very little. Given his history of stress-related health problems, this was a tense situation for the one man who could not spend any time in the hospital in June 1944. All the thousands of decisions, orders, meetings, and requests gave way at this time to a single final decision that he had to make.

Camped out in a trailer near Portsmouth on the English Channel, Eisenhower agonized over the final order to launch the assault. He had to do that on the basis of incomplete knowledge about the weather in the English Channel. An optimistic report by his senior meteorologist convinced him to put the vast force in motion, targeting June 5. But then the weather turned bad, very bad. Eisenhower, who was already feeling "the intensity of these burdens," was forced to reconsider his decision.[62] Meeting with his commanders in Admiral Bertram Ramsay's office in Southwick House, Ike heard that there would be overcast skies that would eliminate his air cover and high winds that would cause disarray in the landing force. He opted for a delay. The next day, Sunday, June 4, the forecast was still dismal, and he called the fleet back for another day of tense delay.

Later in the day, the forecast changed again. This time it looked more promising. A predicted break in the weather reopened the issue and sparked a new debate. Eisenhower polled his commanders. Air Marshal Trafford Leigh-Mallory was pessimistic about the odds, and even Ike's deputy and close confidant Tedder was not optimistic. General Montgomery was ready to go, as was Admiral Ramsay. With a divided house, Ike rolled the issue around in his mind.

Worried, reflective, feeling the terrible weight of the moment, Eisenhower decided to launch the greatest fleet in history and attack early on June 6. This was the single most important decision of his military career—and he knew it. Professional careers seldom turn on a single event. Lawyers win some cases and lose others, but they normally continue in their profession until their retirement. Surgeons lose a patient from time to time, but they continue to practice. General practitioners and nurses toil away for decades, treating patients one at a time, healing or presiding over death, without a single outstanding test of their ability to understand, prevent, or cure disease. For the military officer in peacetime, the same conditions normally applied, as they had for both Ike and General Marshall until December 1941.

In wartime, however, military careers are hostage to single, cataclysmic events. As are the lives of their soldiers. All too many of those events are beyond the control of any commander. Eisenhower's long army career, his reputation, and his role in history were all on the line in June 1944. If the weather turned nasty, as it easily could, or if the Germans responded with greater force than anticipated, as they could, Eisenhower's decision would be a footnote to failure in the next generation's textbooks. Feeling the immense pressure, Eisenhower wrote the following note and placed it in his billfold:

> Our landings in the Cherbourg-Havre area have failed to gain a satisfactory foothold and I have withdrawn the troops. My decision to attack at this time and place was based upon the best information available. The troops, the air and the Navy did all that Bravery and devotion to duty could do. If any blame or fault attaches to the attempt it is mine alone . . .

If a single document had to be used to define Eisenhower's character and leadership, it would be this message, which he was prepared to use if the invasion failed.[63]

Since failure was obviously on the Supreme Commander's mind, we should reflect for a moment on the consequences if the invasion forces had been disrupted by a mighty storm or driven by the German tanks and infantry back into the English Channel.[64] It clearly would have had catastrophic political, social, and even economic ramifications that would have been of far more significance to Europe and the United States than any military or political leader's career. At that time, the military situation in Europe was lopsided. The most significant action was taking place in eastern Europe, where the Soviets were launching their giant spring offensive on five fronts. Soon Stalin's armies would crush Germany's Army Group Centre and advance more than 300 miles toward Berlin. Those German divisions that were not surrounded would retreat in good order, but retreat would be their common fate. Their counterattacks would be blunted, their losses severe. Many of their most experienced divisions would be destroyed in titanic battles that involved more than 6 million German and Soviet soldiers and unbelievable casualties.[65]

The Soviet summer offensive decided the political fate of eastern Europe, and a D-Day failure would have left western Europe open to Soviet influence and perhaps Stalin's control.[66] By the end of the summer of 1944, his armies were only 400 miles from Berlin, capable of seizing Germany's capital, conquering the industrial Ruhr, and standing astride the economic heartland of Europe.[67] In Washington, among those planning the war, there had been "an occasional expression of foreboding" over the USSR's role in the postwar settlement.[68] But the overriding concern was "the task at hand": winning the war.[69] Eisenhower was not the only American leader who forgot in 1944 the lessons they had learned from reading Carl von Clausewitz's *On War*.

A D-Day failure also would have had significant political consequences in the United States and Britain, where voters were eager for success in a war that already seemed far too long and deadly. Would the democracies have chosen new leaders after Roosevelt and Churchill replaced

Eisenhower and retired British Chief of Staff Alan Brooke? That seems unlikely. But I am certain that both FDR and Churchill thought about it as the invasion forces sailed in early June. Throughout the campaigns in North Africa, Sicily, and Italy, both FDR and Marshall had been forced repeatedly to deal with political controversies over the progress of the war. Churchill's British opponents were vigorous and alert to any hint of failure on the part of a prime minister who was also serving as minister of defence.

Everyone had something to worry about, and those who were most honest about the odds were most pessimistic. But even an honest pessimist such as Ike was compelled by his role as a leader to convey optimism to his commanders and troops. He had done that in the previous weeks while visiting as many of the units headed for Normandy as his schedule allowed. He had a unique talent for bridging the enormous gap between the Supreme Commander and the soldiers, sailors, and airmen who were headed into combat. Of all those going across the Channel, the paratroopers were in greatest danger. Their mission was especially chancy, and Air Marshal Leigh-Mallory had predicted a disaster for the airborne troops. Ike disagreed. But it was no accident that on the night before the invasion he took a short drive north from Portsmouth to visit the 101st Airborne Division. Disappointed as usual by not finding any paratroopers from Kansas, he nevertheless chatted with the men and their officers in a casual manner that gave no clue to the anxiety churning his stomach. He told General Marshall that "the light of battle was in their eyes." After spending the day with his own eyes on the weather, he finally went to bed after midnight and awaited the great event.[70]

A Precarious Venture

Suddenly there was nothing for Eisenhower to do except wait. Amid tremendous air and naval barrages, the landings began on June 6. Since the Allies had been able to break the German codes, their intelligence units had substantially better information on the enemy than either Rommel or Rundstedt had on the landings.[71] The Allied information was not perfect. Neither Eisenhower nor Bradley knew, for instance, that the

German 352nd Division had moved into the area behind Omaha Beach, where the US 1st Infantry Division was attempting to land. Encountering a difficult terrain and fierce German resistance, the American attack stalled on the beach. At Utah Beach, the US VII Corps moved quickly inland, as did units from the British Second Army and the Canadian forces that were pointed toward the French city of Caen.

By the end of the day, three of the landings were successful, and only Omaha Beach—where Eisenhower's old friend General Gerow was in command—remained in doubt. The casualties were high both among the paratroopers and among the soldiers attempting to land at Omaha Beach. Landing craft were swamped. Communications collapsed. Tanks and artillery were lost to the surf and to mines buried in the sand. German machine gun and mortar fire from the high ridges above the beach kept the soldiers scattered and unable to form effective units. Confusion mounted, and wounded men drowned as the tide rose.

Most military officers become hardened to death. Generals Bradley, Montgomery, and Patton had a utilitarian, somewhat withdrawn perspective on casualties.[72] Like epidemiologists, they counted casualties but seldom were concerned with an individual death. Eisenhower seems never to have developed the same type of hard external shell when confronted with the deaths of the men he had sent into combat. On D-Day, he had many deaths to ponder, and he would later give eloquent expression to his thoughts. For the moment, however, all he could do was wait, worry, and report from time to time to Marshall and the Combined Chiefs of Staff.[73]

Despite the losses at Omaha, the beach was finally secured, and the US soldiers began pushing inland.[74] Air bombardment and naval fire had once again tipped the balance toward the invading army, and on June 7 Ike was able to survey the beachheads from the minelayer *Apollo* and discuss the advances with Bradley and Montgomery.[75] The Supreme Commander could see the armor and artillery pouring ashore as the Allied forces started working their way through the hedgerows and German defenses that slowed their advance. With each move forward, field by field, their officers were braced for a German counterattack in force.[76]

Eisenhower and his commanders anticipated a major tank assault that would attempt to split their armies and drive the Allies back into the water. They knew that Germany had the potential to create a crushing Allied defeat. They could not help but imagine the Dunkirk II that the British had long feared.

What neither Ike nor Montgomery nor Bradley could really understand, however, were the conflicts and confusion that continued to disrupt the German high command. Before the invasion, General Rundstedt and General Rommel disagreed sharply over the basic strategy for resisting the landings they knew were coming. Rundstedt favored the war of mobility that had accounted for Germany's greatest triumphs since 1939. Unable to predict exactly where the Allies would land, he would hold his powerful panzer divisions back from the beaches and then use their concentrated force to destroy the invaders. The most likely place for the landings, Rundstedt thought, was to the east of Normandy, near Calais, not far from Dunkirk. There the Channel was narrow, and successful landings would give the Allies an opportunity to outflank his forces in France. Convinced by his own reasoning, Rundstedt held his 15th Army near Calais to resist the invasion.

Rommel disagreed. He thought the best defense in this case would be at the waterfront. There, he reasoned, the Allies coming ashore would be at their weakest. They would not have the artillery and armored forces that could only gradually be landed and moved up from the beaches. They could be defeated piecemeal before they had an opportunity to build up their units and mount successful thrusts into the interior, where their superior numbers would ultimately dictate a German withdrawal. Rommel did his best to strengthen the beachfront defenses, even to the extent of using soldiers in construction activities. Some of his green troops could instead have benefited from further training.[77] This was all the more important because the units in France were receiving many inexperienced replacements. German manpower was severely strained by 1944. Supplies as well as labor were frequently unavailable. Rommel thus struggled to improve his German version of the Maginot Line, but the coast was long and much of the planned work could not be completed before June 1944.[78]

Rundstedt's strategy centered on a massive panzer counterattack of the sort that was a major and persistent concern of Eisenhower and his fellow officers. Ike had in mind all of the things that had gone wrong in North Africa, Sicily, and especially Salerno. All the landings in the Mediterranean had succeeded, but the resistance in Normandy was more formidable and the stakes were much higher. Delays in landing armor and artillery and in taking port facilities were worrisome as the Allies warily looked for the German onslaught. There were tactical counterattacks, but the full-bore counteroffensive never came.

Rundstedt tried, but he had many more problems than Eisenhower did as the invasion unfolded. Deceived about Allied intentions, he left the Fifteenth Army waiting for General Patton to lead his forces across the Channel to the beaches near Calais. This was never part of the Allied strategy. Patton was actually waiting in Britain until he could bring his Third Army into the battle in Normandy. There were other divisions that Rundstedt might have added to his force, but they could be moved from Norway and the Eastern Front only on direct orders from Hitler, and on June 6, Hitler was not ready to give those orders. There were also reserve forces in France—the formidable 12th SS Panzer Division and the Panzer Lehr Division—and Rundstedt promptly sent them into battle. Or he thought he did.

The German high command (OKW) delayed carrying out Rundstedt's order until they could receive Hitler's confirmation. But the Führer was sleeping and OKW did not want to wake him up, so they lost a day getting started. Then the German divisions could not move in the daytime because of Allied air superiority, so another day was lost. At this critical turn in the battle for the beaches, that time was all-important. When the Germans finally did attack Montgomery's forces, the Canadian and British armies had cleared the beaches and were able to resist an attack that was weaker than it could have been if Hitler and the OKW had mustered all of their available divisions against the landings. Later, Hitler realized that he had made a mistake and tried to bring a greater force into the campaign in the west. But the crucial hours had passed.

This was the third great blunder Hitler made. Paradoxically, all three mistakes worked to the benefit of Eisenhower, who truly hated the Führer in a personal and visceral manner. The first and most catastrophic error was the invasion of the Soviet Union, which tied up the bulk of Germany's divisions on the Eastern Front. No Allied invasion could have succeeded if even half of the German divisions on the Eastern Front had been in France. The second fateful blunder was to ignore Rommel's proposal and leave the German divisions in Tunisia, where they were surrounded and forced to surrender. The third was to divide authority in the west between Rommel and Rundstedt, leaving the latter's armies too weak to defeat the Allies when they were most vulnerable, during their first few days clearing the beaches. When the invasion began, General Rundstedt was forced to fight with fewer than half of the divisions he needed to repel the Allies. Left with virtually no air support, his soldiers were riding bicycles into combat because Eisenhower's bombers and the French resistance had destroyed so many of the rail connections and made daylight travel on the roads perilous.[79]

Grinding

Within a week, Bradley's First Army and Montgomery's combined British and Canadian divisions were solidly established in Normandy, but neither could break through the German defenses to the interior. Initially Monty's 21st Army Group made the most progress, pressing forward toward Bayeux, some miles west of their primary goal, the important transportation center of Caen. Then the German defense stiffened as Rundstedt's reserve divisions came into action. When Montgomery delayed his next thrust toward Caen, Eisenhower became impatient, but there was actually very little Ike could do to get his armies pressing forward on either front.[80]

Frustrated in Normandy, Eisenhower also found himself sinking into a second disturbing encounter with French military leadership. This time the challenge came from the imposing Charles de Gaulle and his French Committee of National Liberation. They insisted on having an important voice in matters of strategy and tactics. While this was a sideshow for Ike, it was all that mattered to de Gaulle and his Committee. Quick to respond to every opportunity and to roar back at every real or imagined slight, de Gaulle soon began to master the situation in France.[81] Eisenhower tried to maintain a reasonable measure of control. He was consistent and thorough, but de Gaulle was brilliant and imaginative. In effect, de Gaulle made himself the sole leader of the French nation and demanded that Eisenhower shape his plans according to the French general's demands. Neither Eisenhower nor Churchill, Roosevelt, Marshall, or the rest of the Combined Chiefs of Staff were able to come up with a successful plan to contain the advances of the forceful French leader.

Ike's problems were compounded by the "Great Storm" that hit the English Channel on June 19. "The whole eastern coast of the Channel is tied up," Eisenhower said, "in the worst weather we have had yet."[82] It delayed Montgomery's attack again, wrecked the ingenious artificial port the Allies had created, and made it impossible for several days to get Bradley the supplies he needed. The campaign's logistical problems were imposing harsh limits on the invasion. The US Army had divisions waiting in the United States to join Eisenhower's forces in Normandy, but they could not get into action until a good working port was available in France. Ike hoped that Cherbourg would solve this problem, but the Germans effectively destroyed the port before surrendering to Bradley's army on June 26. It would be months before Cherbourg would be fully operational.

At this decisive turn in the campaign, Eisenhower looked to Montgomery for a breakthrough. The British commander of ground forces launched a full-scale air and ground attack aimed at capturing Caen and pushing into a countryside more suited to a war of mobility. On June 25, Montgomery was confident: "I will continue battle on eastern flank till one of us cracks and it will not be us."[83] Determination, optimism, and careful planning were not enough, however, to achieve victory on that eastern flank. By this time Germany was able to muster enough panzer and infantry divisions to stall Montgomery's attack. The resulting stalemate was reminiscent of Sicily, and Montgomery's performance began to attract intense criticism. Ike's deputy, Tedder, and other air commanders began to call for a change of leadership in the ground campaign.

Relations between the leaders of the air and ground forces had always been tenuous, but now they became hostile.

While Ike was never comfortable with Montgomery, he worked once again to preserve a sense of unity.[84] He was well aware that Britain's manpower shortage was cutting deeply into its ability to provide replacements for men lost in combat.[85] It was reasonable to assume that this had something to do with Monty's failure to press ahead with great force. But Eisenhower realized that an attempt to replace Britain's leading war hero would weaken the alliance. He refused to abandon his conciliatory approach to the Allied campaign. Certainly he was prepared to be decisive if he thought the Allied cause was being weakened by blunders in leadership or policy.[86] But in this case, Ike simply switched his strategy and tactics to favor emphasis on a breakthrough by Bradley.[87] In effect, he gave Montgomery the assignment of holding down German divisions and defending Bradley's flank. This, of course, was the exact opposite of the positions the two commanders had been in during the Sicily campaign. At that time, both Bradley and Patton had been outraged over assignments they thought were insignificant. Now, however, Montgomery could not complain about a situation he had created.[88]

To add some firepower and aggressive leadership to the campaign, Eisenhower brought Patton and his new Third Army into action in Bradley's newly formed Army Group. By that time, the Allies had almost a million men in Normandy. Ike needed them to push forward quickly, get out of the seemingly endless hedgerows, and make full use in open country of his advantages in armor and airpower. Patton—despite all of his obvious flaws—was the general for that job. There was a big risk in trying to get Patton and Bradley to work together. Bradley had once served under Patton, and reversing those relationships could generate tensions even when two officers liked each other. In this case, Bradley had developed an intense hatred of Patton and his showmanship. Still, Eisenhower correctly calculated that Bradley would bite his tongue and play it by the book. The two generals would never be friends, but Ike thought they could work together.

But first they had to get untangled from the hedgerows. Artillery did not do the job. The Germans were too deeply dug into their positions. Bombing failed, as did frontal tank attacks, à la Kursk. Ike visited the front and sent a gloomy report to an impatient General Marshall: "The going," Ike said, "is extremely tough, with three main causes responsible. The first of these, as always, is the fighting quality of the German soldier. The second is the nature of the country. Our whole attack has to fight its way out of very narrow bottlenecks flanked by marshes and against an enemy who has a double hedgerow and an intervening ditch almost every fifty yards as ready-made strong points. The third cause is the weather. Our air has been unable to operate at maximum efficiency and on top of this the rain and mud were so bad during my visit that I was reminded of Tunisian wintertime."[89] Hoping to change the situation, Ike established tactical headquarters in Normandy.

Bradley was even more impatient than Eisenhower with his First Army's progress. He became impatient as well with his officers when they were unable to break the stalemate. They could not fall short in combat for any reason, and rain, mud and hedgerows were inadequate excuses. The turnover rate became high as Bradley and his army struggled to fight through German forces that proved just as effective defending the hedgerows of Normandy as they were in the mountains of Italy.[90] Eisenhower's D-Day warning—"Your enemy is well trained, well equipped and battle hardened. He will fight savagely"—proved all too true, and the First Army's losses mounted steadily.[91] Like Montgomery, Bradley was forced to delay his major offensive.

Instead of reflecting on a successful invasion and the decision he had made to launch the landings, Eisenhower was left fretting in July 1944 over a campaign that seemed locked in neutral.[92] His friend George Allen told him he was "the most popular idol of the world," but Eisenhower was not concerned about adulation.[93] He was worried because his forces had yet to break the back of Rundstedt's army. Eisenhower had not lost faith in Bradley and Patton. He had a clear and well-grounded concept of what General Montgomery's forces were likely to achieve in the weeks to follow. But what he did not have was assurance that his Normandy campaign would mark a critical turning point on the Western Front, the sort of decisive victory the Soviets had already won in the east.

Stalemated and frustrated, Eisenhower recognized that "now as never before opportunity is staring us in the face."[94] He hoped for "great results."[95] But as late as August 2, he and General Marshall were extremely nervous about the failure to achieve a breakout. Eisenhower reported, "We are attacking viciously in an effort to accomplish our purpose before the enemy can be successful in establishing new and strong lines." Still, Ike said, the battle was "raging" and he could not predict the outcome.[96]

Eight

Generals Eisenhower, Omar N. Bradley, and George S. Patton meet at Bastogne in 1944.

Tested Again

As late as August 2, 1944, it was still unclear whether Eisenhower, his commanders, and his ground and air forces were going to defeat the German divisions in France. Would attrition give way to a war of maneuver that would enable the Allies to sweep past Paris and drive the remaining German divisions back to the Rhine? On the surface, Eisenhower was optimistic—even about Monty's torturously slow progress toward the strategic rail center of Caen. But he was nervous enough to "forget" to keep Marshall and the Combined Chiefs of Staff well informed about the campaign. "My excuse," he wrote, "is that in my anxiety to push events the matter had merely slipped my mind."

Leaving aside the highly improbable possibility that General Marshall slipped Eisenhower's mind, we can nevertheless feel certain that Ike was experiencing anxiety. His report was stuffed with the vigor and movement the campaign lacked: They would "roll up the enemy forces." His ground commanders were in complete agreement about their strategy and tactics. They would "pin down and destroy" German units. They would "exploit rapidly to the southward into good tank country." They would "drive rapidly," "thrust forward," and "destroy the bulk of the German mobile forces."[1] The future tense abounded. The Supreme Commander's anxiety about his army's progress through the hedgerows had clearly overcome his penchant for precision in the written word.

All of those words could not change the reality that his offense was bogged down. "Over a stretch of such days," one infantryman said, "you became so dulled by fatigue that the names of the killed and wounded they checked off each night, the names of men who had been your best friends, might have come out of a telephone book for all you knew. All the old values were gone, and if there was a world beyond this tangle of hedgerows . . . where one barrage could lay out half a company like a giant's club, you never expected to live to see it."[2]

The war had become a study in contrasts. On the Western Front, the Allies' armies were struggling over yards of muddy ground. On the Eastern Front, the Soviet columns in the Baltic campaign were lopping off miles as they gave the German army little chance to settle into defensive positions. As the Soviets pushed toward Riga, Germany's Army Group North was in danger of complete collapse.[3]

Breakouts

Eisenhower, tense and troubled, did not have an opportunity to spend much time contemplating the Soviet campaigns. He was focused tightly on the grinding progress Bradley's army was making and on the weather in northern France. Bad weather periodically took away the Allies' major advantage in airpower, leaving Germany's armored units room to counter the offensive. Ike, now a more forceful and focused leader, brushed aside Churchill's repeated efforts to prevent the invasion of southern France. The war in the west, Eisenhower knew, was not going to be won in the Mediterranean. But it could be lost if the Allies spread themselves too thinly in the hedgerows.[4]

Suddenly, however, the strategy Ike and Marshall were defending was reaffirmed where it most counted—on the battlefields of France. General Bradley gave the Allied forces the breakthrough they had been struggling to achieve since D-Day.[5] Now the Supreme Commander's plan to bring General Patton—the American master of mobile warfare—into play looked all the more prescient. Ike had held an incredibly impatient Patton in England while the first stages of the landing took place and the war in the hedgerows inched forward. Patton had long been bitter about what he accurately perceived as Ike's willingness to accept British strategy and tactics in the North African, Sicilian, and Italian campaigns. Mollified to some extent by Eisenhower's support after the infamous slapping incident, Patton's critique of the Supreme Commander had blossomed again while he sat stewing in England, away from the action.[6] Bradley sometimes echoed these complaints about Ike's leadership.[7]

Eisenhower was, however, absolutely certain that in action Bradley as well as Patton would continue to provide the invasion force with strong, effective leadership. That would leave Ike the slack he needed to hold the Allied command tightly together, to ensure that every day the ground forces had the air support and the supplies and ammunition essential to a rapid advance, and to deal as effectively as possible with the brilliant, irrepressible General Charles de Gaulle.[8]

With a touch of cunning, Eisenhower could handle Patton and Bradley, but he was still not Machiavellian enough to manipulate de Gaulle. Having mastered the intricacies of French indecision in North Africa, Eisenhower was unprepared for the decisive, energetic advances of de Gaulle. Unlike Eisenhower—and, for that matter, President Roosevelt—de Gaulle was fixated on France's future and his role in shaping that future. His imperious manner and clever maneuvers left Ike longing for an ally who would be less demanding and less aggressive about those demands. Then, Ike thought, he could get on with the central task of winning the war in the west.

How far Eisenhower was from winning in France was emphasized when the Allies created and then botched a good chance to capture a significant number of German troops in the Falaise Gap. Ike was optimistic as Patton pushed forward, outflanking the Nazi forces blocking Montgomery's army.[9] Monty was consistent. He employed the methodical tactics he had used in Sicily.[10] Perhaps concerned to hold down British casualties, or perhaps just sticking to the approaches that had won him fame in North Africa, Monty left the gap open for the German retreat. Eisenhower was upset, but he chose not to change the Allied command structure at this crucial point in the campaign. He played by the book and quickly sent Bradley and Patton on a new mission, pushing toward the Seine and Paris.[11]

Now Patton's tanks began to move forward at a pace that resembled Soviet operations on the Eastern Front. Encouraged by their success, Eisenhower did all he could to feed them the fuel and ammunition they needed to remain on the assault across the Seine. He refused Montgomery's request to stop Patton's advance and concentrate his attack through Monty's Army of the North. This was the same type of request Ike had received from Montgomery in North Africa and Sicily. Both men were entirely consistent: Montgomery wanted everything, and Ike gave him a small part of what he wanted. Under pressure and running out of patience with Monty, Eisenhower continued to a remarkable degree to be the conciliator who kept patching the alliance together and pressing toward Germany. None of the commanders was happy and yet none was in open rebellion, which suggests that the compromise was close to optimal.[12] And all the while, Ike's hand was being strengthened by the mounting evidence that the British could no longer replace their losses.[13]

The New Order

On September 1, 1944, Eisenhower and the Combined Chiefs of Staff (CCS) made a fateful change in the command structure. Monty would no longer be the top ground commander. Eisenhower had finally taken back the role he had lost when he was sandbagged at Casablanca. With Ike leading, Montgomery now headed a strengthened Army Group of the North and Bradley a Central Group, which included Patton's Third Army. Bradley's large force would absorb General Jacob L. Devers's Seventh Army, which was pressing rapidly up from the south. The second invasion through the south of France was working just as Eisenhower and Marshall had planned. "Rapid" became the word of the day. Eisenhower used it five times in his message to his commanders, only once replacing it with "swiftly." For General Marshall and the other chiefs, he carefully catalogued enemy losses: "The equivalent of five Panzer divisions have been destroyed and a further six severely mauled, including one Panzer Grenadier division. The equivalent of twenty infantry divisions have been eliminated and a further twelve very badly cut up and have suffered severe losses." The German army had lost more than 200,000 prisoners of war and an equal number of soldiers killed or wounded. It was, Ike said, a "great victory." There were signs, he suggested, that Germany was "nearing collapse."[14]

To take full advantage of this promising situation, Eisenhower wanted to keep control of the air forces that had so far given his troops a decisive edge. He made it clear that those forces should include the Allied Expeditionary Air Force (for close tactical support) and, when needed, the US Strategic Air Force and Bomber Command, whose main task was attacking Germany's industry and oil supplies. He had fought hard to keep both of those air commands under his supreme authority. He was opposed to any changes, but not to the point of threatening resignation. The CCS responded by shaving one corner off his supremacy. They yielded to the continued pressure from the air commanders by pulling the strategic bombing units out of Eisenhower's control.[15] Ike grumbled. Even Supreme Commanders can get the blues. But he told Marshall, "I have calmed down everybody and I assure you that I can make the system work."[16]

By late September 1944, making the system work involved matters more mundane than the debate over strategic bombing. The question of whether the British and American bombers could by themselves force Germany to surrender would be settled in battle, without debate. Meanwhile, however, the Allied advance was running beyond the capacity of its supply lines to provide essential fuel and ammunition to the ground forces. "Our greatest difficulty at the moment," Ike explained to Marshall, "is maintenance. We have advanced so rapidly that further movement in large parts of the front even against very weak opposition is almost impossible. We are now concentrating on complete destruction of the enemy in Belgium while pushing the siege of Brest and thrusting out our flanks in the Moselle. The closer we get to the Siegfried Line the more we will be stretched administratively and eventually a period of relative inactivity will be imposed upon us."[17]

Inactivity was anathema to Patton and General Courtney Hodges (First Army), as well as General Bradley. Like Eisenhower, they were willing to gamble on their ability to squeeze supplies out of the existing network and push ahead to the Siegfried Line, Germany's last formidable defense.[18] Patton and General Hodges drove toward the Rhine but were forced to stop when their supplies ran out.[19] Despite serious counterattacks, Patton's men "captured about 9,000 prisoners and knocked out 270 tanks."[20] They failed, however, to push into Germany, to break the West Wall, and to open the way to Berlin.

Patton fumed over the stalemate, while Montgomery continued to badger Ike over authority in the ground war. Over and over Monty demanded all of the supplies and insisted that all of the other attacks had to be stopped to ensure that his 21st Army could launch a fierce attack straight through the Ruhr and on to Berlin. He also wanted the command structure returned to the one that had existed on D-Day. He would then depose Ike and take hold of all the ground forces. This was a fantasy— even more so because his army had failed to open the port at Antwerp that offered the only realistic chance to improve the supply situation. Nothing that Ike said or did mollified the British general; Monty was certain that his strategy was correct. But Eisenhower was now convinced that Montgomery's progress to the Rhine would be slow regardless of how much support he received.[21]

At this point in the campaign Ike's optimism faltered a bit as German resistance stiffened. The attempt in the north to use an airborne operation, Market Garden, to gain a bridgehead across the Rhine failed.[22] Insofar as Market Garden was also a cunning attempt to get Montgomery moving faster, it was a double failure. "From the outset," historian Carlo D'Este writes, "Market Garden was a prescription for trouble that was plagued by mistakes, oversights, false assumptions, and outright arrogance."[23] The airborne divisions landed successfully. But they encountered German forces that were more effective than they had anticipated. When the British armored units failed to link up with the troops landed by parachute and gliders, the Allied effort to force their way across the Rhine collapsed. All of the principals and a host of historians would argue over the responsibility for the failure, but the issue was actually very simple. By his own choice and the decision of his bosses, military and political, Ike was now the top ground commander. Whether he acknowledged it or not, he accrued every victory and every defeat—large or small. This included Market Garden.[24]

It was apparent by the end of September that there would probably be some more defeats and disappointments. Nazi Germany was not collapsing and the German army was still a well-trained, disciplined force. "We have a long ways to go here," Eisenhower wrote, "because of the intention of the enemy . . . to continue the most bitter kind of resistance up to the point of practical extermination of the last of his armed forces."[25] He worried about "a nasty little 'Kasserine' if the enemy chooses at any place to concentrate a bit of strength."[26] But his major concern was getting supplies moving so his forces in the north, center, and south could push ahead into Germany. He thought about the port at Antwerp constantly. Without supplies, the Allies were not ready for "the deep drive into Germany."[27]

When Eisenhower was not worrying about supplies or Monty's endless suggestions, he had a deskful of other problems to consider. He was forced to take note of the internal politics in France, including the role of the communists—subjects on which he had very little to say.[28] After the Quebec Conference (September 12–16, 1944), he also had to start thinking about the problems of the impending occupation, and he noted nervously that the proposed settlement had chipped away for the second time at some of his authority as Supreme Commander.[29] He began as well to think about actually meeting the Russian forces and avoiding problems.[30] And he worried that if Soviet pressure in the east was reduced, it might complicate his campaign.[31]

Stalin's Strategy

On August 17, a Soviet soldier planted a red battle flag on the German frontier in East Prussia, and Stalin's forces continued to chop at German strength all along the front.[32] Stalin never lost sight of his main goal: to envelop and grind down the Wehrmacht's divisions. Rail centers were important, as were roads and waterways. But the Soviet general staff and its sole leader focused throughout on the destruction of Germany's military forces in the east. By the fall of 1944, the Soviets calculated that they had eliminated ninety-six German divisions and twenty-four brigades.

They had killed or captured 1.5 million enemy soldiers. Rumania and Finland had been forced out of the war, and the Soviets were steadily pressing in on Budapest.[33] Between August and October, German casualties exceeded their replacements by nearly half a million. Like Britain—but more critically—Germany was simply running out of men.[34]

Still, there were 3 million troops and 4,000 tanks resisting the Soviet advance. Germany could bring at least 2,000 planes into combat in the east.[35] The Soviets recognized that the resistance in the northern wing of their advance through East Prussia would be especially fierce, so they looked to the south for a softer target. But here, too, the German army fought skillfully in retreat, and the front stabilized as the Soviet drive lost momentum. Stalin was impatient to reach the Nazi capital, but Marshal Georgy Zhukov convinced him that further attacks would yield only casualties.[36] Stalin had twice as many men and three times as many tanks as the Wehrmacht, but he nevertheless put his forces temporarily on the defensive. Along the entire front, the Red Army paused to rearm and regroup for what its leaders and certainly its soldiers hoped would be the final thrust into Germany.[37]

A Deadly Interlude

Ike, too, was regrouping and rearming in the West. The approaches to the vital port of Antwerp had finally been cleared of German defenders, and supplies of fuel and ammunition were beginning to be restored.[38] His November campaign had, however, ground along more slowly than he planned, and even General Patton, the master of mobility, was only creeping ahead—that is, when his Third Army was moving at all. Germany's West Wall held up as the weather worsened and tied down Allied air support. In early November 1944, Eisenhower's armies and the Soviets were an equal distance from Berlin, but it was already clear that neither would be able to defeat Germany that year. Their armies were at rest. The situation was so quiet that General Montgomery returned to England in mid-December to spend Christmas with his son.[39]

What neither Montgomery, Ike, Bradley, nor their intelligence officers knew was that Hitler had made a crucial decision that would shortly change their Christmas plans and the lives of many of their soldiers. Threatened in both the east and the west, Hitler and his generals had been forced to decide which front most needed support. The generals made the decision that Eisenhower and the CCS anticipated: Germany was most threatened from the east, and additional divisions were needed there to counter the next great Soviet offensive. The German staff anticipated an attack all across the front in December, and Colonel-General Heinz Guderian recommended an immediate move to counter the Soviet offensive.

But Hitler refused once again to accept the advice of his experienced generals. Instead, he wanted extra divisions in the west to mount an attack in force that could catch the Allies off guard, cut off Montgomery's army in the north, and stop the Allied offensive along Germany's West Wall. The Führer and Heinrich Himmler, commander of the SS and the Replacement Army, predicted that the Soviets would not attack in force. Germany had time, they thought, and could move troops back after their anticipated success against the Allies. For the present, Hitler decided to pull twenty-five divisions into his latest and wildest plan to save the Third Reich.[40]

On December 16, the German army struck in the Ardennes and set out to split the Allies, retake Antwerp, and deal a deadly blow to Eisenhower's forces. Ike, the ground commander, was surprised by the size of the attack. There had been an inkling of evidence when German divisions moved to the west from the Hungarian and East Prussian fronts. But Eisenhower was optimistic about the strength of his Allied force—as many as eighty-seven divisions and 6,000 tanks—and was convinced that the "enemy is badly stretched on this front."[41] He might as well have been talking about his own forces, which were aligned across a broad front and spread very thinly across the Ardennes.[42]

When the Nazi forces struck, Eisenhower tried to set in motion flanking attacks from both sides of the German salient. What he first saw as a "rather ambitious counterattack" had become by December 18 "a major thrust through the Ardennes."[43] Ike brought Patton, master of the unplanned battle, into play from the south, driving his Third Army toward the vital crossroads at Bastogne. There the 101st Airborne Division and a scattering of other units held their ground, surrounded by the enemy. Moving with unusual speed, Patton swung into an attack on the German flank with three divisions. When the skies cleared on December 23–24, air raids on the German armor weakened their advance, and Patton's 4th Armored Division reached Bastogne on the twenty-sixth.[44]

Eisenhower's original concept of the Allied response in the Ardennes involved an envelopment of the Nazi forces, with Montgomery's 21st Army pressing down from the north of the salient. To facilitate that part of the campaign, he gave Monty authority over the American forces operating on his side of the German offensive. Once again, however, Ike was disappointed with the outcome. As in Sicily, as at Caen and the Falaise Gap, Monty was slow to move, always preparing but never pressing with the urgency that Eisenhower sought.[45] If the Supreme Commander needed further evidence to support his decision to mount two major drives against Germany instead of concentrating only on Montgomery's northern offensive, the battles of December 1945 provided Ike with everything he needed to know. He could not, of course, frame the issue in public in those personal terms. Monty was Britain's national hero. Ike still had to do everything he could to hold the alliance together, as he had from the beginning of his service as Supreme Commander. He continued to nudge Montgomery, as he had before, about taking the port at Antwerp.[46] But the British field marshal was not a man to be eased out of his deeply planted habits of mind and command.

Ike's smooth exterior and conciliatory approach to leadership were now about to crack. The Supreme Commander's patience had limits, and he had grown tougher about those limits as the war progressed. Neither Bradley nor Montgomery was able to deliver the crushing blow Ike had hoped for. As the front stabilized, the "Bulge" was still there. So was Monty's constant badgering. Unable to let go of the issue, Monty sent yet another message to Eisenhower proposing that he command both his 21st Army Group and Bradley's 12th Army Group. The tone of the message was almost as infuriating as the content, and Ike finally exploded. He prepared to take the issue to the CCS and, in effect, give his bosses the choice between Montgomery and himself. Only the intervention of

Montgomery's talented chief of staff kept the two leaders in their respective positions.[47] Montgomery apologized and backed down. But the issue did not evaporate. It would hang over the campaign and the histories of the war like a deadly industrial smog. British arguments in the CCS kept the question alive, but Ike remained securely in control of a campaign that would shortly continue on a broad front.[48]

The assault from the west now, for the first time, was running into the same sort of manpower shortages that the British and Germans had been facing for many months. Replacement troops were not always available. Eisenhower began to look nervously to his own soldiers in noncombatant positions: he proposed an "immediate and drastic comb-out here of able bodied men." He scrounged off an Italian campaign that appeared to be going nowhere, and he looked to France, Poland, and Belgium. He also sought volunteers among the more than 100,000 African Americans doing "back-breaking manual work" for the armed forces on the "docks, in depots and on roads." He said that "in existing circumstances I cannot deny the Negro volunteer a chance to serve in battle."[49] Many did.

The End Game

Nervous about his sluggish campaign and the intensity of German resistance, Ike gazed to the east with an aroused interest. Panzer units could move rather quickly between the Eastern and Western Fronts, and he longed for a new Soviet offensive that would, he reasoned, cut down the flow of German soldiers away from the Oder River and westward toward the Rhine. He now thought it was "essential" to know if a Soviet offensive was in the works and, if so, when it would start. He sought coordination with an associated power he tended to consider a virtual ally.[50] After consulting with Marshall and the CCS, Eisenhower established a liaison with the Soviets and wrote his first message to Joseph Vissarionovich Stalin, a leader who would have a dramatic impact on Ike's career.[51]

That impact suddenly took a new form on January 12, 1945. Following plans that had been set since November 1944, the Soviet offensive that Hitler had discounted as a bluff began with massive force, concentrated now across a shortened front. Along the Warsaw-Berlin axis, Stalin and the Stavka had concentrated 163 infantry divisions and more than 6,000 tanks. With a five-fold advantage in manpower and armor, the Soviets drove relentlessly toward the Oder River and the German frontier.[52] The entire Eastern Front, from the Baltic through Hungary, was under assault by the Red Army, and the Wehrmacht no longer had sufficient forces to resist the attack. The campaign was so massive that coordination proved as serious a problem for the Soviets as it was for Eisenhower and Bradley in the Ardennes.

At first there appeared to be no problems with the Soviet advance, which exceeded Stalin's expectations. The Soviet tank and infantry forces, preceded by awesome artillery barrages, pressed forward rapidly across the Vistula River. Driving hard toward the German border, Marshal Zhukov's assaults quickly penetrated the German defenses, pressing twenty miles forward in a day. As Eisenhower had anticipated, he benefited from the advance when Hitler began to move units back from the west to the east. Stalin also benefited when the Führer inexplicably moved the most powerful panzer army to the defense of Hungary, leaving the center of the front weakened. By late January, the Soviets were attacking on the German frontier.

Outgunned and outmanned, a German army that seemed close to collapse nevertheless continued the type of fierce counterattacks that all of the generals of the Allies and associated powers, Eisenhower included, had learned to respect. Now, however, the counterattacks no longer achieved their objectives. By the end of January, Soviet forces were slightly less than fifty miles from Berlin. Ahead of schedule, they had outrun their supplies of both fuel and ammunition. Their forces were worn down by the rapid advance and losses in battle. Soviet manpower for replacements was at last becoming a problem. Marshal Zhukov and Marshal Ivan Konev had to stop, consolidate their positions, and rearm their forces. Stalin grew cautious, concerned that Germany might launch an attack like the one dealt to the Allies in the Ardennes.

The first major counterattack came in Hungary in mid-February, as did a fierce stroke on Zhukov's exposed northern flank. Fighting desperately for the defense of their homeland and people, the German panzers cut deeply into the Soviet forces. But, lacking the element of surprise and weakened by the long grinding Soviet offensive, the counterattacks were soon slowed and then stopped with frightful losses on both sides. It was now evident that Germany could no longer effectively resist on the Eastern Front.

To the west as well, the German army was frayed and weakened. Threatened by encirclement, the German forces in the Ardennes had withdrawn after delaying the Allied offensive by about six weeks.[53] Ike was pleased to see the Eastern and Western Fronts now developing in unison. If the Russian offensive was "strong and sustained" and the weather was good, he told Marshall, he thought his armies could defeat the enemy without additional troops. He "would be justified in expecting quick success only after we have closed the Rhine throughout its length, concentrated heavily in the north and staged a definite supporting secondary attack somewhere to the south of the Ruhr." He needed "the ability to maneuver. For example, the ability to advance also on Frankfurt and Kassel, rather than to rely on one thrust in the north."[54]

News of Soviet success encouraged Ike to speed up his campaign to breach the Rhine in the north. At first Montgomery's attack moved ahead quickly.[55] But Bradley's First Army moved even faster after capturing a railway bridge intact at Remagen and pushing a substantial force across the river.[56] As Patton pressed forward with infantry and armor, he was able to breach the West Wall and continue his characteristic rapid advance.[57] He crossed the Rhine in a surprise attack on March 22.[58] Eisenhower reported to the CCS that although he was "continuing to plan for and to be ready to meet stern resistance, it is my personal belief that the enemy strength on the Western Front is becoming so stretched that penetrations and advances will soon be limited only by our own maintenance."[59] Eisenhower was justified in pausing at this point to reflect with satisfaction on the accomplishments of the broad front strategy he had promoted, defended, and was now bringing to a successful conclusion.[60]

Following his breakthrough in the center, Ike pushed forward with what he knew was the final campaign for his Allied armies.[61] He informed Montgomery—who had advanced across the Rhine in the north—that he was returning the American Ninth Army to the control of Bradley, who would make the major thrust into Germany.[62] Eisenhower's decision—his own Machiavellian moment, reminiscent of his encounter with MacArthur in the Philippines—brought down a new hailstorm of British protests But to no avail. Neither Montgomery, nor Brooke, nor even Churchill could persuade Eisenhower to change his strategy.[63] Already the leading American hero of World War II, he was now truly supreme.[64]

Even in that lofty position, he continued to have problems that could not be solved. One of them involved the Eastern Front. He had opened communications with the Soviets and had informed Stalin that the Allied drive into Germany would point toward Leipzig, not Berlin.[65] Stalin had replied that his armies were also driving toward the center and not the German capital. But he was lying. He was lying both about the timing and about the objectives of the next Soviet campaign. He approved the plans for an early Soviet push to Berlin on the same day he sent his message to Eisenhower.[66] This was the first serious lesson Ike had in dealing with Stalin and his Soviet government, and there is no evidence that he ever forgot what he learned.[67] One could date Eisenhower's experience with the Cold War from this exchange and the Allied rush to seize the German rocket bases before they fell to the Soviets.

For Ike, these long-term strategic considerations were still less important than the final victory over Germany. The zones of occupation had already been staked out, and he was fully prepared for a peaceful meeting between his Allied armies moving east and the Soviets moving west. Patton had advanced rapidly after crossing the Rhine, splitting the German defenses.[68] There was no possibility that Ike would abandon his strategic plan for a race with the Soviets to reach Berlin. He had made his position clear: "That place has become, so far as I am concerned, nothing but a geographical location, and I have never been interested in these. My purpose is to destroy the enemy's forces and his powers to resist." To the CCS he explained, "Berlin as a strategic area is discounted as it is now largely destroyed and we have information that the ministries are moving to the Erfurt-Leipzig region. Moreover, it is so near to the Russian front that once they start moving again they will reach it in a matter of days."[69]

Ike was now concerned about evidence of "Soviet suspicion on this question of zones of occupation." He wanted to avoid any misunderstandings as their forces met in Germany. He wanted *"firm prior"* agreements on these issues.[70] In the meantime, he continued to give the Soviets accurate reports on his operations through the military mission to Moscow.[71] The anticipated meetings took place, without incident, on April 25; indeed, the Soviets came prepared to bestow decorations on their American counterparts.[72] By May 4, the Supreme Commander had the firm agreement he sought from the Soviets, who had followed Stalin's plan and already entered Berlin.[73]

German resistance ended on May 7, 1945, when Eisenhower received the surrender of all German forces on behalf of the Allies and their associated powers. Ike was formal but brisk and unyielding. His respect for German military prowess had morphed into bitter hatred for the Nazi regime and all those who supported it. He could never forgive the officers who had ordered the slaughter of American prisoners of war in the Ardennes. Nor could he forget the horrors he had encountered in his visit to a German concentration camp.[74] Earlier, in Italy, he had questioned the policy of unconditional surrender, but in Germany he implemented it with relentless vigor.

At last his authority was unchallenged, but his responsibilities had actually multiplied as the Allies swept toward victory. There were more and more populations to feed, more trouble over occupation zones, more undisciplined soldiers and officers to create problems.[75] Supplies were short and shipping continued to be a bottleneck. There was still a war to be won in the Pacific, but now he could, ever so briefly, enjoy the great victory in Europe.

Invited to speak in London at the Guildhall on June 12, 1945, Eisenhower gave an address that said a great deal about the quality of his leadership and the quality of the man. He had just received the Freedom of the City of London from Lord Mayor Sir Frank Alexander. Speaking before Prime Minister Winston Churchill and his cabinet, Eisenhower praised the accomplishments and lamented the sacrifices of those who had served under his command:

Humility must always be the portion of any man who receives acclaim earned in blood of his followers and sacrifices of his friends.

Conceivably a commander may have been professionally superior. He may have given everything of his heart and mind to meet the spiritual and physical needs of his comrades. He may have written a chapter that will glow forever in the pages of military history.

Still, even such a man—if he existed—would sadly face the facts that his honors cannot hide in his memories the crosses marking the resting places of the dead. They cannot soothe the anguish of the widow or the orphan whose husband or father will not return.

The only attitude in which a commander may with satisfaction receive the tributes of his friends is in the humble acknowledgment that no matter how unworthy he may be, his position is the symbol of great human forces that have labored arduously and successfully for a righteous cause. Unless he feels this symbolism and this rightness in what he has tried to do, then he is disregardful of [the] courage, fortitude, and devotion of the vast multitudes he has been honored to command. If all Allied men and women that have served with me in this war can only know that it is they whom this august body is really honoring today, then indeed I will be content. . . .

No petty differences in the world of trade, traditions, or national pride should ever blind us to our identities in priceless values.

If we keep our eyes on this guidepost, then no difficulties along our path of mutual co-operation can ever be insurmountable. Moreover, when this truth has permeated to the remotest hamlet and heart of all peoples, then indeed may we beat our swords into plowshares and all nations can enjoy the fruitfulness of the earth.[76]

For a moment in history, Europe and Ike could contemplate truth, peace, and fruitfulness. But in the years to follow, that moment would fade, and swords as well as plowshares would continue to be Dwight David Eisenhower's central concerns.

Part III

Becoming the Leader of the Free World

Nine

A Republican poster from the 1952 presidential election. Courtesy of the Library of Congress.

Duty, Honor, Party

In 1943, in the midst of the brutal, slow-moving Italian campaign, Ike began to hear stories about his great potential for political office. He could be president of the United States. Or maybe vice president, serving with FDR. By D-Day he was an American hero, and after the German surrender he was *the* leading American military hero of World War II. As his reputation soared, Eisenhower heard over and over and over again that he should seek high office in America. His efforts to dissuade his admirers were unsuccessful. He had a war to win, and he was consistent and determined in denying political ambitions. But the thought had been planted and would not go away. His admirers made certain of that.

By the summer of 1945, of course, he had more to worry about than political entanglements at home. As the military governor of the US Occupied Zone of Germany, he had all the political entanglements he could stand in western Europe. He had millions to feed and too few ships to supply the food and fuel that were needed immediately. There were survivors of the Holocaust to be taken care of and survivors of Nazi occupations to be helped. He had to find a means of dealing with the black markets that quickly developed in areas where commodities and currency were scarce. He had suddenly been transformed from a military officer into a political leader, and he quickly discovered that the unity inspired by the war against Germany would not carry into the postwar settlements.

He had to move the Allies into their zones of occupation and be certain the three zones were transformed, quickly, into working units of government. He had to establish a new team because many of his experienced officers were sent to the Pacific to finish the conquest of Japan. Others were sent home in honor of their service in the war. His enlisted men were also eager to leave Europe and get home to their loved ones. Families quickly began to turn up the heat on the nation's political leaders to bring the soldiers home and integrate them into civilian life as soon as possible. Initially, however, Ike did not even have all the ships he needed to transport troops being discharged from the army.

While he continued to enjoy a good working relationship with the British, the French promptly began to create problems for Eisenhower. They were initially upset with the zone of occupation carved out for them. Their pride hurt by France's minor role in the great victory, they sought retribution from Germany in matters large and small. Eisenhower had to juggle their requests while doing his best to see that he was not starving any civilians, even those whom the Allies and the Soviets had just conquered.

At first Ike approached the Russians as comrades in arms. He got along well with Marshal Zhukov, who had emerged as the Soviet's leading general by the end of the war. Eisenhower admired what Zhukov and his armies had achieved, and he wanted American soldiers to get along better with the Soviet troops: "I hope that we can do something toward indoctrinating our own people so that they may understand something of what the Russians have been through. They have not had our great advantages in sanitation, education and, of course, there is always the great language bar to real social contact. But the Russians have contributed mightily to the winning of this war. They have produced good soldiers and brilliant generals and, moreover, they are naturally a friendly race."[1]

Eisenhower hoped—as had President Roosevelt and to some extent Prime Minister Churchill—that good personal relationships between leaders and followers would be translated into good working relationships on the ground. Ike visited and was honored in Moscow in August 1945.

But when he attempted for a second time to cooperate with the Soviets in an even-handed way, he soon began to learn the limits of personal relations where national interests and deep-set ideologies were concerned. The Soviets were determined to exact revenge on the Nazis, to weaken German industry, to rebuild the Soviet economy, and to position the Soviet empire for the ultimate victory over capitalism that Marx and Lenin had foretold.

Like most Americans, Eisenhower was slow to acknowledge the full measure of Stalin's intentions in Europe. He continued to refer to the people as Russians, not Soviets. His optimism was understandable. The surrender had gone relatively smoothly. The Soviets were, quite reasonably, concerned when entire German units rushed away from the Red Army in order to surrender on the Western Front. The Soviets had also been worried about Germany signing a separate truce with Eisenhower's forces. But Ike adhered strictly to his political guidelines, and the two armies met without further problems.

Soon, however, there were difficulties in Yugoslavia, more questions about the Soviet unwillingness to exchange information, and ripples over the occupation of Czechoslovakia. Ike's visits to Czechoslovakia, Poland, Belgium, Holland, Italy, and France left him pondering why "all of these countries are very much afraid of Russian intentions."[2] In these regards, he still had a touch of Abilene in his outlook on the world, but that would soon give way to a new brand of realism about US-Soviet relations. He was willing to send a supportive message to the National Council for American-Soviet Friendship, but Eisenhower's "friendship" was clearly under pressure in Europe.[3]

He nevertheless left Europe to take over his new responsibilities as General Marshall's replacement as the army's Chief of Staff, still hoping that the United States and the Soviet Union would find a way to maintain peaceful relations. He was nervous about "our complete ignorance of what is going on in Russia and [Soviet-]occupied Germany."[4] But after Stalin backed down and removed his troops from Czechoslovakia, Eisenhower left Europe believing that, as Chief of Staff, he would be the leader of what would continue to be a peacetime US Army.

Chief of Staff

There was little that he needed to learn about his duties as Chief of Staff of the United States Army. But he did have to shift from being Supreme Commander of an Allied force with a single overriding goal to being top commander of a single service with many goals. That office made him the army's strategist, administrator, advocate, and head lobbyist. But Eisenhower was not interested in those last two jobs. He never became a single-minded advocate for his service. His experience in Europe and the example of General Marshall helped him keep the national interest at the top of his list of priorities now that he was one among equals on the Joint Chiefs of Staff. His responsibilities were broad, but his years with General MacArthur had left him with a long list of specific things the army's leader should do and not do. He knew, for instance, that he had to keep the army out of the kind of embarrassing conflict he had experienced when the Bonus Army marched into Washington, DC, in the 1930s.

There was potential for embarrassment as the Bring Back Daddy organization pressed a highly vocal campaign to get as many American soldiers as possible out of uniform and at home. Eisenhower reminded the public that the army still had worldwide responsibilities. In spite of his gentle message, the furor continued for a time before the discharges undercut the cause. Through the entire media episode, Ike managed to keep his public reputation intact. He had learned in Europe that at times it is what you do not say that works to your political advantage. His repeated efforts to muzzle his explosive friend Patton and his dealings with the British press had stamped home a lesson that helped ease him through the demobilization controversies.

There were now much bigger issues on his plate: atomic weapons, rockets, and the potential threat posed by an aggressive Soviet empire. He was still trying to maintain friendly relations with Marshal Zhukov. But the pressure of Soviet expansion could not be ignored. As early as January 1946, war plans were under discussion.[5] The Soviets were aggressively pressuring German scientists and engineers to move to the Soviet zone of occupation in Germany.[6] There were problems in a divided Korea.[7] And there was at least one war scare in the United States, in March 1946. But Ike tossed cold water on FBI director J. Edgar Hoover's panic about the news that the USSR's ships were all suddenly clearing American harbors.[8] Eisenhower demanded firm evidence of a Soviet military buildup behind the lines in Europe. Of course the evidence did not exist, and the issue disappeared. Nevertheless, by this time his goodwill toward the "Russians" was giving way to concerns about what the "Reds" were going to do next.[9]

Eisenhower was not a belligerent Cold War warrior. He had seen too many young men die in combat already. But he now clearly understood that the USSR had long-term goals that were a threat to America, its democratic system, and its most important allies. Limited by the reduced manpower of the army, Eisenhower was nevertheless still thinking in terms of a traditional war along the lines of World War II.[10] He was optimistic about the capability of the US forces currently in Europe, but he thought the government should be preparing the American people to understand the tense situation the Soviet Union was creating.[11] Firmly convinced that America's "self-interests can be served only by a long period of peace," Eisenhower was determined to find means short of war for handling the Soviet pressure.[12]

Essential to the peace, he thought, was the unity of the Anglo-American alliance. He had struggled to preserve a united front through four years of war and endless bickering on both sides. Unity would be no less important, he reasoned, in the years ahead and in particular in the resistance to Soviet aggression. In September and October 1946 he revisited Europe in part to energize the alliance that had survived the end of the war and a British Labour government that was less suspicious of Stalin's plans than Churchill had been.[13]

Gradually Eisenhower developed a long-term Cold War strategy. He decided that atomic weapons would certainly be used to resist a Soviet attack.[14] He was relatively quick to respond to technological changes that had important military implications: born in an age of horses and buggies, he had learned to respect and understand the new technologies that were rapidly changing America and the rest of the developed world. If nations were so foolish as to allow a third world war to take place, he realized, it would not feature the trench warfare of World War I or the mass tank attacks of World War II. In the new age of rockets and atomic (and then nuclear) weapons, military tactics and strategy had to change. Above all, he wanted to avoid situations that might lead to that dreadful outcome. He was convinced, for instance, that a radical approach to US national security might well provoke the Soviets to fear America's "offensive intent."

Overestimating the enemy, he said, "may reduce our own capability of developing that economic strength of the US and other free nations which might constitute the more effective deterrent to Soviet and Communist expansion." He sought "emphasis on strengthening the economic and social dikes against Soviet communism rather than upon preparing for a possibly eventual, but not yet inevitable, war."[15] In the wake of the 1947 Truman Doctrine, which extended US aid to Greece and Turkey, Eisenhower became more negative about Soviet intentions. Still, he was restrained: "Although we must never lose sight of the constant threat implicit in Soviet political, economic and military aggression, we must remember also that Russia has a healthy respect for the power this nation can generate."[16]

That power, he reasoned, would be multiplied by unity. Through his stint as Chief of Staff, he tried never to press for policies or programs that favored the army over the other two services. Months of hard struggle over strategy, missions, and resources did not break his determination to stick to his version of an ideal national security plan for the Joint Chiefs of Staff. His political gyroscope continued to be oriented to the national interest, not the parochial interests of the army. He was dismayed by the fact that interservice rivalry blocked his efforts to achieve the unity he had worked to create in Europe during the war.[17] The battles of the budget, however, brought out the worst sort of rivalry between the services. He ended his three years as Chief of Staff lamenting that the Joint Chiefs had become "little more than an agency for eliminating from proposals and projects inconsequential and minor differences—a body of 'fly speckers.'"[18]

What he had finished was a thoroughgoing lesson in interest-group politics.[19] It was a bitter lesson for Ike. He still found it difficult to ac-

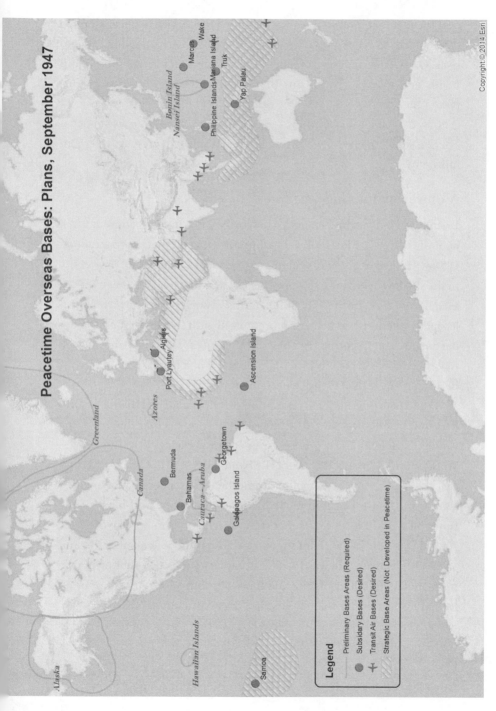

Peacetime Overseas Bases: Plans, September 1947

Alaska

Greenland

Canada

Bermuda

Bahamas

Curacao – Aruba

Georgetown

Galapagos Island

Hawaiian Islands

Samoa

Azores

Port Lyautey

Algiers

Ascension Island

Bonin Island

Nansei Island

Marcus

Wake

Philippine IslandsMariana Island

Truk

Yap Palau

Legend

- Preliminary Bases Areas (Required)
- ● Subsidary Bases (Desired)
- ✈ Transit Air Bases (Desired)
- ▨ Strategic Base Areas (Not Developed in Peacetime)

Copyright© 2014 Esri

Source: *The Papers of Dwight David Eisenhower: The Chief of Staff IX*, p. 2297. Map by James E. Gillispie, Curator of Maps at Johns Hopkins University.

cept the fact that interest groups—including the services—never stopped their efforts to reshape public policy to favor their immediate objectives. Once a decision was reached, Ike thought, all parties should join hands and move forward. But that was not the way interest groups played the game of politics. This central aspect of America's twentieth-century democracy aroused his temper. He continued to brood about it after he set forth on a new venture as the president of a great American university.

A University Interlude

Eisenhower had begun his service in North Africa in the shadow of Chief of Staff George C. Marshall. He had finally escaped that comparison on D-Day. He would begin his tenure as president of Columbia University in the shadow of Nicholas Murray Butler, who had been president of the school from 1902 until 1945. Butler, a marvelously energetic former philosophy professor, had been deeply engaged with the disciplines, the departments, and the ordinary affairs of Columbia. He found time as well to write, dabble in Republican politics, and win a Nobel Peace Prize for his leadership of the US peace movement.

While Ike's international reputation certainly matched that of his predecessor, Eisenhower had little interest in the intellectual content of the various disciplines and no interest whatsoever in their political squabbles. Working with Thomas Watson of IBM and the rest of the Board of Trustees, Ike made some attempts to strengthen the school's endowment.[20] But he was not a talented or dedicated fund-raiser, and most of the funds he brought in were to support the special programs he favored. He started this new job with an inappropriate vision of academic life and an ill-chosen team. He was too conservative for a faculty that primarily resonated to liberal ideologies and for a city with a long history of intellectual leadership on the left side of American political discourse. Ike was not just a fish out of water. He was a fish that was going to be fried in the political debates and gossip that raged around the university at Morningside Heights. Nothing in Eisenhower's experiences had prepared him for the leadership of this institution at this time.[21]

He did not, however, lack determination. Nor was he inflexible. He tried for months to provide Columbia University with the kind of leadership that had served him and the Allies well in Europe and Washington. He was most effective in dealing with the university's Board of Trustees. They trusted him, liked him, and helped him solve some of the school's worst economic problems. He was also able to muster support for two of his pet undertakings: the Conservation of Human Resources Project, which stemmed from his concern with America's problems in providing manpower during the war,[22] and the American Assembly, which was supposed to give the nation a new brand of intellectual discussion and orientation.[23] Civil debate, Eisenhower reasoned, would help Columbia and the United States avoid the types of intense conflicts that were tearing apart many of the postcolonial nations.

What Ike's brand of leadership could not provide to the university, however, was a set of common goals that would appeal to and draw together the faculty and students. The disciplines, each of which had its own goals, methodologies, cultures, and leaders, worked against unity of the sort that Ike sought. They were in most regards just like the interest groups that provoked his ire in Washington. For many faculty members it was dangerous to even think about intellectual consensus and a common purpose. If you were dedicated to transforming America's brand of democratic capitalism into an entirely different system—as some faculty members were—the Eisenhower brand of compromise and conciliation was simply a surrender to the already powerful individuals and organizations that had long been the ruin of America.

Ike was in a trap. His situation got worse rather than better as he heeded once again the call to national duty. The disunity that had dismayed him as Chief of Staff had grown worse, and the secretary of defense, James Forrestal, asked President Truman to appoint Eisenhower as informal chairman of the Joint Chiefs in an effort to achieve a workable truce over the budget. "The talents of Ike," Forrestal wrote, "in terms of the identification of problems and the accommodation of differing views, would be highly useful. . . . Specifically, what I had in mind was inviting him to come down, only with your approval, of course, to sit with us for a period of three or four weeks. I should like, if it were possible, to have him named by you for that interim period, and to preside over the Joint Chiefs, but if that were impossible an informal basis would be second best."[24]

Shocked by the Soviet blockade of Berlin a few months earlier, Eisenhower had already committed himself: "I believe that the time has come when everyone must begin to think in terms of his possible future duty and be as fully prepared for its performance as possible."[25] Although he was still president of Columbia University, his trips to Washington began at once. As Ike quickly discovered, however, neither he nor the secretary of defense—nor, for that matter, President Truman—had the authority to force the services to cooperate, to agree on strategy, or even to line up behind a single budget. "All have found it easy to run to congress & public with personal ideas & convictions," he recorded in his diary. "We will not have unification until the Sec. of Def. is made very powerful—power to appoint & fire, among other things!"[26] Persuasion failed. The threat of a national "disaster" did not faze the leaders of the services. This was the type of classic interest-group struggle that could and frequently did lock down American government and foster justified criticism of democracy.

Eisenhower retained his faith in the American version of democracy, but his struggles in Washington during these years left him bitterly opposed to certain basic features of twentieth-century American politics. He was bitter enough to be willing to return to active service if it was necessary to untangle and reorient the Joint Chiefs of Staff. He was not naive in that regard. But he wanted very badly to give the country a government that stressed the national interest and that placed specific, overriding constraints on the military services. He thought in 1948 and 1949 that the United States was unnecessarily endangering its national security in the Cold War because it lacked a strong commitment to compromise and cooperation at all levels of government. He emerged from his brief career as informal head of the Joint Chiefs with some new ideas about America's defense and about the lobbying groups—service and otherwise—that swarmed Washington.[27]

He continued to fume about the situation in Washington, while quietly building up the team of businessmen who would support his political career—when and if the opportunity arose. He was now sufficiently Machiavellian to push that project forward while vigorously denying any political ambitions. The telling evidence was his repeated refusal to remove himself once and for all from the field of contenders for the presidency of the United States. He did not want to be sandbagged again. He did not want to become a politician. But he wanted to be president.[28] So he worked with a network of Republican friends and political advisors who were just as calculating as he was about the odds that he would someday be living in the White House. Accustomed as some of his close friends were to betting large sums on the turn of a card, they were not men to waste their time on obvious losers. They saw a bright future for Eisenhower, a future beyond military service and well beyond Columbia University. They turned out to be just as shrewd about politics as they were about business.

Before that bright Republican future could unfold, however, Ike was pulled away to answer yet another call to military duty in Europe and Washington during a severe Cold War crisis. In June 1950, communist North Korea had attacked America's ally, South Korea, and President Truman and the United Nations responded quickly and forcefully. US air, sea, and ground forces joined the battle. In western Europe, increasing tension between the USSR and the West had prompted the creation of a new alliance, the North Atlantic Treaty Organization (NATO). While the United States joined the alliance, the American people were seriously divided—as was Congress—about this new entanglement in European affairs. Two world wars had left many Americans wary of involvement and, like most Europeans, weary of war.[29] It would be no simple job to weld together an American and European force that could realistically stand against the powerful land forces and airpower of the Soviet Union. President Truman sent Eisenhower to guide damage control on the all-important European front.

NATO

As Supreme Allied Commander, Europe (SACEUR), for NATO, Eisenhower took on a task that played to his great strengths as a leader. His abiding vision of unity and his conciliatory approach to authority meshed perfectly with NATO's goals. The reputation he had earned in the defeat of European fascism made him the ideal spokesman for the new alliance. Unlike his appointment at Columbia University, he took on this new job with a clear vision of what should be accomplished and how, exactly, it could be done. Everything in his career had prepared him to build a NATO force, develop a realistic strategy, and persuade his commanders and their men and women to devote their energies to the common cause. He was a unifier, and NATO badly needed unity.

Lost lives in World War II, lost money, and lost determination all deeply undercut the effort to unify and rearm the West. One essential part of Eisenhower's task was to encourage the NATO nations to provide the forces and equipment that would be needed if they were to create a realistic defense force. "This whole problem," he wrote, "dissolves itself into one of morale, and there is going to be a lot of skillful and energetic work take place before there will begin to develop a morale that will be effective in these troublesome times."[30] He launched that effort with a quick tour of eleven nations in January 1951.[31] Everything that he had learned about leadership between the North African landings and the German surrender quickly came into play. He was optimistic in the face of massive pessimism. He was well organized and precise in confronting disorganization and fear. He inspired cooperation at a time when each of the new allies was still struggling with its own particular postwar economic and political problems. It was Eisenhower at his best.

After returning to the United States and reporting on his trip, Eisenhower and Mamie settled in France for this next tour of duty. NATO headquarters were in Paris, and while there Eisenhower began slowly and sometimes awkwardly to build a core team around his close friend and chief of staff, General Alfred Maximilian Gruenther. He and Gruenther were the puzzle masters as they pulled together a staff that could both salve national feelings and get the job done.[32] They had to put up with a good bit of what Ike called "balderdash."[33] His forceful rhetoric was (as it had been in Normandy) applied to situations characterized more by stasis than strength: they had to clear away the "underbrush," he said, and get along with the "real business of chopping wood."[34]

By the spring of 1951, he and Gruenther had laid by a good pile of wood. They had the team they needed and the general outlines of the military organization they would create.[35] Morale in Europe seemed to be improving, and Eisenhower saw considerable potential in the new NATO Defense College for building up "common doctrine" among the forces in the alliance.[36] Solidarity, he knew, would not grow organically: "It will not develop among peoples unless their leaders take constant and positive action. . . . So . . . a constant concern of leadership should be to see that differing national attitudes and policies toward Iran or Indo China, or Korea or India, or any other subject, do not become such bitter issues between NATO nations that we tend to fall apart. The Soviets will certainly not fail to give us enough opportunities to make this mistake."[37]

The Soviets certainly did. And the great Allied victors of World War II frequently resembled newlyweds as they squabbled over money, pride, bureaucratic fumbles, and security classifications.[38] Eisenhower worried that the nations of western Europe would be unable to muster an adequate defense force without first achieving greater unity as a "U.S. of Europe."[39] Unity was elusive, however, as the allies struggled over what to do about Germany. For Eisenhower, this was a decisive issue. NATO—he repeated again and again—needed German economic and military support if it was going to provide a bulwark against expansion of the Soviet empire. To his diary he said, "As of this moment, we ought to be showing Germany how definitely her national interests will be served by sticking and working with *us*!"[40] As always with Ike, the French were a problem. Despairing and reaching for a "spectacular accomplishment," he supported the creation of a European army. He hoped that "some very plain down-to-earth talks" might ease the French toward the European "amalgamation" he sought.[41]

By the fall of 1951, Eisenhower's headquarters had "established a practical command framework, integrated the forces which have already been committed to the Allied Command, initiated necessary training programs, and coordinated such defense plans as could possibly be executed with the limited forces within sight at present."[42] Much remained to be done. Even the US military had yet to accommodate to a NATO-led, transnational defense strategy for Europe, and Eisenhower found it necessary to rebuke the Joint Chiefs over war plans that were entirely US-centric.[43] It was still unclear whether a British intelligence officer serving in NATO would, in fact, have access to all of America's intelligence information. In practice, national frontiers and policies were more rigid than the theory of the NATO alliance presupposed.[44]

In western Europe, the economic situation always dictated delay.[45] The Dutch, the French, the Danes, and the British were all having financial difficulties supporting rearmament for the NATO defenses.[46] The move toward greater European political and economic unity gave Eisenhower hope that the favorable economic results from consolidation would soon create an environment conducive to military progress. But as late as the end of 1951, he was still outwardly positive and inwardly uncertain.[47] Britain's position was still nebulous, and Eisenhower concluded that his friend Winston Churchill "no longer absorbs new ideas; exhortation and appeals to the emotions and sentiment still have some effect on him—exposition does not."[48] Actually, the British prime minister gave some ground on the idea of a European army, but he did so grudgingly, and Eisenhower was not satisfied with the support NATO was receiving from the European nation he knew was absolutely essential to its success. By January 1952, Eisenhower was still pressing for unity, urging faster action, and looking forward to the creation of a force sufficient to stop a Soviet invasion short of the Rhine.[49]

A Republican on Maneuvers

By that time, however, he was increasingly distracted by those who had him lined up for a new and even more demanding job in the United States.[50] The drums calling for him to run for the presidency of the

United States had been beating since 1943. Sounding lightly at first, then with steadily growing intensity, the presidential *Bolero* was by the spring of 1952 crashing with deafening intensity around Ike and his staff in Europe.

Eisenhower, the thoroughly professional soldier, appeared to be of two minds about politics. He was an apostle of the democratic process. But at the same time he was contemptuous of the endless struggles with interest groups that had no sense of the public interest, and he was repulsed by the preening and posing that seemed all too common at every level of government. He said he was "violently negative" about politics.[51] He wanted "no part" of the nation's "domestic struggles."[52] He fiercely and finally refused to be sucked into "the political groupments and political struggles in America."[53] Or so it seemed.

While denying any political ambitions, he had worked carefully and cautiously to build an effective network of Republican supporters. These were men with money and political clout. They were men who did not waste their time on third-party candidates or other obvious losers. They understood the probabilities of drawing to an inside straight in poker or of investing in a new enterprise. They understood how to run companies and newspapers. They put their money on Eisenhower and initially respected his oft-repeated insistence that he could not—either legally or morally—state any party affiliation while serving as Supreme Commander of NATO's military forces.

So they did the best they could to persuade the general to declare his candidacy and unleash the hounds of fund-raising and vote-getting. Paul Hoffman pleaded with Ike over dinner.[54] Lawrence Whiting and Clarence Francis added their voices to the chorus,[55] as did George Whitney, chairman of J.P. Morgan & Company.[56] Editors, industrialists, and politicians begged Eisenhower to save the country, and along the way to save the Republican Party from another in a two-decade-long string of defeats. Truman's success in 1948 had seared the conservative mentality.

Ike was not immune to flattery, and he developed a fantasy outcome that would put the boy from Abilene in the White House without any danger of being embarrassed and without a grimy campaign either for the nomination or for the presidency. He would be nominated and elected by acclaim in a true people's revolution against the nation's "planned economy and Socialistic trends."[57] As he quietly pondered "bridges that are a long way ahead," he mused with his brother Milton about an outcome "bordering on the miraculous."[58]

Still wishing to avoid controversy, he began to correspond in code with his close friend General Lucius Clay, now retired and chairman of the board at a large firm.[59] Clay became the linchpin in the effort to ease Ike into the battle for the nomination and the ensuing campaign. Neither Clay nor Eisenhower's other confidants were thinking about anything "miraculous." But they could already taste a sweet victory in the election of 1952.

Finally, in the spring of 1952, Eisenhower asked President Truman to relieve him as Supreme Allied Commander, Europe, as of June 1. There were impending political responsibilities, he explained, and he anticipated a nomination "for high political office." He retired from the US Army on May 31, 1952.[60] After a tour of the NATO members' capitals, he was relieved from active duty as SACEUR effective June 1.[61] He was, at that point in his career, the unappointed but universally acclaimed leader of those European nations dedicated to protecting democratic capitalism and opposing the further expansion of the Soviet empire.

In parting, he reflected on his months as Supreme Allied Commander: "With many others I share the conviction that America's interests and the peace of the world require that Western Europe be kept outside the Iron Curtain. Moreover, I believe this can be done, given a readiness to cooperate effectively among all nations of NATO. In spite of the great distance remaining between these nations and their goals, they have achieved, thus far, a marked degree of success in the task of building a viable defense structure in this critical region."[62] This would be an essential part of the record on which he would run for the Republican nomination for the presidency.

Aspirations for High Office

Suddenly, almost frighteningly, Eisenhower's career was thrown back in time to 1941, before he had been selected to lead the Allied forces invading North Africa. At that point he had been only one of several who might have been chosen for that post. Now in 1952 he was in a similar situation when he became a candidate for the Republican nomination for the presidency. The early favorite was Senator Robert Taft, son of President William Howard Taft. The senator had been leading the Republican opposition to the New Deal in his home state of Ohio and the nation through the 1930s and the Second World War. Beloved by the solid right wing of the Republican Party, Taft was a tough opponent, especially for a novice in party politics.

Ike had long been nervous about his "meager voting record"[63] and the possibility that some of his "personal and business affairs" might occasion criticism.[64] He and his supporters knew all too well that he had much to learn about leadership in American politics. He had an unparalleled reputation for military service and a personality that glowed through his interactions with individuals of all ages, nationalities, and races. But he was a beginner at dealing with wily political opponents, lobbyists, and that part of the media oriented toward either Senator Taft or the Democratic Party. That included much of the media. Television was a hurdle to be cleared rather than an opportunity to maximize on his justly famous smile. Deals had to be reached, and from time to time his instinct for a simple set of principles would need to give way to expediency.

Determined to win, Ike took a crash course in American politics from advisors who had the experience he lacked. His brother Milton, who had years of experience in Washington politics, helped. George A. Sloan of the International Chamber of Commerce began to feed Eisenhower position papers on aspects of economic policy.[65] Eisenhower dutifully studied the issues and worked out his positions in more detail than had been the case in his career to date. He was armed with a solid set of principles, but not the kind of information that Senator Taft could muster.

Meanwhile, Ike was trying to learn how to be an effective speaker. He failed at his first major effort in his hometown, Abilene, the single place in America most friendly to Eisenhower, its war-hero son.[66] But as his campaign progressed, he stopped trying to read his speeches and gained confidence in his ability to reach out and establish rapport with those in his audience. He actually became a good campaigner—much to the relief of his team. In the nominating convention, he defeated Taft by a narrow margin, produced in part by the type of political maneuvering he disliked.[67] By that time, however, he had begun to look upon the 1952 campaign with some of the same crusader mentality he had developed in World War II. Once again, he was a man with a national and international mission.

Throughout the 1952 campaign against Democrat Adlai Stevenson, however, he was as much a follower as a leader. He still felt like a novice at politics, and he was right. He was more passive than he had been at any time since the Casablanca Conference in January 1943, when he almost lost his command. So when it came time to select a running mate, he followed the lead of his closest advisors and agreed to anoint Richard Nixon, a darling of the right wing of the Republican Party. Ike did not know Nixon very well. But he soon learned—painfully—to respect Nixon's political savvy. Charged with accepting covert funds from a rich men's slush fund, Nixon countered in September with a tear-jerking TV speech in which he used his wife, Pat, and his dog, Checkers, to sway the audience to his side. It worked. Eisenhower, who had been hesitant about keeping Nixon on the ticket, was boxed in—as he had been repeatedly by Charles de Gaulle. Nixon stayed on the ticket, and the campaign that Ike had labeled a "crusade" against corruption in government limped ahead.

Equally telling of Eisenhower's combination of fierce ambition and passivity was a speech that he gave in Wisconsin and a paragraph that he excised from his remarks. Senator McCarthy had attacked George C. Marshall, one of the two men who had done the most to build Eisenhower's career as a military leader. Simple loyalty and honesty required a public rebuttal from Ike. Responding to this moral challenge, he drafted a spirited defense of a man whose loyalty to the United States had been displayed over a long and brilliant career in challenging times. But the politicians would not have it. Going soft for a moment that he would have years to regret, Eisenhower cut the defense of Marshall out of his speech. But alas for Ike, the spot would not disappear. The speech had already been distributed, and the newsmen, to their delight, pounced upon the paragraph that had been excised. It made the news and cost Eisenhower the friendship of George C. Marshall, who afterward seldom spoke with his former protégé. What price victory?

But what an overwhelming victory it was. Eisenhower swept the election and pushed the Democratic Party out of the White House for the first time since 1933. Ike brought in 55 percent of the votes and 442 of the nation's 531 electoral votes. Turnout was unusually high, as it had been in the primaries. Equally important were the victories in the House of Representatives and Senate—both of which were now in Republican control. A nation nervous about the war in Korea and the potential for the Cold War to slide into an atomic disaster elected the man they associated with victory in World War II. A nation nervous about corruption in Washington and the growth of an intrusive administrative state elected a conservative president they trusted to clean up, to slow down, maybe stop, or perhaps even reverse the growth of the federal bureaucracy. Eisenhower's decision to follow the course charted by his political advisors was successful, if not always pleasing to Ike. Now, as thirty-fourth president of the United States, he would be back in an executive position in which the leadership skills he had mastered as Supreme Commander in World War II, as Chief of Staff of the US Army, and as NATO's Supreme Allied Commander, Europe, would all come into play.

Dwight Eisenhower firmly believed in something that people routinely referred to as the "public interest." This was an idea, a goal, that he thought existed beyond and was far superior to partisan politics, interest-group politics, ethnic politics, and the self-aggrandizement on display so often in Washington. This was a Platonic concept held by a normally Aristotelian and sometimes Machiavellian leader. It was linked tightly in his mind to democracy and to the right kind of leadership. Now he would have four years—and maybe even eight—to put those ideas to the test of practice and power.

To carry forward this study of his leadership, we will focus on the two most important aspects of his presidency: his effort to lead the nation and the world toward peace, and his closely related effort to provide Americans with a reasonable measure of prosperity. Characteristically, he would seek these goals by avoiding extremes and following the middle way.

Ten

Ike meeting with his cabinet at Camp David in November 1955. From left: John Foster Dulles, Eisenhower, and Ezra Taft Benson, with Charles Wilson in the background. Used with permission of the Associated Press. © 2017 The Associated Press.

Pursuing Prosperity

In January 1953, Dwight Eisenhower became the leader of an American economy that faced three major challenges. One stemmed from a postwar settlement that had laid the foundation for a second globalization of the world economy. The first, British-led globalization of the late nineteenth century had been destroyed long ago by the First World War and the retreat in the 1920s and 1930s to nationalism, then to autarky, and finally to war again. Now the United States had replaced Britain as the informal overseer of the global movement, but in 1953 it was still not at all clear that America would be up to this task. There were serious internal struggles over trade policy and international competition, struggles that frequently tied Congress in knots and made it difficult to frame coherent policies.[1]

A closely related challenge involved America's capacity to generate the productivity gains and basic innovations that had powered the nation's growth since the nineteenth century.[2] Many learned analysts thought that the second industrial revolution had run out of gas. The leading industries of that amazing era, they concluded, would no longer provide America with new investment opportunities or the country's consumers with the new goods and services they had come to expect. There was serious discussion in the late forties and early fifties of stagnation or, even worse, stagflation—a devastating combination of slow growth and high inflation.[3]

The third problem was easier to understand but still difficult to solve. It stemmed from a combination of accumulated federal obligations, the ongoing expenditures for the war in Korea, and the added expenses of a major military buildup. The 1953 deficit would be $6.5 billion—an amount that would foster inflation if Congress ended the Korean War program of price controls.[4]

These challenges had global as well as national implications. Since 1945, the United States had been the bulwark for the capitalist nations arrayed against the Soviet Union and its allies and client states. The United States was also providing essential support for the new array of international institutions—the United Nations, the International Monetary Fund, and the World Bank—designed to prevent the kind of economic nationalism and beggar-thy-neighbor autarky that had led the world toward war in the 1930s. Meanwhile, America had pumped substantial Marshall Plan subsidies into the effort to spur western Europe's postwar recovery.[5]

In the new president's mind, the links between these international programs, the nation's foreign policy, and the success of its domestic economy were crucial and self-evident. He fully understood that one of his most important tasks was to guide the world's largest industrial economy by working with Congress to craft policies that would help to keep business profitable, hold down unemployment, control inflation, and promote growth. These were awesome goals. To some considerable extent, they were conflicting goals.[6] They were a formidable challenge to the new administration and its leader.

They were especially challenging because nothing in Eisenhower's long army career had prepared him for this new role. In the aftermath of World War I, he had developed an economic mobilization plan for the War Department, but his understanding of and interest in America's very large, very complex economy was shallow. He sought and received advice about industry from investors such as Bernard Baruch. But he appears not to have developed any particularly salient ideas that would help him in 1953. Even during the Great Depression of the 1930s he had given little thought to what made America's capitalist system tick—or not tick.

Many of his experiences as a professional soldier were, however, relevant to his tasks in the White House. He had learned how important it was to operate within the given political context and to draw upon the best professional expertise available in that setting.[7] He had learned from painful personal experience how easy it was to get into economic trouble and how important it was to avoid getting trapped in that way. Ike knew that he would have to build an effective team and provide them and the nation with an appropriate vision of America's past, present, and future. In the realm of economic policy, he was not entirely prepared to do all that in 1953. As president, he was in effect sent back to school, and his performance would provide a good test of his ability to learn on the job and give effective leadership to his administration.

A Collage of Economic Ideas

While lacking formal training or knowledge of the economy, his mind was filled—as most of ours are—with random economic ideas.[8] Many of these traces of thought were rooted in his personal experiences. Some of the ideas had been gathered long ago as he was growing up in Abilene, Kansas, when he was far more interested in football than finance. His family, as we have seen in previous chapters, was poor and money was always tight. Life near the railroad tracks was not easy, and Ike and his brothers were familiar with hand-me-down clothing. It may sound quaint or even humorous to you, but my sense is that it was not easy or fun when one of the younger brothers had to wear a pair of secondhand women's shoes to school. All of that was distant by 1953, but Ike's early life left him sensitive to the impact the economy could have on those Americans whose incomes were low and relatively fixed. There were many Americans who had shared these experiences in the 1930s.

His own career and those of his brothers convinced Eisenhower that even the poorest Americans could better their income and status if they got an education and worked hard. The best road to progress and upward mobility for white Kansans of that era was through the professions. Ike's father had worked hard, but, lacking the right kind of education and career, he was stuck for much of his life in the American nightmare, a detour on the highway of American dreams. David could barely support his family and certainly could not help his sons pay to attend a college or university. Later, long after Ike left Abilene, David completed his degree through a mail-order school and at last made it into a white-collar job. But finishing his education was an afterthought to a long career spent performing the kind of labor that garnered little respect and even less income in an advanced, urban society.

Ike's older brother Edgar had charted a far better course at the University of Michigan and in the legal profession. He had quickly achieved the material success and status that had eluded their father. Edgar was not the only brother in the Eisenhower household who had successfully scaled the capitalist ladder. To one degree or another, along one path or another, all of the brothers had pushed their way up in a society that seemed happy to reward the right mixture of intelligence, self-discipline, and ambition.

After young Dwight had launched his military career, he had also learned something about the perils of debt. Like much of the working class and many middle-class Americans, Eisenhower periodically wanted to buy more than he could afford.[9] He had suffered an embarrassing episode when he did not have enough cash to buy the uniforms he needed to serve in his first post. Later, his career was endangered when he misled the army about expenses for a son who was not then living with him. He emerged from these experiences with a visceral opposition to debt. In that sense, he resembled the average American in the 1950s, but he was an anomaly in a Republican Party that included many businessmen and women who built their fortunes by using debt successfully.

Postgraduate Training in Economic Policy

To help Ike translate his core ideas into specific economic policies, his team of shadow supporters for the presidency had begun introducing him to the major economic issues facing the United States. They had started this informal course of postgraduate training long before he actually announced his decision to run for office. Some of the economic grooming had been informal: it popped up in the conversations he had when he was playing bridge with businessman Ellis D. Slater or *New York Herald Tribune* publisher William E. Robinson. It arose in his frequent dealings at Columbia University with business leaders such as Thomas Watson of IBM.[10] The more formal phase of his economic education was initially handled by George A. Sloan, a director at the United States Steel Corporation. Sloan's approach was gentle. It began at a dinner with Ike, Mamie, and Mr. and Mrs. Sloan in 1950.[11] Then Sloan visited Ike in Paris and tried to nudge him toward a run at the presidency.

Sloan also reported on the possibility of a major economic downturn, provoking the following response from the general: "When people are out of work, bewildered, and see their families enduring privation, they instinctively turn to the greatest temporal force of which they know—the government—for relief. In doing so, it is easy enough to forget that all powers of government must always be carefully and intelligently limited or it is certain to become the master of the people who have set it up. In other words, catastrophes of the kind we are now describing become the occasion for weaving into governmental organization, procedures, and functions a net in which is caught an increasing portion of the individual political and economic liberty which is the basic characteristic of our system."[12]

Would Eisenhower allow the people to sink or swim? No. "These things could be thought about in advance—they could be studied and the intellectual climate so developed that, in time of emergency, *the individual would get all the help he needed* but without permanent damage to the essentials of representative government."[13] Obviously, the Great Depression of the 1930s and the New Deal programs prior to World War II were front and center in Ike's mind.

Although at that time he was preoccupied with the situation in Europe, Eisenhower said he was grateful for Sloan's report "on the American scene." He asked for additional "interesting condensed reports." There was little chance that Sloan would not respond positively to that request, as he was now deeply engaged in the process of easing Ike into the presidential campaign. Further reports followed from those Eisenhower referred to as "my friends."[14] They were, of course, much more than that. They pressured Eisenhower to speak more specifically to "the issues," rather than the principles the general was expounding.[15] On matters of national security in the Cold War, Eisenhower had in mind both a general statement of strategy and specific measures to implement that strategy.[16] But he left his domestic policy more abstract than Sloan and his colleagues felt would best serve the purposes of the fast-approaching political campaign. As it turned out, Ike was able to win both the nomination and the ensuing campaign without committing himself to a specific set of economic policies. That quickly changed, however, after he won his sweeping victory in the election and began to marshal his new administration.

Getting Up to Speed

In preparation for that momentous transition, the president-elect quickly put together a team. Because he lacked a solid background in domestic policy, Ike's choices for his economic advisors were extremely important. His secretary of the treasury, George M. Humphrey, who came out of Ohio and the Taft wing of the Republican Party, brought good business sense to the table and a tendency to focus very tightly on taxes. Similar input with a similar tilt came from budget director, Joseph M. Dodge, and from Gabriel Hauge, who was the president's special assistant for economic affairs. Economist Arthur F. Burns, the new head of the Council of Economic Advisors, played a different role. He put the president in touch with the work being done at the National Bureau of Economic Research and with the Keynesian economics that had swept into America following World War II. It was a measure of Eisenhower's respect for Burns and also of the president's weak background in economics that he allowed Burns to select the other two members of the council.[17]

Together, this team helped the president frame the specific policies set forth in his first State of the Union message to Congress (February 2, 1953). The address was important because it placed before the legislature, the nation, and all those foreign observers attuned to developments in the United States an economic program that would guide the administration's next four years. With some minor adjustments, Eisenhower would promote the same basic programs in his second term. Four central themes emerged. First was the need to achieve economic growth through greater *efficiency* in both the public and the private sectors. Second was the closely related need to promote *innovation*, the "creative initiative in our economy." Along with the "economic health and strength" created by achieving the first two aims would come *equality of opportunity*. That would be buttressed by the "safeguards against the privations that too often come with unemployment, old age, illness, and accident"—that is, the *economic security* essential to life in "a complex industrial economy."

Very soon, Eisenhower began to give specific form to this vision for America's economic future. The generalizations characteristic of all political campaigns gave way to very detailed policy proposals. Economic growth, Eisenhower said, could be achieved in several very precise ways. For starters, they needed to get rid of price controls, reduce the government's debt, and balance the budget.[18] By stabilizing the economy, his administration would be able to promote the innovations that would flow from "the free play of our people's genius for individual initiative." The national effort to achieve efficiency would start with the federal government and ripple to the private sector: "We are concerned with the encouragement of competitive enterprise and individual initiative precisely because we know them to be our Nation's abiding sources of strength."[19] This plan left Ike supporting the traditional antitrust policy and leaning hard against both those pressing to cut taxes quickly and those who wanted to continue spending as usual. On these bedrock issues, he had to be tough. On taxes, for instance, there was at first hardly any room for the kind of compromises his conciliatory approach to leadership normally favored.

This program, he was certain, would not interfere with his administration's efforts to see that Americans would also have the economic security they needed and the equity they deserved. He thought that economic growth without a good measure of security could not be successful over the long term in a democracy. He was not a leveler—a reformer determined to eliminate inequality. Like most Americans, he assumed that equality of opportunity would suffice to bring to the top those deserving strivers who—like his siblings—had worked their way up from the other side, the poor side, of the railroad tracks.

Realities of Economic Growth

The first battleground was fiscal policy. He initially had immense power to shape the legislative decisions on taxes and spending. He knew it, and he used that power with his own closest advisors and with the Republicans who controlled Congress. He managed to hold taxes at the abnormally high level set for upper-income individuals and corporations during the Korean War crisis. Feeling pressure in his own party on the tax issue, he noted in his diary: "I believe that the American public wants security ahead of tax reduction and that while we can save prodigious sums in the Defense Department without materially hurting our security, we cannot safely, this year, knock out enough to warrant an immediate tax reduction." He feared "another deficit of extraordinary size . . . [that] would be most inflationary in its effect."[20] The end of the war in Korea and the adoption of a new defense strategy enabled Ike to nail down his most important economic accomplishment: a balanced budget in 1956. He achieved that objective while dealing with numerous issues that he considered sideshows to the nation's main economic features.

One of those dangerous sideshows was provided by the volatile senator Joseph McCarthy. Ike had been badly burned in the campaign when he sacrificed his friendship with George Marshall in order to avoid a public spat with McCarthy. Now the president adopted a passive strategy for dealing with McCarthy's wild, inaccurate charges that communist spies had infiltrated major American institutions and were threatening the republic. McCarthy was a dangerous demagogue whose charges played on people's fears about the Cold War struggle with the Soviet Union. Refusing to bring more attention to McCarthy, Ike worked quietly, covertly, and effectively to undermine the senator from Wisconsin. By taking this course, Ike left the American people without the kind of forceful public leadership they needed on this issue. Ultimately, however, Eisenhower's strategy was successful and McCarthy was defeated in 1954, leaving the president an opportunity to concentrate on what he considered to be the vital issues before the nation.[21]

He had much to do on these other fronts. As if to punish the president for his fiscal accomplishments, the congressional elections in 1954 had left him burdened with a Democratic majority in the House of Representatives. That called for additional compromises, but Eisenhower proved adept at working with Congress, even with liberal Democrats who had a more expansive attitude toward debt than Ike did.[22] The reward for those necessary compromises and for the grinding effort to reduce federal expenditures came with another balanced budget in 1957. Eisenhower would enjoy his third and last balanced budget in 1960, an accomplishment that was neither well understood nor appreciated during the presidential campaign that year, when Vice President Richard Nixon ran against John Kennedy.

To Eisenhower, however, these budgets were of vital importance: they helped to create the relatively stable economic environment that he believed was the essential context for promoting secular economic growth. They also gave the administration maneuvering room when it had to weather downturns in the business cycle, as it did during a brief recession in 1953–1954, again in 1957–1958 with a deeper and longer recession, and finally to a less challenging decline in 1960–1961.[23]

With the assistance of a Federal Reserve Board that accepted Ike's emphasis on preventing inflation, the administration survived these recession challenges with its basic strategy intact. While Eisenhower formally respected the Fed's autonomy, he worked closely with chairman William McChesney Martin to keep the government united and focused on controlling inflation first and then promoting balanced growth.[24] The most serious challenge to this policy was in 1957–1958, when unemployment reached 7.6 percent despite a 3 percent rate of inflation. Still, the administration held the line. In peace, as in war, Eisenhower relentlessly sought the middle way through compromise and cooperation within his administration, within the government, and within the entire American society.

The president tried to promote efficiency in both the public and the private sectors. Without changing the statutory missions of the federal agencies, he called for and received reduced budgets.[25] This negative approach to increasing productivity by simply cutting an agency's budget was not likely to yield good results over the long term, but it was about all that a chief executive could do in the short term. In the private sector, his major initiative was a fundamental improvement in America's transportation infrastructure. In 1956, Eisenhower signed the bill creating and funding a national highway system, which the president linked to national security. His personal experience with America's poor highways in 1919 gave him ample reason to press hard for a federal investment in transportation efficiency that was more consistent with a liberal, New Deal ideology than with a Republican perspective on political economy.[26]

More consistently conservative was his effort to rein in the agricultural subsidy program. From his perspective, all that he was doing was bringing agricultural policy into line with the changes that had taken place in this sector of the economy during the years since the Great Depression. Agriculture from the late 1930s through World War II and into the 1950s had experienced revolutionary changes in productivity and organization. Innovations in breeding and mechanization were matched by economies of scale in corporate farming.[27] Still, the political pressure to preserve the subsidy system created under the New Deal was intense, and after eight years of struggle, the expenditures on control were just as high as they had been in 1953. The interest groups and their friends in Congress won this fight—the worst defeat of Ike's eight years in office.[28]

What was missing from Eisenhower's initial approach to the economy was an aggressive effort to promote in business the kinds of innovations that were—with substantial, long-established local, state, and federal support—transforming agriculture. With regard to business, the central assumption of the first Eisenhower administration was that after the federal economic house was in order, private initiatives would take hold and produce the innovations that would prove the "stagnationists" wrong about America's economic future. To some considerable extent, Eisenhower and his closest advisors were still deeply invested in and interested in the great firms that had given the United States a leading edge in the second industrial revolution. One of the major symbols of this mind-set was secretary of defense Charles "Engine Charlie" Wilson of General Motors. Wilson famously elided the differences between GM and the national economy: "What was good for our country," he proclaimed, "was good for General Motors, and vice versa."[29]

For the most part, Eisenhower initially agreed with this simple formulation. While the administration's budgets included support for basic research at the National Science Foundation and the National Institutes of Health, agricultural research, and government purchases of advanced equipment (including, in particular, computers), the Eisenhower concept of political economy was at first more passive than active.[30] There were of course "spillovers" from the national security program.[31] Government purchases had for some years been an important form of support to the computer industry.[32] But this was not a planned program to encourage innovation. Eisenhower's strategy assumed that once the government had balanced the budget and had begun to create a business-friendly environment, the private sector would on its own generate the innovations that would sustain American growth. In 1954, Ike carefully analyzed the economic problems confronting him: they ranged from the farm problem and public electrical power to drought and disaster relief. The need to promote innovation through scientific and technological advances was not on the list.[33] The president meant what he said when he championed "the free play of our people's genius for individual initiative."

Then, strangely, inadvertently, miraculously, it actually happened. The geniuses were many and for some years they worked far away from the media's gaze. But the wellspring of America's third industrial revolution had already begun to flow in 1947 when Eisenhower was the army's Chief of Staff. Contrary to economic logic and common sense, the foundational innovation came from a giant, pervasively regulated, heavily bureaucratized corporation. The Bell System's discovery, the transistor, had quickly acquired a national and international reputation. But the transistor was popular only among those firms, individuals, and government organizations that had something very specific to gain from a new type of electronic switching device. AT&T made the invention available through reasonable licensing contracts, and by the mid-1950s the dynamics of the third industrial revolution, the digital revolution, were taking hold in the United States. At Fairchild Semiconductor and a few other firms, the transistor evolved into the integrated circuit and laid the technological base for what would shortly become California's Silicon Valley— America's digital heartland.[34] This was more "genius for individual initiative" than even Ike could have wished for in early 1953.[35]

The Eisenhower administration's role in this stunning economic transition remained unchanged until the Soviet Union sent Sputnik into orbit in 1957. Congress, the media, the public, and America's allies were shocked by the Soviet accomplishment.[36] The United States had long been protected by the Atlantic and Pacific Oceans, but now those natural barriers seemed less formidable and isolation a dwindling option. Eisenhower remained calm. He was confident that the Soviet satellite was not a threat to America's national security. But he decided that his administration had to take a more positive and visible position on scientific and technical change and had to do that quickly.[37]

Changes came tumbling out of the White House.[38] Ike spoke to the nation on "science in national security" and announced that he had appointed a new advisor, Dr. James R. Killian Jr., of the Massachusetts Institute of Technology, as his special assistant on science and technology. New appropriations followed. One created the Advanced Research Projects Agency (ARPA, later the Defense Advanced Research Projects Agency, DARPA) in 1958, a defense organization whose mission included the promotion of public-private innovations that would strengthen America's leadership in high technology.[39] The administration was, in effect, laying the foundation for the public science-and-technology infrastructure that would in a few years develop the Internet and support other innovations in digital technology.[40] It would be some years before the innovations in electronics would begin to have a major impact on the national economy, but by 1960 it was already evident that America's private sector was not about to become stagnant.

What, then, was Eisenhower's record on economic growth? The aggregates are impressive without being overwhelming. The average annual growth rate of real gross domestic product (GDP) over the eight years that he was president was about 2.5 percent. The economy was keeping ahead of an expanding population. GDP per capita increased, as did the workforce, which grew from 63 million workers to almost 70 million. Women had been joining the workforce in increasing numbers since World War II, and that important trend continued. The number of female workers went up by 3.8 million during Ike's eight years in office. Private investment was up by 39 percent, and all this took place while the inflation rate was held to an average of about 1.4 percent. There was no appreciable change in income distribution, so the major gains in equality that Americans had realized during World War II were sustained.

We do not have figures on the rate of increase in start-up firms, but we do know that a series of successful and important new businesses got going during these years. Most impressive was Fairchild Semiconductor, in part because it was the training ground for the executives who went on to found Intel in 1968. Other firms organized during the Eisenhower administrations included Thermo Electron (today Thermo Fisher Scientific), Semtech, and Tyco International.[41] By the end of the 1950s, America had a set of private and public institutions that would enable it to lead the world into the next phase of the digital revolution. Ike's confidence in the "people's genius" was amply rewarded.

Along the way to this conclusion, not all of the economic news was favorable. Capitalism is a restless system, and Eisenhower had to contend with the three recessions mentioned earlier. The cyclical downturns in 1953–1954, 1957–1958, and 1960–1961 all inspired intense fear that the economy might be sagging back into a major depression. The memory of the 1930s had not yet been erased from the minds of most Americans of working age, including President Eisenhower.[42] Two of the recessions were, however, relatively mild: the unemployment rate peaked at slightly over 6 percent in 1954 and 6.8 percent in 1960. More serious was the 1957–1958 recession, which pushed unemployment to a peak of 7.6 percent. In all three cases, the combination of Federal Reserve monetary policy, automatic stabilizers, and the administration's fiscal policy worked to cut off potential downward spirals.[43] On average, unemployment hovered around 5 percent for the entire eight years of the administration. It was a thoroughly "middle way" style of capitalism.

Less successful was Eisenhower's encounter with foreign trade. Here he hoped to maintain liberal trade policies that were consistent with his concept of the creative role competition played in fostering economic progress. Paradoxically, however, problems arose because of the success the United States was achieving in stabilizing the free-world economy and encouraging economic recovery following World War II. Japan was enjoying a surge of economic development supported by the United States. President Eisenhower continued that support through both of his administrations. For reasons linked to Cold War national security, Ike saw Japan as the United States' bulwark in the Pacific, just as Germany was an essential ally in Europe. When, however, Japanese exports to the United States shot up, he found it necessary to negotiate a series of "voluntary export restraints" with Japan. These agreements temporarily relieved the pressure on particular American firms. But they were not a solution to America's encounter with fierce global competition and were inconsistent with Eisenhower's emphasis on the long perspective in economic policy.[44] He left that problem in the lap of the next president.

Realities of Economic Security and Equity

To Eisenhower, there was no serious conflict between policies that supported economic growth, innovation, and efficiency and those that provided Americans with greater security and an enhanced sense of equity. He was not concerned about the high taxes paid by upper-income groups even though they were a core element in the Republican Party. Controlling inflation was more important to him than reducing the taxes paid by wealthy individuals and large corporations. "It would be most unfair," he explained in 1953, "to grant tax relief to one group when we cannot yet afford to grant it to all."[45] Insofar as the Eisenhower and Federal Reserve blend of fiscal and monetary policies held down inflation, they provided a greater measure of security to all those citizens with fixed incomes.

Many Americans were attempting to live on their monthly social security payments, and Eisenhower understood how difficult that could be. His brother Ed, however, was far to the right of the middle way. Ed resented entitlements and attacked the entire social welfare system as a government giveaway that should be curtailed. Still attempting to be the dominant older brother, Ed was full of suggestions about everything from defending the Constitution to making Supreme Court appointments. Ike—certain that he and not Ed had been elected president—was at first patient with his obstreperous older brother.[46] But in November 1954 Ike finally exploded. "The Federal government cannot avoid or escape responsibilities," he wrote to Ed, "which the mass of the people firmly *believe* should be undertaken by it. The political processes of our country are such that if a *rule of reason* is not applied in this effort, we will lose everything— even to a possible and drastic change in the Constitution. This is what I mean by my constant insistence upon 'moderation' in government. Should any politician attempt to abolish social security, unemployment insurance, and eliminate labor laws and farm programs, you would not hear of that party again in our political history."[47] As if to add a final, forceful period to that verbal blast, the president supported another expansion of the social security system and was able to sign the measure in August 1956.[48]

Throughout his two administrations, Eisenhower backed a variety of new programs where he could see a real need for federal action. That continued to be more important to him than an abstract principle about getting the federal government out of activities that should be left to the states. He worked hard to reduce federal involvement where he thought it was unwarranted, but he added to the government's responsibilities when he was certain it would serve the national interest. Fending off the right wing of the Republican Party and suppressing his own constitutional misgivings, he promoted increased federal involvement in education and the construction of a massive federal road system. Ever mindful of the right wing of the Republican Party, he downplayed the liberalism by stressing the national security aspects of the road system.[49] Eisenhower also made no effort to change the congressional policy of using the surplus in social security to fund other programs.

Eisenhower gave substantial consideration to providing Americans with equality of opportunity. He never mistook that for equality of outcomes. He was too experienced in the ways of the world to seek the sort of absolute equality communist leaders frequently touted as an advantage of the socialist system. But where opportunity was concerned, he moved quickly and forcefully to establish his position. Convinced that education played a powerful role in opening the way to jobs and promotions for Americans, Ike was willing to use the federal government's resources to promote school construction in kindergarten through twelfth-grade education.[50]

Ike understood that African Americans were blocked from the education they deserved and the job opportunities they needed. In 1954, the Supreme Court overturned the state laws that had kept African American and white children in separate and distinctly unequal schools.[51] That, for Eisenhower, was now the law of the land. While privately he would have preferred a more moderate step forward, he did not question his responsibility for enforcing the law. He tried to establish racial equality where he had the authority to act. In matters of civil rights, Ike was something of a convert. During his long career in the military from 1915 through D-Day, he had never officially or informally complained about policies on racial segregation in the army. In the latter stages of the war in Europe, however, he had insisted that African American soldiers should be allowed to volunteer for combat duty.[52] In this limited case, he had been successful in changing the policy.

In 1953, however, he moved quickly and forcefully to open opportunities for African Americans. He eliminated segregation in Washington, DC, and pushed forward with the desegregation of the military—a policy that President Truman had begun in 1948.[53] Seeking a more decisive change, he worked closely with Democratic leader Lyndon Johnson to push through Congress the first civil rights act of the twentieth century. Fierce Dixiecrat opposition prevented the passage of a truly formidable measure. So the Civil Rights Act of 1957 fell short of what was needed to protect African American voting rights and opportunities for education and employment. But it broke ground for later, more powerful measures and was a step toward federal support for the development of a society that eventually might not discriminate against people of color.[54]

In 1957, when Governor Orval Faubus of Arkansas challenged federal authority by employing the state's National Guard to block court-ordered integration of the high school in Little Rock, Eisenhower moved decisively to defend federal authority. He tried first to avoid a confrontation that he knew Faubus could not win. But when discussion failed, the president ordered a stop to the obstruction of justice, federalized the state's National Guard, and sent troops from the 101st Airborne Division to enforce the court order. For Eisenhower, this struggle had at least three major dimensions: he was concerned about the damage it did to America's reputation abroad; he was incensed by the direct, senseless challenge to a federal court; and he was now and would remain deeply concerned about equality of opportunity through education.[55]

Eisenhower's Style of Prosperity

When Eisenhower turned over the White House to President John Fitzgerald Kennedy in January 1961, he gave the new Democratic administration an American economy that was in better shape than the one Ike had received from Truman in 1953. The economy was well attuned to the "middle way" philosophy of government. The budget had been balanced in 1960, and the recession of 1960–1961 was relatively mild. With recovery, the economy would be positioned for another surge of growth and more advances in the new digital technology. That would not satisfy President Kennedy, Vice President Johnson, or their economic advisors, who would seek to close the gap they saw between the economy's potential and its performance.

Eisenhower and his team, however, would leave office satisfied that they had achieved most of their long-term goals in the realm of political economy. In his last economic report to the Congress, on January 20, 1960, President Eisenhower described an economy that had achieved record-breaking levels of production, income, and employment. By avoiding "speculative excesses and actions," he thought, the United States would be able to maintain a low rate of inflation and still have "the basis for a high, continuing rate of growth."[56]

Above all, Ike and his team had given the nation an economy that was suited to a Cold War that was likely to last longer than any of them would be alive. He had recognized from the beginning of his first administration that America's economic strength would be crucial to an ultimate victory in the struggle against communism. Over his eight years in office, he had never lost sight of that goal. In 1956, Soviet premier Nikita Khrushchev had threatened to bury the United States and its allies as the communist economies surged ahead. By 1961, Eisenhower had shown the Soviets just how difficult that would be.

Eleven

President Eisenhower with Soviet premier Nikita Khrushchev during a tense period in US-USSR relations.

Pursuing Peace

No American president comes into power with a clean slate, the *tabula rasa* of academic discourses and philosophical meanderings. In the twentieth century, all came into power faced by a bewildering complex of organizations (both private and public, national and international), individuals, deeply planted cultures, and expectations about the new leader. For President Eisenhower this complex included a war that had not been going well, a series of dangerous enemies, a rapidly shifting military technology, and a loosely jointed empire of client states, overseas possessions, a base system, and the military services—that he had been struggling to bring under control through the entire postwar era.

In office, Eisenhower quickly set out to develop a grand strategy that would, if successful, guide this complex array of institutions and individuals and achieve America's primary goals. As he understood those goals, they were above all the peace and stability that would enable the US economy and democratic society to thrive. Along the way, he had to deal with residual resistance to internationalism and to beat back one attempt to limit his authority in foreign affairs. But he was successful in handling both of those problems and in maintaining his strong leadership role at home and abroad.[1]

As Ike knew, the United States would benefit little from major changes in the world. It would be nice if the United Nations, the World Bank, and the International Monetary Fund were able to put all of the underdeveloped nations on the path to economic growth. It also would be nice if various authoritarian governments would become democratic. But Eisenhower understood that the "free" world probably would never be entirely free of autocrats, and he was experienced enough to recognize that some of them could actually help him achieve his primary goals. It sufficed if they remained reliable allies or truly neutral bystanders in the great struggle at the heart of international relations in the 1950s.[2]

The Cold War with the Soviet Union, its empire, and the new Chinese communist government threatened to destabilize the world's political economy through stealth or internal revolutions if possible and through force if necessary. Unlike the United States, the communist nations had much to gain through change. Their ideology and national interests fed the desires of the revolutionaries seeking to overturn colonial powers throughout the world. As the empires of America's allies gave way to socialist-nationalist regimes in Africa and Asia, the United States was forced to deal with a world increasingly hostile to its democratic capitalist creed.

Eisenhower remained convinced that "only in collective security was there any real future in the free world."[3] To Ike, it was self-evident that America's national security could not be successfully defended without a collective system of alliances, anchored in western Europe and the United States. His quest was for unity: greater military and economic unity in Europe, political and military unity in Asia, and unity within the government in the United States.[4] This goal kept slipping away from him. But in leading at home and abroad, he sought it all the more vigorously. "Clearly," he told a friend, "there are different ways to try to be a leader. In my view, a fair, decent, and reasonable dealing with men, a reasonable recognition that views may diverge, a constant seeking for a high and strong ground on which to work together, is the best way to lead our country in the difficult times ahead of us."[5] These were not just talking points. He relentlessly applied that formula at home and abroad, with his own party and with the Democratic opposition.

Worried about America's position in the world, he quickly set out to develop a new strategy that would serve the United States over the long term. Soviet hostility had taken on a new face in the age of atomic weapons, jet aircraft, and powerful missiles. The United States had ended the war against Japan with two atomic bombs and had, for a brief time, enjoyed a global monopoly on these terrifying weapons. But the Soviets had closed the atomic gap by 1949, and there was every reason to believe that they would acquire a thermonuclear weapon soon after the United States tested its hydrogen bomb in 1952. Eisenhower understood that the destructive force of the new weapons changed forever the manner in which military force could be deployed and national interests defined and defended.[6] The strategic and tactical implications of the new age were as yet ill-defined, but Ike was determined to clarify this situation for the nation's friends and enemies.

In Washington, DC, there was thus much to worry about in 1953. Even America's best friends seemed to be inching to the left, toward the USSR and away from the United States. In Ike's view, America had already weathered "eight post-war years of suspicion and fear," and the international situation appeared to be getting even more threatening.[7] Within NATO, the British had nationalized major industries and created a formidable welfare state that made American leaders nervous. Similar changes were taking place in France, and in Italy there appeared to be some chance that the communists would come to power through democratic elections. All of Eisenhower's earlier efforts to strengthen NATO seemed to be in danger from within. With whom would Americans trade if Europe slid further toward a socialist or communist future?

For help in dealing with these threats, Ike did the first thing any leader must do promptly and well: he built a national security team. He well understood that "success is going to be measured, *over the long term*, by the skill with which the leader builds a strong team around him."[8] The process—as with the team for domestic policy—was almost completed before the end of November 1953. The linchpin was John Foster Dulles, who had worked closely with the president-elect through the campaign. As secretary of state, Dulles would bring to the new administration his worldwide contacts and his long experience in foreign relations. Defense would go to America's leading industrialist in the 1950s, Charles Wilson of General Motors. Eisenhower's legislative liaison (and later chief of staff) would be Major General Wilton B. "Jerry" Persons; in 1954, Colonel Andrew J. Goodpaster would provide staff support and would gradually assume an important role in handling national security issues.

The new team's contribution to policy came soon after Ike's inauguration. Then consultation and a formal internal process of planning—Project Solarium—gave the newly elected president the grand strategy he would implement for the United States. Ike hoped that strategy would survive through his next four years in office and maybe beyond his presidency.[9] He would continue to support the general policy of containing communist power initially drafted under President Truman; Ike was committed to "the basic truth that only in collective security was there any real future in the free world."[10] He would attempt through overt and covert means to keep pressure on the communist regimes and would use the threat of thermonuclear war to block Soviet expansion into areas considered vital to America's interests. The covert, Machiavellian elements of international policy would be developed gradually by the Central Intelligence Agency. The well-publicized military version of the Eisenhower strategy was the "New Look," with its emphasis upon strategic aircraft, missiles, and atomic, then nuclear, weapons.[11]

Eisenhower rejected the Truman administration's effort to build up the country's traditional forces. As he explained to a Republican congressman from Kansas, "Our plan for national security, in contrast to earlier programs, envisages a long-range undertaking capable of continuing national support. It seeks to avoid the exceedingly costly, demoralizing, short-range effort premised upon an imaginary date of maximum danger and incapable of being sustained for a prolonged period. It will provide us with solid military force based on a dynamic economy, both capable of rapid expansion in an emergency."[12]

His goal was to avoid that "emergency." World War III would, Ike had realized, not be fought with massive arrays of tanks or battleships. There would be no trench warfare, no advances from mountain chain to mountain chain, no encirclements or tactical withdrawals. There would not be time for all that. As he explained in 1955: "Due to the destructiveness of modern weapons and the increasing efficiency of long-range bombing aircraft, the United States has reason, for the first time in its history, to be deeply concerned over the serious effects which a sudden attack could conceivably inflict upon our country. Our first objective must therefore be to maintain the capability to deter an enemy from attack and to blunt that attack if it comes."[13] Such a war would be over quickly and would result in the most horrific loss of life and destruction of urban civilization that anyone could possibly imagine.[14]

For the next four years and then for a second term, Eisenhower would have his hand on one of the two triggers that could launch that destruction on world civilization. If confronted by a full-scale Soviet nuclear attack, would he have pulled the trigger? We will never know. But this was the man who gave the order to attack the Continent on D-Day. He was, I believe, fully prepared to make the decision called for by the strategy he had now formulated for his country.[15]

The Korean Contradiction

The Cold War had forced the United States and its allies to become deeply involved in the affairs of states with which most Americans were unfamiliar. That was certainly true of the Korean War, which was being fought in a distant country that few Americans had visited and very few understood. Japan (now America's ally) had occupied and exploited Korea for many years. Since 1945, however, Korea had been an independent nation, divided between a communist North and a capitalist South, the latter linked to the United States. In 1950, North Korea launched a nearly successful invasion in an attempt to unify the nation. Pushed back by US forces armed with UN authority, the North was on the edge of total defeat when the Chinese army entered the war and drove General MacArthur's forces back to the 38th parallel. The result was a stalemate and seemingly endless—and fruitless—negotiations over an armistice. This was the sorry mess that awaited Eisenhower after his election in November 1952.

As president, he recognized that he had to solve the nation's "Asian problem" as soon as possible.[16] In the campaign for the presidency Ike had promised to go to Korea—a statement widely interpreted to mean that he would quickly settle a war that had already cost America thousands of casualties. He went in December 1952 as president-elect. The trip was a good opportunity for Eisenhower to discuss policy and formulate positions with his growing team of advisors, but it yielded no quick breakthrough in the negotiations. The ongoing battles produced no breakthroughs, either, and they continued to result in heavy American casualties.[17]

In South Korea—as in France during World War II—Eisenhower had to deal with a determined, nationalistic leader who had his own agenda for the settlement. Syngman Rhee, the president of the Republic of Korea (ROK), sought unification of the nation on his terms. Since this could not be achieved by the ROK army, Rhee insisted that the United States carry the war forward to total victory. Ike was perturbed. He found Rhee to be "highly emotional, excitable and threatening."[18]

As Eisenhower realized, Rhee's goal could be achieved against the combined North Korean and Chinese forces only by using nuclear weapons. The unwillingness of the Truman administration to authorize General MacArthur to employ these weapons had yielded a unique civil-military struggle that MacArthur, predictably, had lost; Truman had replaced the storied victor of the Pacific War in 1951. Ike was also opposed to using nuclear weapons, believing that this would be likely to broaden the struggle, engulfing Japan and ultimately the USSR in a general war.[19]

In the strategy that emerged from the Solarium discussions and in President Eisenhower's carefully reasoned approach to America's national security, the unification of Korea was simply not worth the risk of a general, nuclear war. Ike's primary focus was on Europe. He wanted to preserve the status quo in Korea and throughout Asia. He wanted to reassure American allies and enemies of his determination to oppose significant communist expansion. So he worked toward a conclusion that would finally be implemented in the summer of 1953. It involved an armistice, which is, all these decades later, still in effect. It left the two Koreas divided. Out of the war came a mutual defense pact between the ROK and the United States guaranteeing that American forces would be used should South Korea be attacked again.[20]

The nuclear threat had been introduced, and it probably helped persuade the North Koreans, their Chinese saviors, and their Soviet backups to accept an armistice. We may never know whether the establishment of nuclear weapons in the Far East—on Guam, one of the distant outposts of the American empire—altered communist thinking about the strategic importance of the ROK. But, viewed from Eisenhower's desk in the Oval Office, the basic goal of the new nuclear diplomacy and the New Look military seemed to have been achieved. And the killing had stopped.[21]

The conclusion was not one that would bring crowds into the streets in America to celebrate the end of the war. I doubt that even America's military leaders had celebratory dinners after the results emerged. Americans were not accustomed to playing to a tie, which is the way the Korean armistice looked from outside the national security establishment. In that regard, it was an accurate measure of what Americans could expect in the next eight years.

The "unconditional surrender" policy of World War II would become a fond memory for veterans and fodder for historians, but the Cold War and the nuclear age had now transformed international relations. Eisenhower was one of the agents of that transformation, as was his strident secretary of state, John Foster Dulles. Dulles's role was to provide counsel, to front the administration, and to inspire a measure of fear about how the United States might use its awesome power. But throughout the Korean settlement, Ike was completely in charge of this crucial step in his diplomacy. He was, by the end of 1953, well on his way to becoming the leader of the free world as well as the United States.

Ike and the Revolutionary Impulse

That new crown on the head of the former Kansas boy would become very heavy in the next few years. Stability turned out to be an immodest goal in a world ripped apart by revolutionary movements. The empires of the British and French were falling apart. Under pressure from socialist-nationalist movements in Africa and Asia, the former great powers were forced to withdraw from their colonies. At times they did so gracefully and skillfully. At times they blundered and battled to the end. Either way, they were compelled to withdraw. When Churchill attempted to defend the empires, Ike noted, "The one truth that he chooses to ignore is that any attempt on the part of the old imperialist powers to sustain by force some of their governing positions . . . would by this time have resulted in resentment, unrest, and possibly bitter conflict."[22] There was an abundance of all three results.

The growing force of the communist movement had a strong influence on this development. A democratic, capitalist ideology had little appeal to revolutionary movements seeking to overthrow democratic, capitalist powers that had long suppressed indigenous peoples. Democracy was a difficult concept to sell when the fight for independence was under way. It was equally difficult to sell when autonomy had been achieved but a new nation was struggling with tribal, religious, or regional divisions.[23] The blend of socialism, communism, and nationalism, on the other hand, had a natural appeal. It was an ideology of change. It had proven results apparent to living people for whom the revolutionary pasts of Britain, France, and the United States were dim and distant.[24]

For Eisenhower, these revolutions posed a series of head-scratching problems. He understood and sympathized with the desires of colonial people to be free and independent. No problem with that. He frequently chided Churchill about his frantic and ultimately unsuccessful efforts to hold the British Empire together.[25] So too with the French in Indochina. But when the revolutions blended into the expansion of communist power in the world, his sympathy was weakened by his own dedication to the containment policy and its Solarium variations. Thus, he continued to support French efforts to maintain their Vietnamese colony, although he would not entangle the United States Army in another Asian land war. He had seen enough of that in Korea. As he explained to Paul Hoffman, "The postwar insurrections that began in Vietnam should have awakened the French to the true situation and to the fate that was almost certain to overtake them unless they should act with respect to colonial peoples in a more enlightened fashion. Instead of that, they undertook the formidable, even impossible, task of subduing an insurrection by force."[26]

He had to return to that issue when at Dien Bien Phu the French maneuvered themselves into a losing position (surrounded, they were in the "General Custer position") against the communist forces. Ike offered help but not salvation, and the French lost their control of North Vietnam.[27] Eisenhower hoped that American support would enable "a free, stable Viet-Nam" in the South to "make a significant contribution to the strength of the Free World." But he knew that would depend upon the ability of their government to attain "wider popular support and a broader representative base."[28]

The Middle East presented a different situation, and Eisenhower was willing to move forward with American power and replace the British when they no longer had the resources to preserve their long-standing domination.[29] In this case, control of oil supplies vital to the American and western European economies was important. Prosperity was the other arm of Ike's grand strategy for America and its allies. He understood the economic underpinnings of national strength, as we saw in Chapter Ten. At one time the United States had produced more oil than it could use. That was no longer the case. America and western Europe needed Middle Eastern oil supplies, and the oil fields had to be kept out of Soviet control. Hence an active engagement that included covert operations to oust an Iranian prime minister who was opposed to US-British policies.[30] Like many such ventures into the internal politics of other nations, Ike's program was a short-term success and a long-term failure.[31]

Eisenhower was not, however, prepared to support every effort on the part of Britain and France to hold the positions they were steadily losing. In diplomacy as in economy, the politics of losing positions seldom gets the attention it deserves. The winners draw historians. The losers often become mere foils to the heroes of the winning side. This is apparent in our studies of the Suez crisis in 1956, which was a decisive measure of Ike's national security policy.[32]

When the British, French, and Israelis decided to invade Egypt rather than accept Gamal Abdel Nasser's decision to nationalize the vital Suez

Canal, they did so over US protests. Eisenhower was furious about the invasion and the dramatic rift it caused in the alliance structure. He urged the British to avoid using force, but he was ignored. He warned the Israelis that the United States would oppose "clear aggression by any power in the Mid-East," but he was ignored.[33] While Nasser was and would continue to be a problem, the Egyptian president was not the sort of problem that called for a return to gunboat diplomacy. As Ike acknowledged, the situation in the entire Middle East was "a terrible mess." The Arab-Israel struggle had "no limit in either intensity or in scope." Unfortunately, even those British and French leaders who had long worked closely with the United States had been oblivious to one of Eisenhower's fundamental principles: "You cannot resort to force in international relationships because of your fear of what might happen in the future."[34]

Under strong pressure from the United States and threats from the Soviets, the Anglo-French-Israeli forces finally ended their assault and restored a tenuous peace.[35] The abortive invasion prompted Eisenhower to announce a new Eisenhower Doctrine for the Middle East and to hurry to rebuild the alliances that were essential to his Solarium policies. Under Ike's new doctrine, the United States increased its economic and military aid to friendly nations in the region, and Congress authorized the president to use force to protect those countries.[36]

The Suez crisis was the most dangerous international conflict of the first Eisenhower administration. It had the potential to create the kind of misunderstandings, mishaps, and nationalistic blunders that Eisenhower feared could inadvertently cause World War III. Staring down his allies was even more difficult for Ike than confronting the nation's enemies was. He worked hard to avoid another such crisis, but events kept undercutting that effort. Forced repeatedly to improvise in both overt and covert operations, he attempted to respond creatively without violating his basic strategy and weakening America's alliances.

Those alliances were strained again during Eisenhower's second term as president. The United States had supported the Nationalist forces of Chiang Kai-shek in the struggle over China and had watched with growing apprehension the rise to power of Mao Zedong's communists and their victory in 1949. The Nationalist retreat to Taiwan left behind an unstable situation that threated to expand into a war, one neither the United States nor China wanted. China was struggling to solidify and strengthen its position at home and in the Far East. The revolution was not really over, as was demonstrated by the tragic experience of the Great Leap Forward in the 1950s and later by Mao's devastating Cultural Revolution.

In the course of formulating the communist regime's policies toward Taiwan and the rest of its neighbors, Mao launched an attack on two small islands, Quemoy and Matsu, within artillery range of the mainland.[37] The Nationalists dug in. They vowed to defend the islands as the first part of a defense of Taiwan, and Eisenhower supported them despite the disapproval of his European allies.[38] After another show of US atomic force, this test of the Solarium policy dribbled to a conclusion in 1961. It left the Nationalists still in Quemoy and Matsu, Mao still searching for the economic strength that would sustain a more aggressive foreign policy, and the allies focused on events in Europe that were much more threatening to America and world peace than anything happening in the Far East.

Europe, NATO, and the Soviet Challenge

Campaign rhetoric seems often to inspire Americans, even though they understand that the promises will seldom be honored once their candidate is in office. Campaign biographies add to the myth, as do the accounts produced by journalists who are swayed to favor one candidate or another. The result is a march toward office with supporters carrying banners that will be dropped quickly as the realities of public office intrude upon the successful candidate. Eisenhower was no exception. There are few exceptions to this rule in American history.

The biggest single campaign promise that came back to haunt President Eisenhower was the Republican national platform in 1952, which echoed Dulles's earlier call for liberation of the peoples of eastern Europe from communist control. This promise—to seek "the genuine independence of those captive peoples"—defied the kind of common sense that characterized Ike's approach to national security. Eisenhower had a good understanding of what the Soviets had accomplished on the Eastern

Front in World War II. They had crushed the bulk of the German army and made it possible for the Allies to succeed at D-Day and in the following campaigns in France and Germany. He had a good understanding as well of the Soviet dedication to an expansion of communism and to control of the communist regimes in eastern Europe. Having been invaded from the west by Germany and long before that by France, the Soviets were not about to roll back to Russia without a fight. It was a fight that Eisenhower could not expect to win. He understood the strengths and weaknesses of NATO all too well.

Why, then, did he run on a platform promising "liberating influences" that would mark "the beginning of the end" for the communist rulers of eastern Europe? That is not too hard to explain. He wanted very badly to be president of the United States. Otherwise, he would not have kowtowed to Senator McCarthy and failed to defend his great friend General Marshall.[39] But that leaves you to ponder why he would allow even a hint of the "rollback" concept into the Solarium strategy. In this case, the only appealing explanation is that he wanted the strategy to inspire as well as guide, and whereas "containment" was an essentially static concept, "rollback" was dynamic and seemed to point toward victory rather than the status quo.

But rollback was a fatuous public relations concept, and its hollowness was revealed with clarity in 1956 when the Hungarian revolt began. The Soviets had practiced for this crisis as early as 1953, when an East German uprising had taken place. They had quickly crushed that movement, and they responded with even greater force to the Hungarian revolution. Stalin had died in 1953, but Stalinism lived on in eastern Europe. The Allies were divided by the abortive Suez invasion that had left the United States and the Soviet Union temporarily on the same side. Without starting World War III, there was virtually nothing Eisenhower could do about Hungary except fume, criticize the Soviets, and go to the UN for a hollow statement of condemnation.[40]

The Soviets had sent 4,000 tanks and thousands of troops into Budapest, dwarfing the forces that NATO had at that time. The situation was horribly reminiscent of the battle of Kursk and other World War II campaigns on the Eastern Front. The balance of power in Europe was still decisively weighted toward the USSR—unless, of course, you added US thermonuclear power to the formula. Eisenhower was unwilling even to consider a nuclear response, howsoever vaguely stated. He did everything possible during his eight years in office to build up NATO's military power. Even during the worst disagreements with his NATO allies, he never left any doubt that the linchpin of the New Look strategy was still the defense of western Europe. It was the one part of America's sprawling empire that clearly would justify a nuclear response to a Soviet invasion. But Eisenhower was determined to ensure that would not be in 1956. He mustered rhetoric against the Soviets on Hungary and blasted his allies into submission over Suez.

There was, however, one part of western Europe that was vulnerable to Soviet pressure, and that, of course, is where Khrushchev pressed forward to explore the level of Eisenhower's determination. The Soviet leader issued what appeared to be an ultimatum: the United States, Britain, and France had to give formal recognition to the communist East German government and pull their troops out of Berlin. The Soviet note specified what would happen and when it would happen if the NATO allies refused to budge. The controversy, which had been going on since late 1958, seemed now to have reached a dangerous junction. On May 27, 1959, Khrushchev said, the USSR would turn over control of access to Berlin to its East German satellite. That would force the Allies either to deal directly with the East German regime or move out of a city they could no longer supply.[41]

Eisenhower and his advisors took this threat seriously. The president was worried "about unexpected developments either through miscalculation or muddling."[42] He nevertheless rejected the advice of the Joint Chiefs of Staff and decided to make three interrelated moves on the US/USSR chessboard. First he set in motion a highly visible if routine replacement of US troops in Berlin. Simultaneously, he moved tactical nuclear weapons to Europe. Finally, he accepted the British suggestion that he press for further discussions by the foreign ministers of the four engaged powers: the United States, the Soviet Union, France, and Britain.

The discussions drizzled toward no conclusion, as did Khrushchev's determination to force the issue. The Soviet ultimatum simply floated away after Eisenhower issued a somewhat softer ultimatum of his own: in 1959, he refused to discuss other issues with Khrushchev unless the Soviets removed "any appearance of a threat or time limit to the settlement" over Berlin.[43] This left the Allies in Berlin and the city still a vulnerable outpost inside the Iron Curtain. But the basic Eisenhower strategy appeared to be working. Time, he was certain, was still on his side.

Meanwhile, Eisenhower had worked hard to counter the threat of a nuclear surprise attack. With Ike, the memory of the Japanese attack on Pearl Harbor in 1941 was very much alive. He had served for years in the Philippines, where the threat from Japan was always under consideration. He was thus unusually aware throughout his eight years as president of the danger of a surprise attack from the USSR. He supported the efforts to develop reconnaissance aircraft, the most famous of which was the U-2, which flew so high that it could not at that time be downed by Soviet antiaircraft fire or fighter planes—even though the overflights of Soviet territory were clearly a violation of international law and common practice.[44] The aircraft were only a temporary answer, so he also signed off on the funding of the rockets and space satellites that could observe Soviet preparations for war on a permanent basis.[45]

The attack never came, and Ike and America could by 1961 celebrate eight years of peace as well as prosperity. It was a wary peace. In 1961, Ike's efforts to prevent a surprise attack would morph into a National Reconnaissance Office responsible on an ongoing basis for ensuring that future administrations would not suffer that kind of attack. By that time, however, it was evident that the Solarium strategy had worked. It would continue to work for the next thirty years, when the collapse of the Soviet Union at last removed from America and its allies the threat of mutual nuclear destruction. The peace would continue to be tenuous, dangerous, and more unpredictable than any American would like. But it did last.

The Mixed Bag of Mastery

Through his entire presidency, Eisenhower had the impression that he was constantly putting out forest fires in the middle of a windstorm. There seemed never to be the time or resources to put out any of the fires completely—or at least to his satisfaction. Neither America's allies nor its enemies were entirely predictable or, for that matter, entirely rational. Above all, they frequently appeared to be willing to take a chance on creating a nuclear Armageddon to gain some relatively minor advantage. The Soviets in the Berlin crisis. The British, French, and Israelis in the Suez crisis. The Chinese, who bombarded two small islands between the mainland and Taiwan. It was enough to make a mature leader ill, and indeed, Ike's stress-related health problems flared up again and again.

His own relatively rational brand of leadership was on full display for eight years: move carefully rather than quickly; keep the long view up front as much as possible; nurture the elements of your national strength; squeeze out the emotion of the moment and explore the facts; prioritize your problems and your resources; stress unity in a common cause; and always give your opponents a way out with their honor intact.

Often this formula did not work very well in dealing with revolutionary movements; given the temper of the postwar world, that was Ike's major shortcoming. While he sought stability in a peaceful world, socialist-nationalist revolutionaries sought radical change in a world that was unlikely to be peaceful until they had achieved their objectives.

To his credit, however, Eisenhower's style of leadership worked very well in great-power relations and in the vital business of governing the United States. He had the advantage of understanding what the bulk of the American people would tolerate, and he respected their opinions even when he disagreed with them. He continued to respect their views when Cold War exigencies seemed to call for actions that were certain to be unpopular in the short run. He recognized that complete transparency in government was both impossible to achieve and undesirable, but he attempted to provide the legislature and the nation's citizens with as much information about foreign policy and national security as could safely be revealed.[46] He had in his long career absorbed enough of the Machiavellian outlook to realize that he could not always be open and would need from time to time to support covert operations.

He could not, of course, tell Americans about the U-2 surveillance flights over the Soviet Union. They provided vital information to a president still nervous near the end of his term about a Soviet surprise attack on the United States. In addition to yielding information, the flights had no doubt inspired caution in Moscow by repeatedly demonstrating to the Soviet leadership how far behind they were in military technology. Thus, Eisenhower authorized the flight by Gary Powers that the Soviets were able to shoot down, much to the embarrassment of the president at the four-power summit with Khrushchev. At first Ike lied about the situation like a little boy in Abilene caught reading some books that he was not supposed to have.[47] That seldom works for little boys, and it did not work for Ike. The summit collapsed, and the president was forced to acknowledge that he had lied and to pledge that the United States would no longer conduct overflights of the USSR. This was clearly a short-term loss for Eisenhower, both in prestige and in international relations. The U-2 incident crushed his hopes and those of America's allies for the summit and weakened the unity Ike had spent eight years building.

Viewed in the long term, the U-2—even its last, provocative flight— was typical of Eisenhower's handling of Cold War relations. The repeated flights that had not been intercepted were an accurate measure of the military gap between the United States and the Soviet Union. This gap was as evident to Khrushchev as it was to Eisenhower and the Joint Chiefs of Staff. By 1960, Eisenhower could well afford to end the flights because he held a hidden ace in the US satellite program. The Soviet launch of the Sputnik satellite in 1957 had accelerated American efforts to develop the intercontinental missiles that would bolster the threat essential to the New Look and, not incidentally, provide the lift needed for effective observational satellites. The intelligence results began to come in as early as August 1960. The satellites gave Eisenhower the vital information that he needed about Soviet military development and potential to launch the surprise attack that Ike had been focused on since 1953 and that Americans had feared since 1957.

As his second administration ended, there were long-term problems left to fester in Latin America and in Iran. Nor had Ike discovered the magic formula for creating a stable peace in the Middle East. But he had given the United States eight years of the most effective leadership in foreign relations that the country had received—or would receive—in the twentieth century. His legacy in January 1961 included a national security strategy that would in a matter of decades bring the Cold War to an astonishing and peaceful conclusion.

Saying Goodbye

Dwight David Eisenhower had served his country with honor since 1915 and had learned along that frequently contentious way how to lead a platoon, a division, an army, an allied force, a nation, and a complex international alliance. His identity and his reputation as a statesman were well established throughout the world. Three days before he left office, he gave a farewell address that summed up some of the lessons he had learned. Cooperation, democracy, sacrifice, balance, the long view, equality, trust, diligence, and devotion to principle would, he said, continue to carry the nation toward its "great goals" of prosperity and "peace with justice." Echoing the New Look, he reminded Americans that there would be constant threats: "Our arms must be mighty, ready for instant action, so that no potential aggressor may be tempted to risk his own destruction."

But then, in one of the most memorable phrases in any of his speeches, he pointed to the danger posed to democracy by "the military-industrial complex." He had struggled to harness that complex for eight years in the White House. Before that, as Chief of Staff and as informal chairman of the Joint Chiefs of Staff, he had wrestled with armed services that behaved like civilian interest groups and industrial interest groups that were never willing to subordinate short-term self-interest to the national interest. There was as well a "scientific-technological elite" that buttressed the military-industrial complex and threatened to warp the country's universities and public policies.

Still an optimist despite these problems and his experiences with war and partisan politics, Eisenhower expressed his hope that the nation would overcome its challenges at home and abroad and would achieve success in its "adventure in free government." He proudly benchmarked 1961, declaring: "America is today the strongest, the most influential and most productive nation in the world." If America used its power "in the interests of world peace and human betterment," the United States would, he hoped, be able "to keep the peace, to foster progress in human achievement, and to enhance liberty, dignity and integrity among peoples and among nations."

He spoke with all of the authority of the premier leader of the free world. He held that position because he had responded creatively to the many changes that had taken place in America and the world in his lifetime. That was the central challenge the boy from Abilene had faced, and it was the challenge the American people and their leaders would face in the years that followed 1961.

Twelve

Ike and Mamie in retirement at the Gettysburg farm in 1966.

The Wise Man

Dwight David Eisenhower helped lead the United States and its allies through their two most threatening confrontations of the twentieth century. One was the war against Nazi fascism. The other was the struggle against the Soviet brand of aggressive, authoritarian communism. In the course of those epic encounters *the boy* from small-town Kansas had become the preeminent leader of the free world and the spokesman for the middle way, a moderate style of conservatism, in the democracies. A master of consensus building and unity, he managed to reduce conflict at home and to prevent the war he most feared. While he did not achieve all of his personal goals as president, he was justified in being proud of the prosperity and peace Americans had experienced in the 1950s. He had certainly earned his long-awaited retirement from public service.

When Eisenhower left office in 1961, he and Mamie retreated to their farm in Gettysburg, Pennsylvania, and contemplated a new life. No longer in office, no longer in power in the federal government, the Republican Party, the US Army, NATO, or the United Nations, Ike thought he might from time to time provide wise counsel to those who now exercised authority. He looked forward to being out from under the hammer of decisions. He had had enough of that, and his long string of serious health problems attested to his relentless attention to duty. But in the course of his military and political careers he had accumulated an immense knowledge of the people, the institutions, and the issues the world faced in the 1960s, and now he had every reason to believe that his advice would be useful to those who wielded power at home and abroad. He would be *the wise man* of American policy.[1]

This was the seventh and the last major shift in his evolving identities, rounding out the transitions that had shaped his capacity for leadership, his selection as a leader, and the type of leader he became. His ability to adjust throughout his career to a changing environment, responsibilities, and associations distinguished him from most of his peers. His shifting identities provide an important part of the answer to the question at the heart of this book: how did a small-town boy from Kansas become the leader of the free world? The boy from Kansas was smart and knew how to work hard. But he displayed little aptitude for leadership and little interest in worldly issues beyond sports, friends, girlfriends, and family—the common stuff of boyhood in Middle America in the early twentieth century, and today as well. His family life decisively shaped his orientation to authority. His father and older brother left him with a streak of anti-authoritarianism that blended with his congenital tendency to have a short fuse. His mother encouraged him to control his temper, to learn to accommodate to authority, and to get ahead in life through education, self-discipline, and hard work. Well liked by his peers, *the boy* left Abilene with a mind-set that was a jumble of conflicting values and perspectives on life. His orientation toward authority had the potential to impose a sharp upper bound on his performance at West Point and his subsequent military career.

His decision to seek an advanced education that neither he nor his family could afford was a crucial part of the answer to our guiding question. Along with the education he received at West Point, he entered a profession—a step that would enable millions of Americans and several Eisenhowers to climb the social mobility ladder in the twentieth century.[2] At the US Military Academy and in his early career as a junior officer, Eisenhower demonstrated a substantial capacity for leadership in teams, in small units, and finally in a wartime position that substantially extended his reach and responsibilities. In his new identity as *the professional soldier*, he was trusted and respected by those who served with him and under his authority. He overcame his profound disappointment about not being sent to France during World War I and performed admirably and resiliently when he was responsible for leading thousands of men training for tank warfare.

There were, however, problems. He was not unusually ambitious and was still somewhat ambivalent about his chosen career. The tensions in his personality were unresolved, and in the immediate postwar era, his anti-authoritarian streak surfaced and threatened for a time to end his professional career. These episodes and his failure to adapt successfully to a postwar army that was particularly conservative indicated that he might never escape his bureaucratic typecasting: a good coach, a good trainer of recruits, but not a candidate for the top ranks of the military service.

Luckily for Eisenhower—and for the United States—General Fox Conner adopted him as a personal and professional project, mentored him, and supported him for years. With Conner's encouragement he became something of a striver, a man determined to get to the top, a candidate for leadership as a general officer. Eisenhower absorbed Conner's lessons, recognized what was at stake, and demonstrated an unusual capacity to turn his career and his life around in order to fit the model that Conner was advocating. Having taught Ike how to be successful in the US Army, Conner steadily used his friendships and his knowledge of the army bureaucracy to advance Eisenhower's career. Conner's continued support was necessary because the US Army changed more slowly than Eisenhower did.

In brief, Ike's reputation substantially lagged behind his capabilities. The army was slow to acknowledge that Major Eisenhower could be much more than a good football coach, much more than a skillful trainer of recruits. Despite Eisenhower's outstanding performance in the Command and General Staff School, the army behaved in a manner that would not surprise those who admire Franz Kafka and the anti-bureaucratic school of thought. Conner, however, was a master

Machiavellian. He outmaneuvered the bureaucrats, pushed Eisenhower ahead, and gave his protégée the entrée and the confidence he needed to enter higher office.

There are, then, major elements of contingency in Eisenhower's ascent. Had he not been able to serve with General Conner in the 1920s, Eisenhower probably would never have emerged from the shadows of a mediocre career in his chosen profession. To his credit, Ike proved to be unusually receptive to Conner's mentoring. He was throughout his career flexible about doctrine, the ordinary stuff of life, while remaining tightly locked down on dogma, his basic values, including his concept of how he should treat those who worked for him and with him.[3] He was deeply committed to being approachable and fair-minded, willing to a fault to cut some slack for the officers and enlisted men and women with whom he served.

There were, as well, larger elements of contingency that influenced Ike's career. In his lifetime, the United States emerged as the world's largest industrial power and began to express that power overseas. Two world wars bracketed the middle phase of Ike's military career and provided him with unusual opportunities to advance in the US Army. Thwarted in World War I, he and Conner were able in the 1920s and 1930s to position him for rapid advancement when America's national security was again threatened.

In the interwar era, he made full use of Conner's guidance, protection, and power. In those years, Eisenhower became an aspiring perfectionist: *the perfect staff officer.* In that new identity, he found himself attached to the army's leading officer, General Douglas MacArthur, who was pleased to have Ike on his team. As his years with the powerful, quixotic MacArthur demonstrated, Eisenhower had almost completely suppressed the anti-authoritarian streak that had stymied his early career. As the leading member of MacArthur's team in the War Department and then in the Philippines, he mastered conciliation under constant stress.

When war threatened in Europe and commenced in Asia, Major Eisenhower looked forward to a new career as a line officer, leading men at war, finally leading men in the field in combat. All he needed at this point in his career was a successful conclusion to his service with Mac-Arthur and an opportunity to break out of the organizational stasis that had characterized the army since the end of World War I. At this crucial divide, he almost lost MacArthur's support, however, and had his first major experience with a Machiavellian leader who sandbagged Ike and taught him a lesson in cunning and duplicity.[4]

Escaping MacArthur without further damage to his career, Eisenhower was soon in a demanding wartime setting that forced him to develop new political and military capabilities, to perform at last as a line officer in combat, and to deal with a complex, rapidly changing context in Africa, then in Sicily and Italy. He was now becoming *the commander*, and in that identity he again demonstrated substantial ability to learn by doing. He became tougher and more demanding of his subordinates; indeed, there was a touch of MacArthur's cunning in the way he handled his two favorite officers, George Patton and Omar Bradley.

In his role as commander, his performance was uneven but ultimately successful in the most challenging American military action since the Civil War. Along the way, he was once again sandbagged—this time by the British at the Casablanca conference. In effect, Churchill and FDR took away his direct command of the troops and left him isolated at the top of his army and somewhat bitter. He swallowed those feelings, however, and continued to learn and to promote Allied unity. He achieved success where it counted, on the battlefields of North Africa, Sicily, and Italy. After the successful D-Day invasion in France, his reputation at home and abroad matched his identity perfectly, and he soon regained his direct command of the men in battle. While he suffered a defeat with Market Garden and a costly near defeat in the Battle of the Bulge, he eventually led the Allies to success on the Western Front. He was now in both identity and reputation *the supreme commander*.

Throughout, he dealt with a long, stressful experience handling General Montgomery, whose contempt for Ike took the supreme commander to the absolute limits of his capacity for conciliation. As the final act in his relationship with Montgomery illustrated, Ike had developed a streak of Machiavellian cunning that would serve him well in the years ahead. After finishing the end game of the war with success, Eisenhower emerged in 1945 with a well-tooled sense of his capabilities as a leader and a well-established reputation as America's most outstanding military officer.

His next challenge was the Cold War between totalitarian communism and democratic capitalism—a titanic, all-consuming struggle that provided the central theme for the remainder of Ike's exceptionally active career. By the time he had served as army Chief of Staff, president of Columbia University, informal chairman of the Joint Chiefs of Staff, and NATO's Supreme Allied Commander, Europe, he was America's premier military professional in a new global age. He had through his career demonstrated an unusual capacity to deal with technological, organizational, and political change. He was comfortable with his new identity as *the statesman*. To an important extent, this identity and reputation placed him above some (but not all) of the short-term anxieties of service struggles, party affairs, and even national politics. It enabled him to take a long-term perspective on America's role in the world and the important links between its domestic and foreign policies.

Elected president of the United States in 1952 and reelected in 1956, Eisenhower was totally dedicated to leading through conciliation and cooperation at home and through an alliance-based, carefully delineated resistance to communist expansion abroad. At times, he found cunning as useful as compromise, especially in his dealings with Senator McCarthy and with some of the problems he encountered in foreign relations. Since he was convinced that time was on the side of democratic capitalism, he was able to implement and defend his strategic version of the containment policy. Constantly challenged by the aggressive, expanding communist empires and by revolutions in the collapsing British and French empires, Eisenhower was able to provide the leadership that kept America's alliances intact for eight difficult, tumultuous years. His covert efforts were sometimes successful in the short term but frequently unsuccessful in the long run. Overall, though, he was able to achieve his major objectives in foreign policy.

As late as 1952, he still had very little experience with domestic politics and thus was forced once again to learn on the job. These experiences were not always successful and were frequently painful to a leader who was never completely comfortable with interest group and partisan struggles. He was, however, able to work easily with the Democratic opposition in Congress and to maintain his hold on a Republican Party that was deeply divided between an ultra-conservative wing and those who supported Ike's policy of the middle way. An ardent believer in democracy, he worked incessantly, skillfully, and to a considerable extent successfully to achieve his two major goals: prosperity for America and a tenuous Cold War peace for the world. By the time he left the presidency, he was indeed the preeminent leader of the free world.

As a widely admired statesman and military leader, he had every reason to expect that in the 1960s, his voice would continue to command respect after he left office. It was not to be. The Kennedy and Johnson administrations used the Eisenhower policies as a foil as they devised more active programs. This was certainly the case in the two areas of policy—the pursuit of prosperity and the pursuit of peace—that Ike had made the centerpieces of his White House years. Both of the Democratic administrations looked to a more powerful and positive federal government to lead, not to follow, the private sector. Both sought to close the gap between what the economy was capable of doing and what it had been doing by following the middle way. They sought as well to give the United States military new capabilities that would enable America to deal more aggressively with the various wars and revolutions taking place on the frontiers of the American empire.

In a less precise but equally forceful way, both new administrations turned away from the Eisenhower leadership style. The Eisenhower people wore hats; the Kennedy/Johnson people wore baseball caps, if they wore anything at all on their heads. The Eisenhower people played golf; the Kennedy people played golf, too, but were better known for their games of touch football. It was a new social order presided over by leaders determined to be more active, more progressive, and more successful than Ike had been. Eisenhower had attempted to strengthen the Republican

Party's center by recruiting a new cadre of young leaders. He had, how-ever, failed to remake or to rebuild the GOP as the party of middle-way leadership.

The fruits of Kennedy/Johnson leadership included a mixed bag of fundamental, lasting reforms and painful problems, some of which are still with us today. The breakthroughs in civil rights and in welfare poli-cies were tremendously important to an American society that had never made a comfortable, thoroughgoing adjustment to the security and equity challenges of urban, industrial life. On the opposite side of the ledger were a debilitating war in Southeast Asia and the great inflation that Ike had feared and sought to prevent throughout the 1950s. Read-ers can balance the books on the fifties and the sixties as they see fit. One can only hope that they give due credit to Ike's special style of leadership and to the prosperity and peace that he believed would ensure a success-ful future for America's democratic society.

Acknowledgments

Research, writing, and publishing are all social activities. Some authors may see themselves as valiant individuals, struggling against the resistance of a bureaucratic society, a university, even a family. In reality, all authors who manage to get their work published benefit from the support of hundreds of individuals and organizations, many of whom seem to be far in the background, almost out of sight. I am no exception to that rule. All of my work—this book included—has benefited from being at Johns Hopkins University, an institution intensely dedicated to serious scholarship. That is certainly true in the History Department, where my colleagues argue in vigorous seminars over ideas and words, over the philosophy of history as well as numbers and sources and ideologies.

The university supported—and successive editors brought to a successful conclusion—the project editing *The Papers of Dwight David Eisenhower* (in 21 volumes). I was an editor or co-editor on many of those volumes, and that experience prompted my interest in Eisenhower, his career, and his distinctive style of leadership. The papers project also left me indebted to all those who, over many years, pushed that effort ahead and along the way gave me the benefit of their ideas about Eisenhower and his times. Particularly important in that regard were co-editor Daun van Ee, Associate Editor Joseph P. Hobbs, and Senior Associate Editor Elizabeth Hughes. I have drawn heavily upon their work in this book. At Hopkins numerous presidents, provosts, deans, and chairs helped me push ahead with the papers and my own research, including the present study of Ike's identity, reputation, and leadership.

Many others helped bring this book to print. A number of colleagues read parts or all of the manuscript and provided me with excellent advice. They included William Becker, Stephens Broening, Robert Brugger, Christy Chapin, Daun van Ee, Steve Hanke, Robert Hogan,

Alan Matusow, Charles Neu, Carl Reddel, and Jeffrey Sturchio. My research assistants and part-time editors were Jessica Ziparo, Laura Veldhuis, and Patrick Gallagher. Morgan Shahan did much to straighten out my endnotes and tighten my prose. In the History Department, I received special assistance from Megan Zeller, Lisa Enders, Jennifer Stanfield, and Rachel La Bozetta.

At the Eisenhower Memorial Library in Abilene, Kansas, I was helped by Karl Weissenbach, Herb Pankratz, James Leyerzapf, Chalsea Millner, and Kim Barbieri. Audiovisual Archivist Kathy Struss researched and helped me find the photographs I needed to provide a visual sense of Eisenhower's progress from Abilene to the White House and then to retirement at Gettysburg, Pennsylvania. James Gillispie, Curator of Maps at the Sheridan Libraries at Johns Hopkins, produced the map that appears in Chapter 9. Thanks to the Eisenhower Memorial Library, to the Library of Congress, to Getty Images, and to the Associated Press for the photographs in this book.

In addition to the backing at Hopkins, I received financial assistance from two other generous donors. The Eisenhower Legacy Council (Ann C. Whitman Committee and Thomas A. Pappas Committee) helped fund my research trips and other expenses. Chairman Eugene Rossides and Executive Director Jeffrey Blavatt kept this project churning ahead from the beginning through publication. The Hogan Family Foundation made it possible for me to have a sabbatical year that was vital to my research and writing. For many years, I have followed and benefited from Robert Hogan's path-breaking research in personality psychology, and I was particularly pleased to exchange ideas with him about leadership and identity.

Johns Hopkins University Press made it happen—on a tight schedule. With Greg Britton, Catherine Goldstead, Julie McCarthy, and William Krause leading the way, the Press did an outstanding job of converting my manuscript into a book. Sue Warga copyedited the text and notes; the notes in particular presented problems that she handled with great skill. Angela Piliouras helped move that process ahead. Tricia

Gesner of the Associated Press helped us clear some of our pictures, the final impediment to publication.

The "foundation" that was most important to this venture was my own extended family. My young daughters Katherine and Emma Galambos helped me reorganize my office and push forward with my writing and editing. They had backup from Jennifer and Denise Galambos, my older daughters, and from Haley Connor, my granddaughter. We were, and miraculously still are, a family firm working on an innovation, for which the author bears full responsibility for any mistakes, infelicities, and inappropriate conclusions that survived this long, social enterprise.

Notes

Preface

1. My apologies to my colleague John G. A. Pocock, whose magnificent intellectual history *The Machiavellian Moment: Florentine Political Thought and the Atlantic Republican Tradition* (Princeton, NJ: Princeton University Press, 2003; orig. 1975) persuaded me to use his title in the study of leadership. Pocock's reference, like mine, is to Niccolò Machiavelli (1469–1527), the diplomat and intellectual who wrote *The Prince* (1532). I am, however, using the expression "Machiavellian moment" to describe personal encounters, not the grand intellectual epoch that Pocock studied.

2. *Oxford English Dictionary*, s.v. "Machiavellianism."

3. The first agricultural revolution, which involved mechanical innovations such as the harvester, took place in the middle of the nineteenth century. The second agricultural revolution, the so-called Green Revolution, occurred in the middle years of the twentieth century and was driven by breakthroughs in agricultural sciences and practices.

4. These numbers and any in the rest of the book are, unless otherwise noted, from Richard Sutch and Susan B. Carter et al., eds., *Historical Statistics of the United States*, vols. 1–5 (New York: Cambridge University Press, 2006).

5. Dr. Daun van Ee became my co-editor on volumes 15–21 of the *Papers*. I am deeply indebted to him for bringing his unrivaled knowledge of international relations, military history, and American domestic history to bear on this extended project. He also provided me with detailed suggestions as he read the draft chapters of this book.

One. Trouble

1. Morris Janowitz, *The Professional Soldier: A Social and Political Portrait* (New York: Free Press, 1960), 11–12, comments: "Among the military the belief in a prescribed career is particularly strong . . . [and] officers who express too openly their desire to innovate or to criticize are not likely to survive."

2. For a recent, exciting exploration of this issue, see Charles E. Neu, *Colonel House: A Biography of Woodrow Wilson's Silent Partner* (New York: Oxford University Press, 2014). Bear in mind that "identity" is the story you tell about yourself, and "reputation" is the story others tell about you.

3. Garry L. Thompson, "Army Downsizing Following World War I, World War II, Vietnam, and a Comparison to Recent Army Downsizing," master's thesis, US Army Command and General Staff College, Fort Leavenworth, KS, 2002, 1–28.

4. On the conservatism of the military, see William Manchester, *American Caesar: Douglas MacArthur, 1880–1964* (Boston: Little, Brown, 1978), 195.

5. See Dwight D. Eisenhower, "A Tank Discussion: *Infantry Journal*," reprinted in *Eisenhower: The Prewar Diaries and Selected Papers, 1905–1941*, ed. Daniel D. Holt and James W. Leyerzapp (Baltimore: Johns Hopkins University Press, 1998), 28–42.

6. At full strength, an American division at that time included as many as 40,000 men and included brigades of infantry, artillery, and other smaller units. Russell F. Weigley, *History of the United States Army* (New York: Macmillan, 1967), 386.

7. Captain D. D. Eisenhower, (Tanks) Infantry, "A Tank Discussion," *Infantry Journal* 27 (1920): 453–458, available from the US Army Military History Institute. Eisenhower had been reduced in rank to captain, which was his rank when he submitted the article. Shortly thereafter, he was promoted to major, as noted above.

8. Dwight D. Eisenhower, *At Ease: Stories I Tell to Friends* (New York: Doubleday, 1967), 173.

9. On Patton's unusual background, see Carlo D'Este, *Patton: A Genius for War* (New York: HarperCollins, 1995); see also Edgar F. Puryear Jr., *Nineteen Stars* (Washington, DC: Coiner Publications, 1971), 1–10. The army reduced Patton to the permanent rank of captain in 1920, but then promptly promoted him to major.

10. D'Este, *Patton*, 289–301.

11. Forrest C. Pogue, "Foreword," in Puryear, *Nineteen Stars*, vii, compared "the flamboyant Patton, the imperious MacArthur, the genial Eisenhower, and the austere Marshall" and said they "are alike in the devotion to duty and their reactions to reversals."

12. Despite the reprimand from Farnsworth, Eisenhower apparently wrote "Tanks with Infantry" in May 1921. See *Eisenhower: The Prewar Diaries*, 35–42, on this document, which is located in the United States Army Military History Institute. The later document was a practical guide to the use of the tank in coordination with the infantry, and its tone was more subdued than that of the article in the *Infantry Journal* (which was intended to convince and convert its readers).

13. Dwight married Mamie Geneva Doud in 1916, and their first child, Doud Dwight, nicknamed "Ikky," was born in 1917. Dwight, who was frequently broke, applied for and received an allowance for Ikky at a time when the child was actually in Denver. Personally, I find it reasonable to believe that

Eisenhower did this because he needed the money and that he understood exactly what he was doing.

14. The army's efficiency ratings provided a record of an officer's accomplishments, progress, and problems, as recorded by his commanding officer. They are an important measure of the organizational or formal reputation of a US Army officer. The categories were universal—as one might anticipate in a military bureaucracy—and the reports tended to sift out the upper and lower tails of the inevitable bell curve. See, among others, Mark C. Bender, *Watershed at Leavenworth: Dwight D. Eisenhower and the Command and General Staff School* (Fort Leavenworth, KS: US Army Command and General Staff College, 1990), 13. See also Carlo D'Este, *Eisenhower: A Soldier's Life* (New York: Henry Holt, 2002), 161–162.

15. Ike's biographers customarily note the large number of demerits he received at West Point and the manner in which he was willing to throw down a direct challenge to one of his instructors. Later, he would have trouble on at least two notable occasions with his superior officers, one of whom would give him the type of rating that could create problems in a military career.

16. This is a special example of what economists call "path dependency." Usually the analysis is applied to institutions, but it can also be used to help us understand individual careers—especially those in bureaucratic organizations. On path dependency, see the original work of Paul A. David, *Path Dependence and the Quest for Historical Economics: One More Chorus of the Ballad of Qwerty* (Oxford: Nuffield College, 1997).

Two. Abilene

1. The population of Abilene was 3,057 in 1900.

2. *Dickinson County News,* November 18, 1909, Eisenhower Library (hereafter EL).

3. C. O. Musser to Milton S. Eisenhower, July 10, 1945, EL.

4. Fred O. Bartlett to George L. McCarty, EL; Jean Edward Smith, *Eisenhower in War and Peace* (New York: Random House, 2012), 5–6.

5. Michael Korda, *Ike: An American Hero* (New York: HarperCollins, 2007), 56–83. Korda provides an insightful analysis of presidential mythmaking as well as an interesting exploration of the problems David experienced in life. Korda also gives a careful description of David's Texas sojourn as an "engine wiper." From page 83: "However much he admired his father—and there was no question that Ike did—there was no getting around the fact that David Eisenhower, despite a college education and an aptitude for engineering, was stuck in a low-paying, menial job."

6. The Eisenhowers' first son, Arthur, was born in 1886, and their second, Edgar (Ed), in 1889.

7. Bela Kornitzer, *The Great American Heritage: The Story of the Five Eisenhower Brothers* (New York: Farrar, Straus and Cudahy, 1955), 29–30.

8. Carlo D'Este, *Eisenhower: A Soldier's Life* (New York: Henry Holt, 2002), 713–714 nn. 33, 38.

9. Korda, *Ike*, 67.

10. D'Este, *A Soldier's Life*, 714 n. 38.

11. Kornitzer, *The Great American Heritage*, 52–54.

12. *Abilene Daily Chronicle*, April 8, 1903, EL.

13. Kornitzer, *The Great American Heritage*, 23.

14. Dwight D. Eisenhower, *At Ease: Stories I Tell to Friends* (Garden City, NY: Doubleday, 1967), 31.

15. Kornitzer, *The Great American Heritage*, 35. Roy Eisenhower, the sixth brother, died before Kornitzer began working on his book.

16. This was in 1906. *Abilene Reflector-Chronicle*, May 1, 1962, EL.

17. Abilene High School yearbook, 1906, and high school grade sheet, 1904–1905, both in EL.

18. The class system also existed in the high school. Little Ike probably noticed that Herbert Sommers, president of the class for four years, was from the north side of Abilene. Dwight may not have cared, but it seems unlikely that he was entirely oblivious to the difference between the middle-class and working-class families in Abilene. For a different view of the Eisenhower family, see Jonathan W. Jordan, *Brothers, Rivals, Victors: Eisenhower, Patton, Bradley, and the Partnership That Drove the Allied Conquest in Europe* (New York: NAL Caliber, 2011). Jordan places the family in the middle class.

19. Abilene High School yearbooks, 1906 and 1907, EL.

20. In the April 28, 1952, issue of *Life*, John "Six" McDonnell, a baseball pitcher who was a local hero, commented on Little Ike's performance in both baseball and football.

21. Abilene High School yearbook, 1909, EL.

22. Characteristically, when they assigned parts for the class play, *The Merchant of Venice*, Big Ike was the Duke; Bruce Hurd, then captain of the football team, played Antonio; and Little Ike was Launcelot Gobbo, the ignorant servant to Shylock.

23. *Abilene Reflector-Chronicle*, May 1, 1962, EL.

24. D'Este, *A Soldier's Life*, 33; Korda, *Ike*, 63, 69. After a series of schisms, one part of the sect became the Jehovah's Witnesses.

25. The reader can follow this process through the yearbooks for Dwight's class in Abilene's high school. The first year, there was an unusually large class of sixty-seven; by 1907, the class was down to forty-five; by 1908, there were thirty-eight students; and only thirty-one made it to graduation.

26. See Mary P. Ryan, *Mysteries of Sex: Tracing Women and Men Through American History* (Chapel Hill: University of North Carolina Press, 2006);

Claudia Goldin and Lawrence F. Katz, *The Race Between Education and Technology* (Cambridge, MA: Belknap Press of Harvard University Press, 2009); and Claudia Goldin, "A Brief History of Education in the United States," in *Historical Statistics of the United States, II* (New York: Cambridge University Press, 2000).

27. Dwight later explained: "I learned to control my explosions in public." Interview with Reiman Moran, August 5, 1965, EL.

28. See note 24 above.

29. High school grade sheets, 1904–1909, EL.

30. The reader may be unfamiliar with rhetoricals, a subject that later evolved into speech or public speaking.

31. Abilene High School yearbook, 1909, EL.

32. Abilene was overstuffed with reminders that you must earn your bread by the sweat of your brow. The motto of Little Ike's class in 1905 was "The palm is not gained without the dust of labor." Abilene High School yearbook, 1905, EL.

33. *Abilene Reflector-Chronicle*, May 1, 1962, EL.

34. When Dwight's younger brother Roy finished high school, he took a course in pharmacy and later went into business running a drugstore.

35. See Swede Hazlett's memo in his letter of May 23, 1944, to DDE, EL. Hazlett's comment had been prepared for the author Alden Hatch, who was writing a book on General Eisenhower.

36. Eisenhower, *At Ease*, 88–90. Also see Evan Thomas, *Ike's Bluff: President Eisenhower's Secret Battle to Save the World* (New York: Little, Brown, 2012).

37. Today you can also get a presidential appointment and/or one from the vice president.

38. See Kornitzer, *The Great American Heritage,* for information on the educations of the Eisenhower brothers. Roy's drugstore was located in Junction City, Kansas.

39. In 1914, David left the creamery for a job at the Home Gas Company. This position was better suited to his desires for a decent salary, better working conditions, and social status closer to the one he had always hoped to have. Four years later, he became a manager. After 1926, David worked full-time with the organization's benefits committee. He retired in 1931. *The Voice*, February 1931, in EL, shows David in that year wearing a snappy bow tie and looking exactly like the middle-class man he had always aspired to be.

Three. Locked In

1. On identity as a personal story—the story we tell ourselves and others—see Robert Hogan, *Personality and the Fate of Organizations* (Mahwah, NJ: Lawrence Erlbaum Associates, 2007), 8–9. See also Robert Hogan and Gerhard Blickle, "Socioanalytic Theory," in *Handbook of Personality at Work*, ed. N. D. Christiansen and R. P. Tett, 53–70 (New York: Routledge, 2013); and Robert

Hogan and Dana Shelton, "A Socioanalytic Perspective on Job Performance," *Human Performance* 11 (1998): 129–144.

2. This, in fact, was the way Eisenhower remembered it in *At Ease: Stories I Tell to Friends* (New York: Doubleday, 1967), 12.

3. Dwight David Eisenhower to Ruby Norman, EL.

4. Michael Korda, *Ike: An American Hero* (New York: HarperCollins, 2007), 91. He had "a reputation for being something between a class clown and a rebel against all forms of authority." Korda's explanation is that he was "bored" by the classes, really only liked athletics, and knew he was never going to be a high-ranking cadet.

5. Edgar F. Puryear Jr., *Nineteen Stars* (Washington, DC: Coiner Publications, 1971), 13, citing "From Plebe to President," *Collier's*, June 10, 1955, 92–93.

6. His yearbook biography called him "poor Dwight" and said he "merely consents to exist until graduation shall set him free." Cited in Puryear, *Nineteen Stars*, 11–12.

7. Carlo D'Este, *Eisenhower: A Soldier's Life* (New York: Henry Holt, 2002), 63.

8. Records 94, Medical Files, Box 4, EL. Eisenhower later added three inches to his height and two pounds to his weight. Eisenhower, *At Ease*, 7.

9. D'Este, *Eisenhower*, 67–71.

10. Lars Anderson, *Carlisle vs. Army: Jim Thorpe, Dwight Eisenhower, Pop Warner, and the Forgotten Story of Football's Greatest Battle* (New York: Random House, 2008), offers considerable detail about Ike's short football career, which the author juxtaposes to the career of Olympic hero Jim Thorpe for dramatic effect. Ike's first injury apparently occurred when he tackled Thorpe in a game that Thorpe and his Carlisle team won.

11. Puryear, *Nineteen Stars*, 17, citing an interview from May 2, 1963. Also see Korda, *Ike*, 104: "It's hard to escape the feeling that after four years as a cadet, Ike approached graduation in a somewhat confused and uncertain state." I agree but would take out the "somewhat."

12. See Puryear, *Nineteen Stars*, 18–20, for an explanation of Dwight's role as team cheerleader, and note that he also got the designations "A.B." ("Area Bird," for walking off violations) and "B.A." ("Busted Aristocrat," for achieving rank and then getting busted).

13. Russell F. Weigley, *History of the United States Army* (New York: Macmillan, 1967), 313–341.

14. Efficiency Reports, 1915, EL.

15. All of the military evaluations of Eisenhower in this and subsequent chapters are available in EL. While they must be used with caution, they provide many insights into the development of his capacity as a military leader and his likelihood for advancement.

16. Eisenhower, *At Ease*, 11–33. If there were further incidents, he apparently did not get caught.

17. Efficiency Reports, EL.

18. On the demands, see Morris Janowitz, *The Professional Soldier: A Social and Political Portrait* (Glencoe: Free Press, 1960), 175–212.

19. Susan Eisenhower, *Mrs. Ike: Memories and Reflections on the Life of Mamie Eisenhower* (New York: Farrar, Straus and Giroux, 1996), 43–49.

20. These incidents are described with care by D'Este in *Eisenhower*, 96–97.

21. Korda, *Ike*, 109, finds a "sea change" here: "a solid, serious determination to devote himself to his profession, as if he had finally accepted the reality of being an officer in the Army." I find less change, but change in this same direction.

22. See especially the efficiency reports by Colonel T. M. Anderson and Colonel Charles Miller in EL.

23. D'Este, *Eisenhower*, 127; Eisenhower, *At Ease*, 136–137.

24. The appointment was, of course, temporary—that is, limited to the duration of the national emergency.

25. Stephen E. Ambrose, *Eisenhower* (New York: Simon & Schuster, 1983) 1:62–65. D'Este agrees and adds more detail to the Camp Colt experience: *Eisenhower*, 127–132.

26. Efficiency Report, July 30, 1919, EL.

27. The Distinguished Service Medal, the second-highest medal in the US Army, is awarded for exceptional service involving great responsibilities.

28. Major Ira C. Welborn, Infantry, to Adjutant General of the Army, April 6, 1920, EL; D'Este, *Eisenhower*, 137; Jean Edward Smith, *Eisenhower in War and Peace* (New York: Random House, 2012), 68–69.

29. Eisenhower, *At Ease*, 157–166.

30. Ibid., 180–182.

31. D'Este, *Eisenhower*, 133. For the impact on the marriage, see Korda, *Ike*, 159; Eisenhower, *Mrs. Ike*, 74, 75.

32. The financial problem that prompted the second threat made its way into his efficiency reports: "Unfavorable Report IGD, 6/17/21, Reference Signing Vouchers for Quarters When Not Entitled Thereto (IG Files)," EL.

33. See, for instance, the efficiency reports by Colonel S. D. Rockenbach, in 1921, and Lieutenant Colonel Leon L. Roach, in 1920, EL.

34. Puryear, *Nineteen Stars*, 3–5.

35. For details in regard to Patton's career, see the excellent biography by Carlo D'Este, *Patton: A Genius for War* (New York: HarperCollins, 1995).

36. Ibid., 274–277, 281.

37. Janowitz, *The Professional Soldier*, 21–37. Janowitz describes a split between military managers and "heroic leaders, who embody traditionalism and glory." He discusses at length the military's resistance to change. Patton was an anomaly; he was a "heroic leader," but he was also (like Ike) an apostle of change.

Four. Epiphany

1. Carlo D'Este, *Eisenhower: A Soldier's Life* (New York: Henry Holt, 2002), 163, dates the meeting to the autumn of 1919.

2. Edward L. Cox, *Grey Eminence: Fox Conner and the Art of Mentorship* (Stillwater, OK: New Forums, 2011), xii.

3. Ibid., xi–xii, 51, 96–97.

4. D'Este, *Eisenhower*, 161ff.

5. Cox, *Grey Eminence*, xvii–xviii. In 1894, 5 of the 109 entering cadets were, like Conner, from Mississippi (ibid., 9).

6. Ibid., xviii.

7. The comparable position in US corporations would be the chief operating officer (COO); this would not become a common position in business bureaucracies until the multidivisional firm began to replace the unitary or centralized firm as the dominant corporate form for large businesses in the 1940s. See Alfred D. Chandler, *Strategy and Structure: Chapters in the History of the Industrial Enterprise* (Cambridge, MA: MIT Press, 1962).

8. While Conner helped Patton along at a crucial stage of his career, Patton's primary mentor was Lt. Col. Le Roy Eltinge. Carlo D'Este, *Patton: A Genius for War* (New York: HarperCollins, 1995), 203.

9. Conner delegated to Marshall most of the responsibility for planning the AEF's offensive against Germany's Saint-Mihiel salient; he also played a leading role in the planning for the Meuse-Argonne offensive.

10. Cox, *Grey Eminence*, 1–6.

11. Mamie left after months of struggling with depression, insects, rodents, and bats.

12. As Ike's biographers delight in pointing out, Eisenhower's high school yearbook predicted that he would become a professor of history at Yale. The closest he came to that position was as president of Columbia University, but by that time he had more contact with the university's board of trustees than he did with its history department. See Louis Galambos, ed., *The Papers of Dwight David Eisenhower: Columbia University*, vols.10 and 11 (Baltimore: Johns Hopkins University Press, 1984). .

13. A brigade and a regiment can include from 3,000 to 5,000 soldiers.

14. Major Mark C. Bender, *Watershed at Leavenworth: Dwight D. Eisenhower and the Command and General Staff School* (Fort Leavenworth, KS: US Army Command and General Staff College, 1990), 6. Bender's study was written to commemorate the Eisenhower Centennial. While I disagree with some of the author's statements about Ike, I am indebted to Bender for his history of a school that played a central role in the professionalization of army leadership.

15. Cox, *Grey Eminence*, 31–32.

16. D'Este, *Eisenhower*, 168.

17. Fox Conner, Efficiency Report, August 31, 1924, EL.

18. Ibid. Also D'Este, *Eisenhower*, 176–177.

19. On the difference between a mentor and a sponsor, see Sylvia Ann Hewlett, "Mentors Are Good, Sponsors Are Better," *New York Times*, April 14, 2013.

20. Michael Korda, *Ike: An American Hero* (New York: HarperCollins, 2007), 168ff. See D'Este, *Eisenhower*, 176–183, for an authoritative account.

21. D'Este, *Eisenhower*, 176–183, citing Boyd L. Dastrup, *The U.S. Army Command and General Staff College: A Centennial History* (Manhattan, KS: Sunflower University Press, 1982).

22. See the discussion of this article in Chapter One.

23. Bender, *Watershed*, 17.

24. Ibid., 21, 24.

25. Ike was only ranked above average on "physical endurance, military bearing and neatness, and tact" and average on "physical activity, which included 'agility' and the 'ability to work rapidly.'" Bender, *Watershed*, 24–25.

26. Korda, *Ike*, 177.

27. Chief of Staff Diary (henceforth "C/S Diary"), September 26, 1929, EL.

28. Efficiency Report, August 9, 1930, EL.

29. Bender, *Watershed*, 26.

30. The memoir won a Pulitzer Prize but, as D'Este notes, it "went largely unread, in no small part because it was as dull and confusing as Eisenhower had predicted." D'Este, *Eisenhower*, 201. For a more charitable view, see Frank E. Vandiver, *Black Jack: The Life and Times of John J. Pershing*, II (College Station: Texas A&M University Press, 1977), 1084–1086. Even Vandiver remarks, "If the book did not rank as great literature, it did deserve admiration as a splendid historical source." I agree with D'Este, not with the late Professor Vandiver, my former colleague (at Rice University) and a talented historian.

31. See Robert D. Cuff, *The War Industries Board: Business-Government Relations During World War I* (Baltimore: Johns Hopkins University Press, 1973).

32. Evaluation, June 30, 1932, EL.

33. Ibid. He continued: "Major Eisenhower is one of the finest officers I know and in general value to the service I would place him near the top of a list of all officers of my acquaintance. . . . He works rapidly and untiringly. . . . He has a keen intellect. . . . Here is a man I should always like to have with me." The assistant secretary of war concurred: "I, too, have the feeling that I should like to keep him with me." Evaluation, July 1, 1931, EL.

34. Evaluations, July 31, 1931, EL. On February 18, 1933, Moseley recognized DDE's three years of service with him: "What a great blessing you have been! . . . You possess one of those exceptional minds which enables you to

assemble and to analyze a set of facts, always drawing sound conclusions and, equally important, you have the ability to express those conclusions in clear and convincing form." While many other officers could pull together and analyze information, "few have your ability of expression," he wrote. Moseley looked forward to promotion for Eisenhower.

35. In 1923, Ike thought his appendix was to blame for his health issues. In an episode that provides a good measure of the lowly state of American medicine, Eisenhower actually persuaded his doctors to remove his healthy appendix, but the surgery did not cure his recurrent gastrointestinal distress. Clarence G. Lasby, *Eisenhower's Heart Attack: How Ike Beat Heart Disease and Held on to the Presidency* (Lawrence: University of Kansas Press, 1997), esp. 23–25, describes and analyzes in detail the evidence provided by Ike's long medical history. Lasby notes: "Back in Washington, where Eisenhower was extraordinarily busy and under stress with an assignment to the office of the assistant secretary of war, his symptoms returned and persisted for several years" (24).

36. Evaluations, November 4, 1931, EL.

Five. Tested

1. The Chief of Staff was the top officer in the US Army and the only officer who was a four-star general.

2. William Manchester, *American Caesar: Douglas MacArthur, 1880–1964* (Boston: Little, Brown, 1978), 7.

3. D. Clayton James, *The Years of MacArthur* (Boston: Houghton Mifflin, 1970), 1:7–11.

4. Ibid., 32–44.

5. Ibid., 75.

6. Cole C. Kingseed, "Dark Days of White Knights," *Military Review*, January 1993, 67–75, discusses some of the low points in the careers of Douglas MacArthur, Eisenhower, and Patton.

7. MacArthur was given to gross overstatements about these campaigns, and some of his accounts need to be divided by 20 (based on his errors in estimates of German prisoners taken in the action at St. Mihiel). James, *Years of MacArthur*, 204.

8. For a precise and skeptical analysis of one of the central military actions that gave MacArthur his reputation, see Robert H. Ferrell, *The Question of MacArthur's Reputation: Côte de Châtillon, October 14–16, 1918* (Columbia: University of Missouri Press, 2008). For the standard version of MacArthur's heroic actions, see, for instance, Geoffrey Perret, *Old Soldiers Never Die: The Life of Douglas MacArthur* (New York: Random House, 1996), esp. 103–109.

9. This was MacArthur's second tour of duty in the Philippines. His first was 1903–1904, when he was serving with a detachment of US Army engineers.

Carol Morris Petillo, *Douglas MacArthur: The Philippine Years* (Bloomington: Indiana University Press, 1981), esp. 64–78, 125–137.

10. See DDE to Elivera Doud, John Doud, Eda Carlson, November 12, 1931, and C/S Diary, December 1, 1931, both in *Eisenhower: The Prewar Diaries and Selected Papers, 1905–1941*, ed. Daniel D. Holt and James W. Leyerzapf (Baltimore: Johns Hopkins University Press, 1998), 201–202, 205; James, *Years of MacArthur*, 462.

11. C/S Diary, June 15, 1932, in *Eisenhower: The Prewar Diaries*, 224–233.

12. See Carlo D'Este, *Eisenhower: A Soldier's Life* (New York: Henry Holt, 2002), 218–224.

13. Donald J. Lisio, *The President and Protest: Hoover, MacArthur, and the Bonus Riot* (New York: Fordham University Press, 1994). Lisio does an excellent job of examining the evidence and providing the reader with reasonable conclusions about the motivations of the major actors in this disgraceful episode. He delineates Ike's role as a "reluctant" subordinate and notes the two major occasions when Eisenhower's advice to MacArthur was ignored (esp. 192–194, 213–214). Lisio draws upon the account in Dwight D. Eisenhower, *At Ease: Stories I Tell to Friends* (New York: Doubleday, 1967).

14. D. Clayton James, a leading biographer of MacArthur, gives the general as much credit as possible, but suggests that he should have reflected on the lessons of *Don Quixote* before attacking the Bonus Army. James, *Years of MacArthur*, 383–414. Perret, *Old Soldiers Never Die*, 154–161, is more charitable to MacArthur.

15. August 10, 1932, *Eisenhower: The Prewar Diaries*, 233, EL.

16. Report and notes, August 15, 1932, in *Eisenhower: The Prewar Diaries*, 233–247. For more accurate accounts of the army's actions and MacArthur's leadership, see Lisio, *The President and Protest*, and Roger Daniels, *The Bonus March: An Episode of the Great Depression* (Westport, CT: Greenwood, 1971), esp. 242–283.

17. The Chief of Staff had no fixed term and served at the pleasure of the president of the United States. An optimistic Eisenhower commented on the November election results: "While I have no definite leanings toward any political party I believe it is a good thing the Democrats won—and particularly that one party will have such overwhelming superiority in Congress." C/S Diary, November 30, 1932, in *Eisenhower: The Prewar Diaries*, 247.

18. C/S Diary, June 15, 1932, in *Eisenhower: The Prewar Diaries*, 224–233.

19. MacArthur apparently kept him working most nights until 7:30 or 7:45. Eisenhower, *At Ease*, 214.

20. Diary, February 28, 1933, in *Eisenhower: The Prewar Diaries*, 247–249. In addition to favoring centralization, Major Eisenhower thought that enhancing world trade was not the way out of the Depression: "We have a greater per capita wealth in natural resources than any other nation. Very well—let's shut

the others out and proceed scientifically to adjust economic activity within our own country so as to enhance the general standard of living to the greatest extent possible." Diary, April 20, 1933, in *Eisenhower: The Prewar Diaries*, 251–252.

21. Stephen E. Ambrose, *Eisenhower* (New York: Simon & Schuster, 1983) 1:83, comments on the friendship and joint activities of the two Eisenhower brothers during the 1930s.

22. Diary, October 29 and December 9, 1933, in *Eisenhower: The Prewar Diaries*, 253–257. As James points out, the relief work done by the army made MacArthur's political ideas and media image important to FDR. See James, *Years of MacArthur*, 442.

23. DDE to General George V. H. Moseley, February 21, 1934; DDE to Isaac Marcosson, March 5, 1934; DDE to General Fox Conner, April 23, 1934; DDE to Captain J. C. Whitaker, May 31, 1934; Diary, April 26, and June 8, 1934. All in *Eisenhower: The Prewar Diaries*, 264–274. Also see James, *Years of MacArthur*, 426–435, 437–442.

24. John S. D. Eisenhower, "Introduction: The Eisenhower Diaries, 1929–1941," in *Eisenhower: The Prewar Diaries*, xxvii.

25. According to his biographer, MacArthur had been intemperate as he struggled with FDR over the army's budget. James, *Years of MacArthur*, 428–429.

26. Later in life, Eisenhower said that his tour of duty at the War Department was the most stressful, unpleasant part of his career in the army.

27. Remembering that *At Ease* was written many decades after these events, it is nonetheless interesting that Eisenhower recalled these developments in these words: "General MacArthur *lowered the boom on me*, so to speak. . . . Duty with troops was my first desire. Psychologists might argue that my wish was simply a preference for the known over the unknown. I do not know. Whatever might have been going on inside me, I was in no position to argue with the Chief of Staff." Eisenhower, *At Ease*, 220, italics added.

28. As his biographer observes, MacArthur had set himself up for this retaliation by not treating President Roosevelt with the respect he deserved. James, *Years of MacArthur*, 428–429.

29. Eisenhower, *At Ease*, 223. For a more charitable view of MacArthur's actions, see Petillo, *Douglas MacArthur*, 173–175.

30. Diary, December 27, 1935, in *Eisenhower: The Prewar Diaries*, 8–9.

31. Diary, January 20, 1936, in *Eisenhower: The Prewar Diaries*, 302, Ike's dour comment was: "We must never forget that every question is settled in Washington today on the basis of getting votes next November. To decide this matter completely in our favor would gain no votes, while to disapprove the request and give the matter some publicity might be considered as a vote getting proposition among the pacifists and other misguided elements of the American electorate."

32. Diary, January 17, 1936, in *Eisenhower: The Prewar Diaries*,301.

33. Petillo, *Douglas MacArthur*, 180–185. See especially Secretary of State Hull's message to Secretary of War Woodring, September 18, 1936, quoted in ibid., 184.

34. DDE to Ord, July 8, 14, 29, and August 13, 1937, in *Eisenhower: The Prewar Diaries*, 340–354.

35. James, *Years of MacArthur*, 484.

36. Diary, January 20, 1936, in *Eisenhower: The Prewar Diaries*, 304.

37. Diary, February 15, 1936, in *Eisenhower: The Prewar Diaries* 306.

38. Diary, September 26, 1936, in *Eisenhower: The Prewar Diaries*, 328. Roosevelt won a landslide victory that cemented the Democratic coalition.

39. Diary, May 29, 1936, in *Eisenhower: The Prewar Diaries*, 311.

40. Diary, January 20, 1936, in *Eisenhower: The Prewar Diaries*, 309.

41. Jean Edward Smith, *Eisenhower in War and Peace* (New York: Random House, 2012), 135.

42. Eisenhower alluded to these meetings in his letter to Ord, September 1, 1937, in *Eisenhower: The Prewar Diaries*, 356–359; by this time, the two men were meeting almost daily.

43. Diary, January 20, 1936, in *Eisenhower: The Prewar Diaries* 304.

44. For the entire plan, see Diary, June 15, 1936, *Eisenhower: The Prewar Diaries*, 312–325.The peso was pegged at 50 cents to the American dollar.

45. Diary, Christmas 1936, in *Eisenhower: The Prewar Diaries*, 329.

46. Letter to Ord, July 29, 1937, in *Eisenhower: The Prewar Diaries*, 345–349.

47. Diary, December 21, 1937, in *Eisenhower: The Prewar Diaries*, 370–372.

48. Ibid.

49. James, *Years of MacArthur*, 525–526.

50. The total number of islands was 7,100, but only 2,000 were occupied.

51. Diary, February 15, 1938, in *Eisenhower: The Prewar Diaries*, 377.

52. Eisenhower received his promotion on July 1, 1936, when he was forty-five years old.

53. For the holes that Ike began to shoot, as well as MacArthur's effort to break the two men apart, see Diary, April 6, 1938, in *Eisenhower: The Prewar Diaries*, 379–381.

54. Diary, June 18, 1938, in *Eisenhower: The Prewar Diaries*, 383.

55. Ibid.

56. See Eisenhower's diary entries from June 26 through July 18, 1938, in *Eisenhower: The Prewar Diaries*, 387–388.

57. These events are covered in the diary entries from July 18 through October 14, 1938, in *Eisenhower: The Prewar Diaries*, 388–409. See also the accounts in Smith, *Eisenhower in War and Peace*, 144–145, and D'Este, *Eisenhower*, 248. And see Kerry Irish, "Dwight Eisenhower and Douglas MacArthur in the Philippines: There Must Be a Day of Reckoning," *Journal of Military History* 74 (April 2010): 439–473.

58. Sandbagging refers to the practice in poker of concealing your hand (with a call) and then striking with a large bet (a raise) after the pot has been increased. It is a perfectly legal way to bet, but the practice is frowned upon in friendly games.

59. Diary, November 10, 1938, in *Eisenhower: The Prewar Diaries*, 410.

60. Ibid., 410–411.

61. Ibid., 410–412. For various opinions on the conclusion of Ike's tour of duty in the Philippines, see James, *Years of MacArthur*, 564–565; Daniel D. Holt, "An Unlikely Partnership and Service: Dwight Eisenhower, Mark Clark, and the Philippines," *Kansas History* 13 (Autumn 1990): 161–162; D'Este, *Eisenhower*, 248–249; Smith, *Eisenhower in War and Peace*, 141–149; Michael Korda, *Ike: An American Hero* (New York: HarperCollins, 2007), 207–227.

62. See, for instance, his diary entry for December 12, 1938, in *Eisenhower: The Prewar Diaries*, 412–413. Exasperated, Ike wrote, "Will I be glad when I get out of this!!" On January 18, 1939, 419: "We don't have policies, we just walk tight ropes!" See also March 9, 1939, 422–424: "I work on academic subjects, because I have no longer power or opportunity to start execution of needed projects."

63. Holt, "Unlikely Partnership," 149–165. Also see DDE to Major Mark Clark, May 27, 1939, 434; June 7, 1939, 435; June 22, 1939, 435–437; June 28, 1939, 437; all in *Eisenhower: The Prewar Diaries*.

64. DDE to Major Mark Clark, October 25, 1939, in *Eisenhower: The Prewar Diaries*, 451–452.

65. Diary, November 15, 1939, 453–454; December 14, 1939, 456; both in *Eisenhower: The Prewar Diaries*.

66. Diary December 14, 1939, in *Eisenhower: The Prewar Diaries*, 456; John S. D. Eisenhower, *Strictly Personal* (New York: Doubleday, 1974), 6, 17.

67. Evaluation, June 30, 1936, EL.

Six. Combat

1. DDE to Quezon, August 8, 1940, EL. This report is an excellent guide to some of Eisenhower's major assumptions about the challenges of military leadership on the borderline before American entry into the war. It is not too difficult to apply some of his ideas about the Philippines to the United States. These include his emphasis on "removing the worthless type of seniors from controlling positions," promoting morale by eliminating "favoritism, neglect or injustice," and establishing the "clean cut administration through established channels of communication and authority" that would "achieve unity of purpose and effort."

2. Diary, September 3, 1939, 445–447, EL. Ike also noted: "I have had some degree of admiration for Mussolini, none, ever, for Hitler. The former has made some tragic, stupid, mistakes. But he at least has seemed able as an administrator, and for a dictator, has abstained from the use of the 'blood purge' in

maintaining himself in power." Eisenhower guessed that Mussolini would stay out of the war. This was Ike's first serious discussion in his diary of what was happening in Europe.

3. Eisenhower called himself a crusader in a letter to his old friend Swede Hazlett: "I do not mean to sound like a demagogue nor a politician. . . . But I do have the feeling of a crusader in this war." DDE to Hazlett, April 7, 1943, Eisenhower, *The Papers of Dwight David Eisenhower: The War Years*, ed. Alfred D. Chandler Jr. (Baltimore: Johns Hopkins University Press, 1970), 2:1081–1082 (hereafter cited as *Papers*). He would later title his book about the war *Crusade in Europe*. See also Ira Chernus, "Eisenhower's Ideology in World War II," *Armed Forces and Society* 23, no. 4 (Summer 1997): 595–613.

4. See, for instance, DDE to Major Mark Clark, September 23, 1939, 447; October 11, 1939, 450–451; October 25, 1939, 451–452. See also DDE to General Walter C. Sweeney, September 27, 1939, 448. All in EL.

5. DDE to Colonel Leonard T. Gerow, October 11, 1939, 449–450, and August 23, 1940, 489–490; DDE to Thomas A. Terry, May 1, 1940, 463; DDE to Brigadier General Courtney Hodges, May 1, 1940, 464. Also see DDE to Lieutenant Colonel Omar N. Bradley, July 1, 1940, 466–467; DDE to Colonel George S. Patton Jr., September 17, 1940, 491–492. All in EL.

6. In a diary entry on September 26, 1940, 493–495, EL, Ike explained that "it has been a constant battle to stay with the outfit."

7. Walter Krueger to George C. Marshall [hereafter GCM], June 11, 1941, in *The Papers of George Catlett Marshall*, ed. Larry I. Bland (Baltimore: Johns Hopkins University Press, 1986), 2:534n.1 (henceforth *Marshall Papers*).

8. See, for instance, Ike to Hugh A. Parker, February 8, 1941, in *Eisenhower: The Prewar Diaries and Selected Papers*, 1905–1941, ed. Daniel D. Holt and James W. Leyerzapf (Baltimore: Johns Hopkins University Press, 1997), 514–516: "Of one thing I'm certain: I'm weary of these eternal staff details. I'd like to get a command of my own, even if just a squad."

9. Notes for Colonel Charles H. Corlett, June 1941, in *Eisenhower: The Prewar Diaries*, 517–520.

10. Ike, who feared that MacArthur might again request his services, urged his friend Wade Haislip (Assistant Chief of Staff, G-1, at the War Department) not to send him "back to gugu land, no matter how wonderful the possibilities may *appear* to be." DDE to Wade Haislip, July 28, 1941, in *Eisenhower: The Prewar Diaries*, 534.

11. GCM, Speech to the Army Ordnance Association, October 11, 1939, *Marshall Papers*, 2:83. In 1939, Marshall replaced General Malin Craig as US Army Chief of Staff.

12. GCM to Major General Walter K. Wilson, October 7, 1941, *Marshall Papers*, 2:631–633. "I might tell you, and most confidentially, that General McNair's greatest concern and that of all his officers is the problem of corps

command. That was the greatest lesson of the Louisiana maneuvers." See GCM to Lieutenant General Walter Krueger, October 30, 1941, *Marshall Papers*, 2:655–657, for part of the political kickback to the changes in leadership.

13. See Chapter Three.

14. Christopher R. Gabel, *The U.S. Army GHQ Maneuvers of 1941* (Washington, DC: Center of Military History, 1992), esp. 185–194. "The thirty-one caretakers, commanders of major units in the GHQ maneuvers who did not win combat commands, gave way to younger, more promising, officers" (187). Also see Carlo D'Este, *Eisenhower: A Soldier's Life* (New York: Henry Holt, 2002), 277–281; Forrest C. Pogue, *George C. Marshall: Ordeal and Hope* (New York: Viking Press, 1963), 162–163; and Cole C. Kingseed, "Eisenhower's Prewar Anonymity: Myth or Reality?," *Parameters* 21, no. 3 (1991): 87–98.

15. Pogue, *Ordeal and Hope*, 92–101. The issue of officer retirements was particularly politicized where the National Guard was involved.

16. Gabel, *GHQ Maneuvers*, 170–184.

17. In October, after the Louisiana maneuvers, Eisenhower had told Gerow: "Things are moving so rapidly these days that I get almost dizzy trying to keep up with the parade." In December, of course, the pace would get even faster. DDE to Leonard T. Gerow, October 4, 1941, in *Eisenhower: The Prewar Diaries*, 547.

18. D'Este, *Eisenhower*, 282.

19. Chaumont is the French community where the American Expeditionary Force had its headquarters in the World War.

20. Eisenhower, *Papers*, 1:5–6, 9. Eisenhower and Marshall agreed that they could probably not protect the Philippines from a full-scale invasion, but they both thought an effort had to be made to "save them." A revised version of the paper, dated December 17, 1941, can be found on 9.

21. Not all the recommendations were strong. General McNair put Eisenhower at the bottom of a list of general officers with potential for higher command positions. D'Este, *Eisenhower*, 282.

22. While Marshall had his problems at VMI, he was the top cadet for military activities, ranking corporal in the second year, ranking first sergeant in the third, and first captain in his final year. He did not so do well in class but managed to push himself up to be fifth by the time he graduated.

23. Forrest C. Pogue, *George C. Marshall: Education of a General, 1880–1939* (New York: Viking Press, 1963), 53. "I tried very hard"; "I was very exacting and very exact in all my military duties; as I gradually developed from the mild authority—almost none—exercised by the corporal, to the pronounced authority of the first sergeant." Also see Edgar F. Puryear Jr., *Nineteen Stars* (Washington, DC: Coiner Publications, 1971), 37. Marshall sought "military distinction" and did not receive any demerits in four years. During this time, he was also very much in love, and often snuck out to see his girlfriend. Luckily for him, he was never caught.

24. Puryear, *Nineteen Stars*, 43–66. General MacArthur had a negative influence on Marshall's career, probably as a result of the latter's association with what was called the Chaumont group around General Pershing. See Chapter Five for the details.

25. On the Eastern Front, see John Erickson, *The Road to Stalingrad: Stalin's War with Germany* (New York: Harper and Row, 1975), esp. 101–249. *Papers*, 1:19–20, 23–31 provides an excellent perspective on Eisenhower's work in support of Marshall during the Arcadia conference.

26. The Churchill Project, Hillsdale College, "Were 'Soft Underbelly' and 'Fortress Europe' Churchill Phrases?," April 1, 2016, https://winstonchurchill. hillsdale.edu/?s=soft+underbelly. Churchill's metaphor involved the alligator, which he said should be attacked on the belly and not on the snout.

27. Marshall apparently threatened to resign over the issue of control over war supplies, but this may have just been a rhetorical ploy. Pogue, *Ordeal and Hope*, 287.

28. Ibid., 261–288.

29. In the course of organizing and reorganizing the War Department, the War Plans Division became the Operations Division, but both names were used for a time. *Papers*, 1:109. Ike replaced his good friend Gerow, who moved on to command an infantry division. In regard to the plans involving North Africa, see *Papers*, 1:137–142.

30. The unity question extended from the top to the bottom of the joint effort. On unified commands see Pogue, *Ordeal and Hope*, 275–282. A fully annotated copy of Eisenhower's December 26, 1941, draft instructions to the Supreme Commander, Southwest Pacific Theater, is in *Papers*, 1:24–31. In January 1942, Ike wrote in his notes: "The struggle to secure the adoption by all concerned of a common concept of strategical objectives is wearing me down"; *Papers*, 1:66. The forces pressing against unity were rooted in national, service, and personal interests that were in conflict. See, for instance, *Papers*, 1:174–176 for an attempt to allocate responsibilities between Britain and the United States. See also the directive to Douglas MacArthur, March 18, 1942, *Papers*, 1:189–192. See DDE to Marshall, March 20, 1942, *Papers*, 1:197–198, on an effort to achieve unity of command between the US Navy and Army in the Caribbean.

31. DDE to Marshall, March 25, 1942, *Papers*, 1:205–208. Also see Pogue, *Ordeal and Hope*, 305–306. For a different version of the respective roles of FDR and Churchill, see Nigel Hamilton, *The Mantle of Command: FDR at War, 1941–1942* (Boston: Houghton Mifflin Harcourt, 2014), 101–135, 254–264, 310–321, 363–370.

32. This was the cross-Channel assault code-named SLEDGEHAMMER (part of the broader buildup named BOLERO). On Marshall's trip to Britain, see Pogue, *Ordeal and Hope*, 302–320.

33. Ibid., 326. The Soviets were maneuvering to get the Allies to launch an attack through France as soon as possible. One part of that effort involved repeated hints that Stalin might reach an agreement with Hitler and leave the war.

34. Marshall put through Ike's promotion to major general in March 1942. See *Papers*, 1:217–218, and Dwight D. Eisenhower, *At Ease: Stories I Tell to Friends* (New York: Doubleday, 1967), 249–250. Despite the advantages of his position, Ike called it a "slave seat." DDE to Patton, April 4, 1942, *Papers*, 1:227.

35. DDE Memorandum, May 30, 1942, *Papers*, 1:318–327.

36. DDE to Marshall, June 3, 1942, and Notes, June 4, 1942, *Papers*, 1:327–328.

37. DDE to Marshall, June 3, 1942, *Papers*, 1:327–28. See also DDE to Marshall, June 6, 1942, *Papers*, 1:331–332.

38. Quoted in Pogue, *Ordeal and Hope*, 339.

39. In 1941, General McNair ranked Eisenhower as his eighteenth choice for command of a division.

40. D'Este, *Eisenhower*, 304–305, describes Ike's first encounter with Montgomery, who told his American visitor that he had to snuff out his cigarette during the briefing. Things did not go much better when Ike first met Brooke (305–306). For the formal ("nice-nice") versions, see *Papers*, 1:318–327.

41. Joseph Patrick Hobbs, *Dear General: Eisenhower's Wartime Letters to Marshall* (Baltimore: Johns Hopkins University Press, 1971), 5–6, emphasizes the influence the evaluations of Generals Pershing and Conner had on Marshall's decision; still, I find the choice startling.

42. DDE, Notes, June 8, 1942, *Papers*, 1:333–334. See also DDE, Notes, June 11, 1942, *Papers*, 1:337: "The C/S says I'm the guy." The appointment was effective June 25.

43. Compare DDE to Marshall, July 7, 1942, 373–376, with July 11, 1942, and July 14, 1942, 378–381. See also DDE, "Conclusions as to the Practicability of SLEDGEHAMMER," July 17, 1942, *Papers*, 1:388–392, and DDE to Marshall and Ernest J. King, July 19, 1942, *Papers*, 1: 393–396.

44. DDE Memorandum, July 22, 1942, *Papers*, 1: 405–406. Marshall and King gave in to the British and learned that FDR already had a North African campaign in mind. Pogue calls his chapter on these events "Marshall Loses a Fight." *Ordeal and Hope*, 321–349.

45. DDE to Marshall, July 23, 1942, *Papers*, 1: 407–414. Ike considered the North African campaign "defensive in character," but he concluded that it was preferable to the other possibilities. Eisenhower called July 22, when the decision was reached, "the blackest day in history," See also Pogue, *Ordeal and Hope*, 348–349.

46. Eisenhower had also been promoted to lieutenant general on July 7, 1942. His title would now be Commander in Chief, Allied Expeditionary Force.

47. Gruenther (USMA 1918) was one of Ike's close personal friends; he had served as chief of staff of the Third Army, the position Eisenhower had held before going to Washington.

48. Lee (USMA 1909), who had extensive experience in the Corps of Engineers, would serve as Ike's logistical expert—a function that imposed unwelcomed, unglamorous, and unyielding constraints upon the progress of all combat units.

49. Smith, who had served with Eisenhower in Washington, became Ike's chief of staff.

50. Eisenhower's evaluation of Bradley would shoot up during the campaign in Tunisia.

51. See, for instance, DDE to Hastings Lionel Ismay, August 6, 1942, *Papers*, 1:444–447.

52. Crucial decisions were being made from early August through early November 1942; see *Papers*, 1:439–658 for the details.

53. DDE to Marshall, August 17, 1942, *Papers*, 1:476–479.

54. DDE to Marshall, June 3, 1942, *Papers*, 1:327–328; DDE to Prichard, August 27, 1942, *Papers*, 1:505–507.

55. See DDE to Marshall, October 17, 1942, *Papers*, 1:622–625, for a careful discussion of the issues and imponderables.

56. See Hobbs, *Dear General*, 12–15, for a good discussion of this problem.

57. The timing of the attack was under continuous discussion; schedules were very tight both for manpower and for supplies. Eisenhower and the Combined Chiefs of Staff gradually pushed back the date of attack. Despite pressure from the president of the United States and the prime minister of Britain, October plans were postponed until Sunday, November 8, when the three-pronged amphibious assault began. See, for instance, DDE to Marshall, September 10, 1942, *Papers*, 1:549–550, and September 12, 1942, *Papers*, 1:555–556.

58. Martin Blumenson, *Mark Clark* (New York: Congdon and Weed, 1984), 76–92.

59. DDE to Marshall, November 7 and November 8, 1942; to Combined Chiefs of Staff, November 8, 1942; to Mark Wayne Clark, November [8], 1942, *Papers*, 2:665–676.

60. Blumenson, *Mark Clark*, 91–96; D'Este, *Eisenhower*, 344–348.

61. DDE to Walter Bedell Smith, November 9, 1942, *Papers*, 2:677.

62. DDE to Combined Chiefs of Staff, November 14, 1942, *Papers*, 2:707–711.

63. DDE to Marshall, November 17, 1942, *Papers*, 2:729.

64. See, for instance, DDE's long, anguished message to Walter Bedell Smith, November 18, 1942, *Papers*, 2:732–736. Ike said, "God knows I'm not repeat not trying to be a kingmaker."

65. DDE to Marshall, November 19, 1942, *Papers*, 2:737–739. On that same day, Ike told Mark Clark, "For two days here I thought I would simply have to go to a padded cell" (2:739–741).

66. The pressure from the media is described fully in Harry C. Butcher, *My Three Years with Eisenhower: The Personal Diary of Captain Harry C. Butcher, USNR, Naval Aide to General Eisenhower, 1942–1945* (New York: Simon and Schuster, 1946), esp. 236–251.

67. The situation became slightly less complex after a Free French assassin killed Darlan in December 1942.

68. George F. Howe, *Northwest Africa: Seizing the Initiative in the West* (Washington, DC: Office of the Chief of Military History, 1957), 89–273, describes in detail the landings and immediately subsequent battles. This narrative account gives a good sense of the difference between strategic plans and the resulting, chaotic action.

69. D'Este's *Eisenhower: A Soldier's Life*, 360–374 (a chapter titled "The Dreariest Chapter in the History of Allied Collaboration") provides an excellent account of the campaign and its problems.

70. DDE to Winston Churchill, December 5, 1942, *Papers*, 2:801–805.

71. Forrest C. Pogue, *George C. Marshall: Organizer of Victory* (New York: Viking Press, 2002), 5, says FDR "imposed no unified plan." Nor did Marshall have a unified position from the Chiefs of Staff (15). With FDR leaning toward the Mediterranean and accepting a delay in the cross-Channel attack, Marshall and Eisenhower were unable to impose their own strategy on the conference (15–31).

72. DDE to Henry Harley Arnold, January 19, 1943, and DDE to Marshall, January 19, 1943, *Papers*, 2:910–911. Merle Miller, *Ike the Soldier: As They Knew Him* (New York: G.P. Putnam's Sons, 1987), 463–464, says Ike was "napping" when this happened. It seems more likely to me that he was worried about being replaced as Supreme Commander. Rick Atkinson, *An Army at Dawn: The War in North Africa, 1942–1943* (New York: Henry Holt, 2002), 303, 327–329.

73. Ike had been digging rather deeply into detailed aspects of the campaign in Tunisia. See, for example, DDE to Kenneth Arthur Noel Anderson, December 14, 1942, *Papers*, 2:840–841; also DDE Memorandum, December 15, 1942, *Papers*, 2:842–844. He was increasing his role as the Casablanca meeting approached. DDE to Combined Chiefs of Staff and British Chiefs of Staff, December 29, 1942, *Papers*, 2:871–873.

74. As recently as December 29, Eisenhower had wanted to appoint Spaatz to head the new Allied Air Force (DDE to Marshall, *Papers*, 2:873–875), but the Combined Chiefs of Staff appointed Air Chief Marshal Tedder instead. DDE to Combined Chiefs of Staff and British Chiefs of Staff, December 31, 1942, *Papers*, 2:879–880.

75. In case you forgot, the first time was near the end of his service with General MacArthur; see Chapter Five. On Casablanca, see Michael Korda, *Ike: An American Hero* (New York: HarperCollins, 2007), 359–363; D'Este, *Eisenhower*, 382–390; Alan Brooke Alanbrooke, *War Diaries 1939–45: Field Marshal Lord Alanbrooke* (Berkeley: University of California Press, 2001), 356–365. With Ike pushed "up into the stratosphere," Alexander would (Alanbrooke concluded) now "restore the necessary drive and co-ordination which had been so seriously lacking of late." For a different perspective on Ike's situation at Casablanca, see Eric Larrabee, *Commander in Chief: Franklin Delano Roosevelt, His Lieutenants, and Their War* (New York: Harper and Row, 1987), 428–431.

76. Two developments on the German side were of overwhelming importance. First was Hitler's decision to pour men and equipment into the defense of North Africa, despite Rommel's advice to the contrary. The second was the struggle between Rommel and Generaloberst Juergen von Arnim to control strategy and tactics in Tunisia. See Martin Blumenson, *Rommel's Last Victory: The Battle of Kasserine Pass* (London: Allen and Unwin, 1968), esp. 179ff.

77. DDE to Combined Chiefs of Staff, February 15, 1943, *Papers* 2:953–955.

78. Eisenhower had commended Fredendall after the landings. DDE to Walter Bedell Smith, November 10, 1942, and DDE to Marshall, November 10, 1942, *Papers*, 2:685–689. As late as February 4, he was pushing for Fredendall's promotion (DDE to Marshall, *Papers*, 2:936–938), even as he expressed concern about what Fredendall was doing to defend the army's southern flank. For Ike's concerns, see DDE to Lloyd Ralston Fredendall, February 4, *Papers*, 2:939–941.

79. "Chronology," *Papers*, 5:105. Eisenhower was with the II Corps on February 13 and 14. D'Este, *Eisenhower*, 391–394; Korda, *Ike*, 365–370. See Blumenson, *Rommel's Last Victory*, for a detailed description of the series of battles and the rationale for Rommel's withdrawal. See also Atkinson, *An Army at Dawn*, 357–392.

80. Andrew S. Grove, *Only the Paranoid Survive: How to Exploit the Crisis Points That Challenge Every Company* (New York: Doubleday, 1999), 3–7.

81. Korda, *Ike*, 365–367; D'Este, *Eisenhower*, 392–394; Blumenson, *Rommel's Last Victory*, 86–87, 120–129; Eisenhower, *At Ease*, 261–263.

82. Eisenhower had dealt with the problem of officers who did not perform well in his message to Marshall, December 11, 1942, *Papers*, 2:827–829, but Fredendall was a more serious and complicated matter.

83. Eisenhower first tried to bolster Fredendall by sending General Ernest N. Harmon to restore order at the front. Carlo D'Este, *Patton: A Genius for War* (New York: HarperCollins, 1995), 460. Soon, though, it became necessary to oust Fredendall and bring in Patton. DDE to Patton, March 6, 1943, *Papers*,

2:1010–1011. Also see D'Este, *Patton*, 460–470. Once Patton had completed his work, he would return to the job of getting ready to invade Sicily and would be replaced in Tunisia by General Omar Bradley. DDE to Marshall, March 8, 1943, *Papers*, 2:1016–1017.

84. Eisenhower later followed Patton's advice and replaced General Ward with General Harmon in command of the 1st Armored Division. DDE to Marshall, April 3, 1943, *Papers*, 2:1066–1067.

85. Pogue, *Organizer of Victory*, 183–187, is kind to both Fredendall and Ike. Eisenhower—like Marshall—let Fredendall down very gently. So much so, in fact, that Fredendall was honored as a hero on his return to the United States for a training mission. See DDE to Fredendall, March 2, 1943, and DDE to Marshall, March 3 and March 4, 1943, *Papers*, 2:1002–1003, 1006–1007.

86. In the midst of the landings and efforts to move toward Tunisia, Eisenhower had continued to advocate the cross-Channel strategy. See DDE to Thomas Troy Handy, November 22, 1942, *Papers*, 2, 760–761: "We still have to defeat the German Armies in Europe. . . . Dispersion must cease!"

87. DDE to Marshall, February 21, 1943; DDE to Combined Chiefs of Staff and British Chiefs of Staff, February 21, 1942, *Papers*, 2:970–974.

88. Blumenson, *Rommel's Last Victory*, 302–304.

89. In Howe, *Northwest Africa*, cf. 514–519 (Médenine) with 401–458 (Kasserine Pass). According to Howe (442), Rommel specifically sought through his attack against the US II Corps to create greater disunity among the Allies. Although the attack stalled, Rommel had certainly sharpened the differences between the British and American forces.

90. D'Este, *Eisenhower*, 395.

91. See D'Este, *Eisenhower*, 402 and Jonathan W. Jordan, *Brothers, Rivals, Victors: Eisenhower, Patton, Bradley, and the Partnership That Drove the Allied Conquest in Europe* (New York: NAL Caliber, 2011), 147–158, for Patton's fierce reactions to this situation.

92. Ike also objected in a more conciliatory tone; DDE to Alexander, March 21, 1943, *Papers*, 2:1055–1057. He continued to put on pressure to increase the objectives of the II Corps; DDE to Alexander, April 2, 1943, *Papers*, 2:1065–1066. For the outcome, see DDE to CCS, April 5, 1943, *Papers*, 2:1075–1077, and Howe, *Northwest Africa*, 543–577.

93. Howe, *Northwest Africa*, 613–668.

94. D'Este, *Patton*, 471–490.

95. For a good example of the disunity created by the tension between the British and Americans, see Howe, *Northwest Africa*, 590–591, 599.

96. See DDE to Marshall, April 24, 1943, *Papers*, 2:1101. Ike was commenting on General Ward's lack of "callousness," but he was clearly talking about his own increasing "callousness." See also DDE to Anderson, June 7, 1943, *Papers*, 2:1178.

97. On April 15, 1943, Bradley took over from Patton, who returned to his main task of getting ready for the invasion of Sicily. For the problems with newspaper accounts that worked against British-American unity, see DDE to Marshall, April 15 and 16, 1943, *Papers*, 2:1089–1093.

98. For the ongoing British-American discourse, see DDE to Joint Chiefs of Staff and British Chiefs of Staff, April 12, 1943, *Papers*, 2:1086–1087.

99. See, for instance, DDE to Alan Francis Brooke, July 3, 1943, *Papers*, 2:1236–1237.

100. DDE to Combined Chiefs of Staff and British Chiefs of Staff, July 11, 1943, *Papers*, 2:1253–1254. On the tragic antiaircraft fire that inadvertently brought down twenty-three troop transports, see DDE to Alexander, July 12, 1943, and DDE to Patton, July 12, 1943, *Papers*, 2:1254–1256.

101. DDE to Marshall, July 17, 1943, *Papers*, 2:1248–1260; DDE to Combined Chiefs of Staff and British Chiefs of Staff, August 2, 1943, *Papers*, 2:1305–1307.

102. For interim reports, see DDE to Combined Chiefs of Staff and British Chiefs of Staff, August 4 and August 16, 1943, *Papers*, 2:1313–1314, 1335.

103. For Ike's evaluations of his officers, including Patton, Bradley, and Clark, see DDE to Marshall, August 24 and 27, 1943, *Papers*, 2:1353–1355, 1357–1358.

104. Hobbs, *Dear General*, 62–70, provides an excellent perspective on Eisenhower's approach to "command and organization."

105. DDE to Geoffrey Keyes, September 27, 1943, *Papers*, 3:1465–1466.

106. D'Este, *Patton*, 521–546, covers the incident in detail.

107. The unity issue was broad—far broader than just British-American relations. Shortly before the invasion of Sicily, Ike had to deal again with the split between de Gaulle and Giraud; see, for instance, DDE to FDR, and DDE to Marshall, both June 18, 1943, *Papers*, 2:1192–1195; DDE to Marshall, June 22, 1943, *Papers*, 2:1207. For some of the rough edges in British-American relations, see DDE to Churchill, August 4, 1943, and DDE to Alexander, August 5, 1943, *Papers*, 2:1318–1320.

Seven. The Decision

1. As quoted in David M. Glantz and Jonathan M. House, *The Battle of Kursk* (Lawrence: University of Kansas Press, 1999), 188.

2. It is important to remember that men as well as "torn-off turrets" were being blown out of the tanks.

3. For the Nobel Prize–winning author's account of his brief service in the SS on the Eastern Front, see Günter Grass, "How I Spent the War: A Recruit in the Waffen S.S.," *New Yorker*, June 4, 2007. Grass was sixteen when he was drafted into the Labor Service.

4. John Erickson, *The Road to Berlin: Continuing the History of Stalin's War with Germany* (Boulder, CO: Westview Press, 1983). See esp. ch. 3, "Breaking

the Equilibrium: Kursk and its Aftermath," 87–135. In regard to the importance of the Soviet victories on the Eastern Front, I am in complete agreement
with David Eisenhower's account in *Eisenhower at War, 1943–1945* (New York:
Vintage Books, 1987).

5. This is one of the two occasions in which I broke my own rule and looked
far into Eisenhower's future.

6. There are no references to Kursk in the Eisenhower papers or in George C.
Marshall, *The Papers of George Catlett Marshall*, ed. Larry I. Bland, vol. 4
(Baltimore: Johns Hopkins University Press, 1996). On the continuing British
pressure to move into Italy, see Gordon A. Harrison, *The European Theater of
Operations: Cross-Channel Attack* (Washington, DC: Office of the Chief of
Military History, Department of the Army, 1993, orig. 1951), 68.

7. See, for instance, DDE to Combined Chiefs of Staff and British Chiefs of
Staff, August 28 and 30 (cables 8660 and 8720), 1943, *Papers*, 2:1361–1367.

8. The compromise reached at the Trident Conference in Washington, DC,
May 12–25, was to limit the number of troops deployed in Italy so as to build up
the Allied force in England. See DDE to Patton, June 4, 1943, *Papers*, 2:1173–1175.
For the ongoing discussion of what would follow the campaign in Sicily, see also
DDE to Combined Chiefs of Staff and British Chiefs of Staff, July 18, 1943,
Papers, 2:1261–1262, in which Ike followed his commanders and advocated an
Italian campaign. He still wanted to stop "nibbling and jabbing in order to
leap straight at the vitals of the enemy." DDE to Churchill, July 18, 1943,
Papers, 2:1262–1263. See also DDE to Marshall, September 14, 1943, *Papers*,
3:1416–1417, in which he said "there can be much room for argument" about the
conquest of all of Italy. The Italian surrender was messy but not as questionable
as the Vichy affair; see DDE to Combined Chiefs of Staff and British Chiefs of
Staff, September 8 and 9, 1943, *Papers*, 3:1404–1407.

9. DDE to Combined Chiefs of Staff and British Chiefs of Staff, September 18
and 30, 1943, and DDE to Walter Bedell Smith, September 19, 1943, *Papers*,
3:1430–1435, 1469–1470. Martin Blumenson, *The Mediterranean Theater of
Operations: Salerno to Cassino* (Washington, DC: Center of Military History,
US Army, 1993, orig. 1969), 15, says: "The most widespread assumption among
Allied planners was that an Italian collapse would move the Germans to
withdraw from Italy." This time, however, Hitler rushed his forces into Italy,
and the Allies had to fight their way north in a brutal campaign that was
expensive in terms of men, matériel, and time.

10. DDE to Combined Chiefs of Staff, September 1, 1943, and DDE to Walter
Bedell Smith, September 2, 1943, *Papers*, 2:1375–1377, 1382; DDE to Marshall,
September 13, 1943, and DDE to Combined Chiefs of Staff and British Chiefs of
Staff, September 15, 1943, *Papers*, 3:1411, 1424–1425.

11. DDE to Combined Chiefs of Staff and British Chiefs of Staff, September 21,
1943, *Papers*, 3:1446–1447. While Ike had always sought unity, he now gave

even more emphasis to the importance of combining the land, air, and naval forces to achieve success in an invasion.

12. Blumenson, *Salerno to Cassino*, 208.

13. Dwight D. Eisenhower, *Crusade in Europe* (Garden City, NY: Doubleday, 1948), 194.

14. See the discussion of the role of the British Eighth Army at Salerno in Blumenson, *Salerno to Cassino*, 138–143.

15. Eisenhower, *Crusade*, 194.

16. DDE, Memorandum for Diary, November 12, 1943, *Papers*, 3:1560–1563.

17. Ike had first played this card in his message to Alexander, March 23, 1943, *Papers*, 2:1055–1057.

18. Chief of Staff George Marshall estimated that when the buildup of Allied forces in France reached sixty divisions, the United States would be supplying forty-two, the British thirteen, and Canada five. Marshall, Memorandum for the President, August 11, 1943, *Marshall Papers*, 4:87–88.

19. Maurice Matloff, *Strategic Planning for Coalition Warfare, 1943–1944* (Washington, DC: Center of Military History, US Army, 1994, orig. 1959), 244.

20. DDE to Churchill, October 9, 1943, and DDE to Combined Chiefs of Staff and British Chiefs of Staff, October 9, 1943, *Papers*, 3:1494–1498.

21. Eisenhower was providing advice to Lord Louis Mountbatten, the newly appointed Supreme Allied Commander, Southeast Asia. DDE to Mountbatten, September 14, 1943, *Papers*, 3:1420–1424.

22. See, for instance, Marshall to Eisenhower, September 22, 1943, *Marshall Papers*, 4:136–137.

23. On the campaign, see DDE to Combined Chiefs of Staff and British Chiefs of Staff, November 4, 1943, *Papers*, 3:1548–1550.

24. FDR announced the decision at the Teheran conference, and Ike was informed in early December. See Marshall to Eisenhower, December 7, 1943, *Marshall Papers*, 4:197–198; DDE to Marshall, December 17, 1943, *Papers*, 3:1604–1607.

25. Churchill, displaying his usual panache, had jumped the gun and told General Sir Alan Brooke that he would have the appointment. Harrison, *European Theater*, 113.

26. For a time, it appeared Marshall would get the appointment; see DDE to Walter Bedell Smith, October 2, 1943, *Papers*, 3:1479–1482. Also see *Marshall Papers*, 4:129.

27. DDE, Memorandum for Diary, December 6, 1943, *Papers*, 3:1585–1589.

28. Eisenhower's attention was increasingly captured by the plans for the cross-Channel invasion, but he did not leave the Mediterranean until the end of December, when he flew back to the United States. He then traveled to Britain in the middle of January 1944.

29. Ike had, among other things, become much tougher about relieving officers who failed to be successful in combat. Compare his earlier treatment of Fredendall with his abrupt dismissal of Major General Dawley. DDE to Marshall, September 19, 1943, *Papers*, 3:1436.

30. Eisenhower quickly assigned leading positions to General Bradley and General Patton. He went far beyond that in attempting to ensure that he would have a deep team that would perform well in combat. See, for instance, Marshall to Eisenhower, February 25, 1944, and March 20, 1944, *Marshall Papers*, 4:317–318, 356–357. Marshall had General McNair combing through his units to find the kind of aggressive, battle-experienced commanders Ike wanted.

31. Marshall to Eisenhower, December 28 and 29, 1943, *Marshall Papers*, 4:210–211, 215–216.

32. It is expected of every author who writes on Ike to have a conclusion about his relationship with Kay Summersby. So here is mine: She was a beautiful, charming former model who became an important member of Ike's immediate entourage, often called his "family." She served along with Harry Butcher, his naval aide; with Sergeant John A. Moaney, a personal aide; and others, who spent a great deal of time with Ike. He relaxed with Kay and without doubt had what was once called a "crush" on her. Were they sleeping together? I doubt it for two reasons: they were seldom alone, and Kay did not mention it in her second book on the subject, done with a ghostwriter when she was dying. See Kay Summersby Morgan, *Past Forgetting: My Love Affair with Dwight D. Eisenhower* (New York: Simon and Schuster, 1975). Kay's earlier account—*Eisenhower Was My Boss* (New York: Prentice-Hall, 1948)—was less explicit and less interesting in regard to its main subject. The only time their relationship might have intruded on Eisenhower's leadership was when he rather foolishly attempted to introduce her to King George, who refused to acknowledge her presence.

33. See Eisenhower to Marshall, February 19, 1944, for an excellent discussion of what Eisenhower called "the initial crisis of the Campaign," that is, the effort to establish a beachhead and the likely German counterattack. *Papers*, 3:1736–1740. The anticipated margin was so tight that the outcome might be swayed by the ability to keep the planned percentage of landing craft actually in operation. In effect, the absence of spare parts for landing craft might undercut the entire assault. Harrison, *European Theater*, 170–171.

34. Early on, Ike told his chief of staff, "There is a very deep conviction here, in all circles, that we are approaching a tremendous crisis with stakes incalculable." January 22, 1944, *Papers*, 3:1672. See the excellent discussion of Overlord planning under General Morgan in Harrison, *European Theater*, 71–79: "General Morgan was always conscious that the Allies, with such limited resources in the early stages, could hope at best for only a slender margin of superiority" (75).

35. Eisenhower to Joint Chiefs of Staff, March 9, 1944, *Papers*, 3:1763–1764.

36. Eisenhower to Combined Chiefs of Staff and British Chiefs of Staff, January 23, 1944, *Papers*, 3:1673–1676.

37. Eisenhower to Marshall, March 10, 1944, *Papers*, 3:1766–1768.

38. Marshall to Stimson, May 16, 1944, *Marshall Papers*, 4:447–450.

39. Eisenhower to W. B. Smith, January 5, 1944, *Papers*, 3:1652–1654; Eisenhower to Montgomery, January 13, 1944, Eisenhower to Joint Chiefs of Staff, January 27, 1944, and Diary, February 7, 1944, *Papers*, 3:1654–1655, 1688–1692, 1711–1713; Marshall to Eisenhower, February 7, 1944, Marshall, Memorandum for Sir John Dill, February 9, 1944, and Marshall to Admiral Leahy and Admiral King, February 9, 1944, *Marshall Papers*, 4:271–275.

40. Marshall to Eisenhower, February 21, 1944, *Marshall Papers*, 4:313–314.

41. The debate is carried forward in Marshall to General Handy, March 14, 1944, Marshall to Winston S. Churchill, March 16, 1944, Marshall to Eisenhower, March 16, 1944, and Marshall to Churchill, April 13, 1944, *Marshall Papers*, 4:341–343, 347, 348–350, 404–405. See also Eisenhower to British Chiefs of Staff, February 18, 1944, *Papers*, 3:1732–1734; Harrison, *European Theater*, 166–174.

42. Eisenhower to Marshall, March 21, 1944, *Papers*, 3:1779.

43. Eisenhower to Marshall, March 21, 1944, and April 17, 1944, *Papers*, 3:1776–1779, 1827–1829.

44. Harrison, *European Theater*, 270.

45. For background, see Eisenhower to Marshall, September 5, 1943, *Papers*, 2:1384–1386.

46. Eisenhower to Marshall, December 25, 1943, goes over this issue; *Papers*, 3:1611–1615. Eisenhower to Arthur William Tedder, February 29, 1944, gives a good sense of how serious the problem was; *Papers*, 3:1755–1756.

47. Max Hastings, *Inferno: The World at War, 1939–1945* (New York: Vintage, 2012), 455–479, provides an excellent overview of the bombing campaign and the powerful sense of optimism in the bomber command.

48. Harrison, *European Theater*, 211.

49. Ibid., 219. The previous plan had emphasized ball-bearing production as the crucial target.

50. Ibid., 185–186, 214.

51. Ibid., 219–220.

52. Eisenhower, "Memorandum," March 22, 1944, *Papers*, 3:1782–1787, gives a good summary from the Supreme Commander's perspective. See also Harrison, *European Theater*, 218–220. And see Max Hastings, *Bomber Command* (Minneapolis, MN: Zenith Press, 2013), 226–236, which reviews with insight all sides of the debate.

53. Eisenhower to Walter Bedell Smith and Tedder, March 31, 1944, *Papers*, 3:1802.

54. On the raids and simultaneous partisan attacks, see Harrison, *European Theater*, 224–230.

55. Eisenhower and Marshall debated at length over the commanders; see, for instance, Eisenhower to Marshall, December 27, 28, and 29, 1943, and Eisenhower to Walter Bedell Smith, December 31, 1943, *Papers*, 3:1622–1624, 1626–1628, 1630–1632, 1647–1648. On the command structure, see Eisenhower to Marshall, April 25, 1944, *Papers*, 3:1830–1832.

56. Eisenhower to Tedder, March 9, 1944, *Papers*, 3:1765–1766; Harrison, *European Theater*, 219–220, 223.

57. Harrison, *European Theater*, 220–223.

58. On the raids and the simultaneous partisan attacks, see ibid.

59. Rommel emphasized the defense at the Atlantic Wall and Rundstedt gave greater emphasis to the counterattacks, but both generals recognized that their armies would have to move forward and probably be repositioned after the invasion began.

60. For an exciting and meticulous account of Eisenhower's last few days before the invasion, see Carlo D'Este, *Eisenhower: A Soldier's Life* (New York: Henry Holt, 2002), 516–529.

61. Eisenhower to Marshall, March 20, 1944, *Papers*, 3:1773–1774.

62. Eisenhower to Marshall, June 1 and 3, 1944, *Papers*, 3:1902, 1903–1906.

63. Eisenhower's "Note" appears in the *Papers*, 3:1908, and is discussed in Harry C. Butcher, *My Three Years with Eisenhower: The Personal Diary of Captain Harry C. Butcher, USNR, Naval Aide to General Eisenhower, 1942–1945* (New York: Simon and Schuster, 1946), 610. Eisenhower apparently told Butcher that he had written a similar note on the occasion of each of the amphibious attacks he had led.

64. It had been understood from the beginning of the planning process that the margin favoring the Allies would initially be very thin. See Harrison, *European Theater*, 74.

65. Erickson, *Road to Berlin*, 154–162. At the Teheran Conference (November 28–December 1, 1943) Stalin had begun to clarify for the Allies exactly what the Soviets would want in the postwar settlement. Stalin was exploiting his new position of strength. He urged the United States and Britain to abandon their efforts to take Rome and put their soldiers in France. Poland and Germany were clearly Stalin's prime interests. His position became even stronger as the Soviet summer offensive ground ahead. By April, little of Ukraine was left in German control. In the south, the Soviet attacks resulted in more than a million casualties for Germany and its allies. Germany lost between twenty-five and twenty-eight divisions when the Soviets crushed Army Group Centre. See Erickson, *Road to Berlin*, 154–162, 187–188, 190–192, 210, 215, 220, 224, 227–229.

66. Ibid., in a chapter aptly titled "Breaking the Back of the *Wehrmacht*: April–August 1944," esp. 191–326.

67. Churchill had already (May 2, 1944) anticipated that the Soviet Union would dominate East Europe and the Balkans; he was assuming, however, that the cross-Channel attack would be successful. See note 5, *Papers*, 3:1844, on the prime minister's remarks at the War Cabinet meeting. For Eisenhower's thoughts on the postwar situation, see Eisenhower to Walter Bedell Smith, May 20,1944, *Papers*, 3:1872–1876. Ike noted, however, that, "we cannot predict what areas will be occupied by our respective armies at that moment."

68. Matloff, *Strategic Planning 1943–1944*, 287–288.

69. Matloff, *Strategic Planning 1943–44*, 497, comments on "the steady resistance of the President and his close advisers to any introduction of political or military bargaining with the Russians."

70. Butcher, *My Three Years*, 560–563. D'Este, *Eisenhower*, 517–529, provides an excellent account of the difficult days from June 1 through June 5. The author says with authority that "June 5 was a supreme test of his generalship and his ability to keep his nerve under the most trying circumstance he would ever face as a commander" (527). Concerned, as always, about unity, Eisenhower had first visited British troops getting ready to invade. Eisenhower to Marshall, June 6, 1944, *Papers*, 3:1914–1915.

71. On Ultra, the code machine that gave the Allies a significant intelligence advantage, see Eisenhower, *Eisenhower at War*, esp. 167–168, 217, 286, 291, 351–352, 384. See also Paul Gannon, *Colossus: Bletchley Park's Greatest Secret* (London: Atlantic Books, 2007), esp. 299–314.

72. General Patton is, in this regard and many others, a special case. He was obsessed with thoughts of his own death—always in combat—and sprinkled his correspondence with his thoughts on this subject. See Carlo D'Este, *Patton: A Genius for War* (New York: HarperCollins, 1995).

73. Eisenhower to Marshall, June 6, 1944, and Eisenhower to Combined Chiefs of Staff, June 8, 1944, *Papers*, 3:1914–1918.

74. Harrison, *European Theater*, 302–384, covers in detail the operations from June 6 through 18.

75. Butcher, *My Three Years*, 571–574.

76. Harrison, *European Theater*, 284.

77. Ibid., 252.

78. Ibid., 264.

79. Ibid., 265.

80. See, for instance, Eisenhower to Montgomery, June 18, 1944, *Papers*, 3:1933–1934.

81. See Eisenhower to Combined Chiefs of Staff, June 9, 1944, *Papers*, 3:1921–1922, on the matter of issuing "supplemental francs" in liberated

areas. In many regards, the French situation resembled the problems in Italy following the surrender. But the French economy was larger and de Gaulle was larger than life.

82. Eisenhower to Marshall, June 19, and 21, 1944, and Eisenhower to Marshall and King, June 20, 1944, *Papers*, 3:1936–1942.

83. Notes to Eisenhower to Montgomery, June 25, 1944, *Papers*, 3:1949–1950.

84. D'Este, *Eisenhower*, 555; Eisenhower to Tedder, June 29, 1944, *Papers*, 3:1960–1961.

85. D'Este, *Eisenhower*, 554.

86. He went beyond "assertive" in his defense of the invasion of southern France and his rejection of Churchill's continued demands for a campaign in the Balkans. See, for instance, Eisenhower to Marshall, June 29, 1944, *Papers*, 3:1958–1960. The excellent notes to this document lay out the tiresome exchanges over this issue. The prime minister lacked a mental fuse that would stop him when he had gone over the limits of human endurance in debate.

87. Bradley's approach to problems was similarly practical. When his tank guns were unable to penetrate the armor of German tanks, he wheeled more effective antiaircraft artillery into his combat teams and continued the action. Eisenhower to Walter Bedell Smith, July 3, 1944, *Papers*, 3:1970–1971; Martin Blumenson, *Breakout and Pursuit* (Washington, DC: Office of the Chief of Military History, Department of the Army, 1961), 45.

88. Eisenhower continued to talk as if he expected Montgomery's forces "to break out into suitable tank country." Eisenhower to Marshall, July 26, 1944, *Papers*, 3:2010–2031. But he was clearly looking to Bradley and Patton for the progress he sought. Meanwhile, he was forced yet again to fend off the bomber command. See Eisenhower to Arthur Travers Harris, July 27, 1944, *Papers*, 3:2033.

89. Eisenhower to Marshall, July 5, 1944, *Papers*, 3:1971–1972.

90. Eisenhower to Walter Bedell Smith, June 16, 1944, and Eisenhower to Marshall, July 27, 1944, *Papers*, 3:1927–1930, 2034–2035.

91. The quotation is from Eisenhower's June 6, 1944, message to the "Soldiers, Sailors and Airmen of the Allied Expeditionary Forces," *Papers*, 3, 1913.

92. Butcher, *My Three Years*, 583, 612–626.

93. Ibid., 580.

94. DDE to Montgomery, July 28, 1944; DDE to Marshall, July 30, 1944; *Papers*, 4:2041–2042, 2043–2044.

95. DDE to Marshall, July 30, 1944, *Papers*, 4:2043–2044.

96. DDE to Marshall and Combined Chiefs of Staff, August 2, 1944, *Papers*, 4:2048–2051.

Eight. Tested Again

1. He apologized to Marshall and the Combined Chiefs of Staff in his cable of August 2, 1944. *Papers*, 4:2048–2051.

2. Martin Blumenson, *Breakout and Pursuit* (Washington, DC: Office of the Chief of Military History, Department of the Army, 1961), 176.

3. John Erickson, *The Road to Berlin: Continuing the History of Stalin's War with Germany* (Boulder, CO: Westview Press, 1983), 310–318.

4. DDE to Marshall, August 3 and 5, 1944, *Papers*, 4:2054–2056; Butcher Diary, August 6–7, 1944, *Papers*, 4:2057–2058. Churchill was not an easy man to brush off; see DDE to Churchill, August 11, 1944, *Papers*, 4:2065–2066.

5. Blumenson covers the campaign in meticulous detail in *Breakout and Pursuit*. See especially 53–77, 175–182, 185–304.

6. Carlo D'Este, *Patton: A Genius for War* (New York: HarperCollins, 1995), 571–615.

7. Jonathan W. Jordan, *Brothers, Rivals, Victors: Eisenhower, Patton, Bradley, and the Partnership That Drove the Allied Conquest in Europe* (New York: NAL Caliber, 2011), 296–316.

8. DDE to Somervillel, August 8, DDE to Combined Chiefs of Staff, August 15, and DDE to Marshall, August 17, 1944, *Papers*, 4:2061–2073.

9. Blumenson, *Breakout and Pursuit*, 305–558; DDE to Marshall, August 9 and 11, 1944, *Papers*, 4:2062–2065.

10. For a different perspective, see Max Hastings, *Overlord: D-Day and the Battle for Normandy* (New York: Vintage Books, 1984), 307–320.

11. For all you need to know about the gap, see William Weidner, *Eisenhower and Montgomery at the Falaise Gap* (Bloomington, IN: Xlibris, 2010). Also see DDE to Marshall, August 17, 1944, *Papers*, 4:2071–2073. There was a serious public relations difference between the British and American commands, and Eisenhower felt compelled to explain to Marshall in detail what was happening in the Supreme Headquarters Allied Expeditionary Force (SHAEF) as well as what would happen on about September 1, 1944. DDE to Marshall, August 19, 1944, *Papers*, 4:2074–2077.

12. See DDE to Montgomery, August 24, 1944, *Papers*, 4:2090–2092, and DDE to Marshall, August 24, 1944, *Papers*, 4:2092–2094, which explain Ike's position very clearly.

13. On August 24, 1944, Ike put it bluntly to Marshall: "The British have already been compelled to cannibalize one division, the 69th, and will have to break up another before the end of the month. Their replacement situation is tight." *Papers*, 4:2092–2094. Ike also compromised with de Gaulle by allowing a primarily French force to march into Paris—a sideshow that was of immense importance to de Gaulle and trivial importance to the war.

14. DDE to Bertram Home Ramsay et al., August 29, and DDE to Combined Chiefs of Staff, August 30, 1944, *Papers*, 4:2100–2104.

15. DDE to Combined Chiefs of Staff, September 9, 1944, and DDE to Marshall, September 17, 1944, *Papers*, 4:2124–2128, 2157–2160.

16. DDE to Marshall, September 17, 1944, *Papers*, 4:2158.

17. DDE to Marshall, September 4, 1944, *Papers*, 4:2118–2119.

18. DDE to Combined Chiefs of Staff, September 9, 1944, *Papers*, 4:2124–2128.

19. Stephen E. Ambrose, *Eisenhower* (New York: Simon & Schuster, 1983), 334–363; DDE to Bradley, September 15, 1944, *Papers*, 4:2146–2147.

20. DDE to Montgomery, September 20, 1944, *Papers*, 4:2164–2166.

21. DDE to Montgomery, September 15, 16, 20, 22, and 24, and October 9, 10, 13, and 15, 1944, *Papers*, 4:2148–2149, 2164–2166, 2215–2217, 2175–2176, 2185–2186, 2221–2225, 2227–2228; DDE to Lee, September 16, 1944, *Papers*, 4:2153–2154.

22. DDE to Robert Elliott Urquhart, October 8, 1944, *Papers*, 4:2214; Cornelius Ryan, *A Bridge Too Far* (New York: Simon and Schuster, 1974); DDE to Bradley, September 23, 1944, *Papers*, 4:2183.

23. Carlo D'Este, *Eisenhower: A Soldier's Life* (New York: Henry Holt, 2002), 613.

24. David Eisenhower, *Eisenhower at War, 1943–1945* (New York: Vintage Books, 1987), 441–500, provides a full explanation of the debates over Market Garden and the controversies it later inspired.

25. DDE to Marshall, September 25, 1944, *Papers*, 4:2186–2188.

26. DDE to Montgomery, September 24, 1944, *Papers*, 4:2185–2186; DDE to Marshall, October 26, 1944, *Papers*, 4:2252–2254.

27. DDE to Combined Chiefs of Staff, September 29, 1944, *Papers*, 4:2199–2202.

28. DDE to Walter Bedell Smith, September 22, 1944, *Papers*, 4:2181–2182. See also DDE to Alphonse Pierre Juin, October 13, 1944, *Papers*, 4:2225–2227.

29. DDE to Marshall, September 25 and October 22, 1944, *Papers*, 4:2186–2188, 2242–2243.

30. DDE to Combined Chiefs of Staff, October 29, 1944, *Papers*, 4:2263–2264.

31. DDE to Marshall, September 14, 1944, *Papers*, 4:2143–2145.

32. Erickson, *The Road to Berlin*, 308–330.

33. Ibid., 429. See especially Chapter 5 "Breaking the Back of the *Wehrmacht*: April—August 1944," 191–330.

34. Ibid., 422.

35. Ibid., 429.

36. Ibid., 424.

37. Ibid., 424–426.

38. DDE to British Chiefs of Staff, October 31, 1944, *Papers*, 4:2268–2269.

39. DDE to Montgomery, December 16, 1944, *Papers*, 4:2350.

40. Erickson, *The Road to Berlin*, 430.

41. DDE to Marshall, December 5, 1944, *Papers*, 4:2335–2336.

42. Hugh M. Cole, *The Ardennes: Battle of the Bulge* (Washington, DC: Office of the Chief of Military History, Department of the Army, 1965), 1–32, 51–444.

See also Eisenhower, *Eisenhower at War*, 554–645, for an excellent discussion of the battle and its outcome.

43. DDE to Brehon Burke Somerville, December 17, 1944, and DDE to Bradley and Jacob Loucks Devers, December 18, 1944, *Papers*, 4:2355–2357.

44. Cole, *The Ardennes*, 445–555; DDE to Combined Chiefs of Staff, December 19, 1944, *Papers*, 4:2358–2359; DDE to Bradley and John Clifford Hodges Lee, December 19, 1944, *Papers*, 4:2361; DDE, Memorandum, December 23, 1944, *Papers*, 4:2371–2376.

45. Cole, *The Ardennes*, 610–614, 668–676; DDE to Combined Chiefs of Staff, December 20, 1944, *Papers*, 4:2363.

46. DDE to Montgomery, December 31, 1944, *Papers*, 4:2386–2388; also DDE's "Outline Plan" of the same date, 2388–2389.

47. John S. D. Eisenhower, *General Ike: A Personal Reminiscence* (New York: Free Press, 2003), 128–131. D'Este, *Eisenhower*, 654–658, also provides an excellent description of the crisis. Montgomery's chief of staff was Major General Sir Francis de Guingand.

48. See, for instance, DDE to Marshall, January 10, 1945 (2 messages) and January 11, 1945, *Papers*, 4:2412–2420, 2422–2423.

49. DDE to Marshall, January 7, 1945, *Papers*, 4:2394; DDE, "Draft," January 4, 1945, *Papers*, 4:2408–2410.

50. DDE to Combined Chiefs of Staff, December 21, 1944, *Papers*, 4:2367.

51. DDE to Marshall, December 26, 1944, *Papers*, 4:2379; DDE to Stalin, December 29, 1944, *Papers*, 4:2384–2385.

52. Erickson, *The Road to Berlin*, 446–447.

53. DDE to Combined Chiefs of Staff, January 20, 1945, *Papers*, 4:2444–2449.

54. 53 DDE to Marshall, January 15, 1945, *Papers*, 4:2430–2435.

55. DDE to Marshall, February 9, 1945, *Papers*, 4:2473–2474.

56. Charles B. MacDonald, *The Last Offensive* (Washington, DC: Office of the Chief of Military History, United States Army, 1973), 208–235; Ambrose, *Eisenhower*, 1:387–388; D'Este, *Eisenhower*, 681–682.

57. DDE to Marshall, March 12, 1945, *Papers*, 4:2521–2523.

58. D'Este, *Patton*, 711–713.

59. DDE to Combined Chiefs of Staff, March 24, 1945, *Papers*, 4:2539–2540.

60. DDE to Marshall, March 26, 1945, *Papers*, 4:2543–2545.

61. For that massive campaign—involving ninety-one divisions—see Mac-Donald, *The Last Offensive*. The German ground strength was nominally eighty divisions, but many of these units were understrength. Despite the strategic bombing campaign, German industrial production peaked in the fall of 1944.

62. DDE to Montgomery, March 28, 1945, *Papers*, 4:2364.

63. DDE to Marshall, March 30, 1945 (2 messages), DDE to Churchill, March 30 and April 1, 1945, DDE to Montgomery, March 31, 1945, and DDE to Combined Chiefs of Staff, March 31, 1945, *Papers*, 4:2559–2563, 2567–2571.

64. We will never know whether Ike enjoyed the fact that Montgomery was now forced into the subordinate position he had happily assigned to the American forces in North Africa and in Sicily. But we do know that Eisenhower was human and given to some of the same emotions all of us have.

65. DDE to John Russell Deane and Ernest Russell Archer, March 28 and 29, 1945, *Papers*, 4:2551, 2557–2558.

66. Erickson, *The Road to Berlin*, 528–529.

67. See Louis Galambos, *The Creative Society and the Price Americans Paid for It* (New York: Cambridge University Press, 2012), 128–130. Also see two important books by John Lewis Gaddis: *The United States and the Origins of the Cold War, 1941–1947* (New York: Columbia University Press, 1972) and *Strategies of Containment: A Critical Appraisal of American National Security Policy During the Cold War* (New York: Oxford University Press, 2005). See also Gregg Herken, *Brotherhood of the Bomb: The Tangled Lives and Loyalties of Robert Oppenheimer, Ernest Lawrence, and Edward Teller* (New York: Henry Holt, 2002), 149–156.

68. MacDonald, *The Last Offensive*, 373–406. As MacDonald notes, between April 5 and 13, the First, Third, and Ninth US Armies had pushed 150 miles across central Germany.

69. DDE to Montgomery, March 31, 1945, and DDE to Combined Chiefs of Staff, March 31, 1945, *Papers*, 4:2567–2571. This question, like so many others involving the war, inspired a cottage industry of debates that much exceeded the amount of thought Ike gave to the question. See, for instance, Stephen E. Ambrose, *Eisenhower and Berlin, 1945: The Decision to Halt at the Elbe* (New York: W. W. Norton,1967).

70. DDE to Marshall, April 15, 1945, *Papers*, 4:2612–2613.

71. DDE to John Russell Deane and Ernest Russell Archer, April 21 and 22, 1945, *Papers*, 4:2632–2636.

72. DDE to Marshall, April 28, 1945, *Papers*, 4:2661.

73. DDE to John Russell Deane and Ernest Russell Archer, April 30, 1945, *Papers*, 4:2664 n. 5.

74. DDE to Marshall, April 15, 1945, *Papers*, 4:2614–2617.

75. See, for instance, the discussion in S. P. MacKenzie, "On the 'Other Losses' Debate," *International History Review* 14, no. 4 (November 1992): 717–731.

76. These excerpts from Eisenhower's address would later appear on the Eisenhower Memorial in Washington, DC. For the entire speech, see the version published in Eisenhower, *At Ease: Stories I Tell to Friends* (New York: Doubleday, 1967), 388–390.

Nine. Duty, Honor Party

1. DDE to Paul Williams Thompson, August 8, 1945, *Papers*, 6:247.

2. DDE to Thomas Troy Handy, October 27, 1945, *Papers*, 6:481.

3. DDE to Lucius Du Bignon Clay (hereafter LDBC), November 8, 1945, *Papers*, 6:521.

4. DDE to LDBC, November 8, 1945, 6:523.

5. See *Papers*, 7:742ff.

6. DDE to Joint Chiefs of Staff, February 4, 1946, *Papers*, 7:823–824.

7. DDE to Joint Chiefs of Staff, February 13, 1946, *Papers*, 7:856–858.

8. DDE to Robert Porter Patterson, March 29, 1946, *Papers*, 7:962–964. Also see John Lewis Gaddis, *The United States and the Origins of the Cold War, 1941–1947* (New York: Columbia University Press, 1972).

9. DDE to Joint Chiefs of Staff, June 7, 1946, *Papers*, 7:1105–1107.

10. DDE to Joseph Taggart McNarney, April 17, 1946, *Papers*, 7:1010–1013. Also see DDE to Chester William Nimitz, June 29, 1946, *Papers*, 7:1157–1159.

11. DDE to Joint Chiefs of Staff, June 7, 1946, *Papers*, 7:1105–1107.

12. DDE to John Sheldon Doud, August 23, 1946, *Papers*, 8:1250.

13. DDE to Willis Dale Crittenberger, September 20, 1946, *Papers*, 8:1312–1313.

14. DDE to Joint Chiefs of Staff, March 12, 1947, *Papers*, 8:1581–1585.

15. DDE to Joint Chiefs of Staff, July 25, 1947, *Papers*, 8:1855–1858.

16. DDE to Walter Bedell Smith, November 28, 1947, *Papers*, 9:2084–2085.

17. DDE to All Members of the Army, July 26, 1947, *Papers*, 9:1867–1868.

18. DDE to James Vincent Forrestal, February 7, 1948, *Papers*, 9:2242–2256.

19. These lessons began early. See, for example, DDE to Rear Admiral Henry K. Hewitt, October 13, 1942, *Papers*, 1:612.

20. David L. Stebenne, "Thomas J. Watson and the Business-Government Relationship, 1933–1956," *Enterprise and Society* 6, no. 1 (March 2005), esp. 45–75, discusses Watson's links to Eisenhower.

21. Travis Beal Jacobs, *Eisenhower at Columbia* (New Brunswick, NJ: Transaction, 2001). See also Joan D. Goldhamer, "General Eisenhower in Academe: A Clash of Perspectives and a Study Suppressed," *Journal of the History of the Behavioral Sciences* 33, no. 3 (Summer 1997): 241–259.

22. DDE to Roger John Williams, September 15, 1948, *Papers*, 10:194–195.

23. DDE to Philip Young, August 14, 1950, *Papers*, 11:1277–1278.

24. DDE to James Vincent Forrestal, November 4, 1948, *Papers*, 10:283–284. Also see Diary, December 13, 1948, *Papers*, 10:365–368.

25. DDE to James Vincent Forrestal, September 27, 1948, *Papers*, 10:230–234.

26. Diary, December 17, 1948, *Papers*, 10:369–371; DDE to James Vincent Forrestal, December 21, 1948, *Papers*, 10:379–386.

27. Diary, January 7, 1949, *Papers*, 10:398–400.

28. See Raymond J. Saulnier, "Recollections of a 1948 Visit with General Eisenhower," *Presidential Studies Quarterly* 24, no. 4 (Fall 1994): 865–867.

29. DDE to Arthur Hays Sulzberger, December 29, 1950, *Papers*, 11:1505.

30. DDE to James Wesley Gallagher, December 30, 1950, *Papers*, 11:1511.

31. Diary, January 1, 1951, *Papers*, 12:5–8.

32. DDE to William Averell Harriman (hereafter WAH), February 24, 1951, *Papers*, 12:64–67. Also see DDE to Harry S. Truman, February 24, 1951, *Papers*, 12:67–68, and DDE to Marshall, March 12, 1951, *Papers*, 12:117–121.

33. Diary, March 2, 1951, *Papers*, 12:83–84.

34. DDE to WAH, March 2, 1951, *Papers*, 12:88–90.

35. Unfortunately, there were still a few bad apples in the barrel. See DDE to Omar Nelson Bradley, March 30, 1951, *Papers*, 12:166–170.

36. DDE to WAH, April 20, 1951, *Papers*, 12:222–227.

37. Ibid.

38. See esp. DDE to Bernard Law Montgomery, April 24, 1951, *Papers*, 12:243–244; DDE to Omar Nelson Bradley, April 28, 1951, *Papers*, 12:248–249; DDE to WAH, May 4, 1951, *Papers*, 12:262–266; DDE to WAH, June 1, 1951, *Papers*, 12:315–319; DDE to WAH, June 7, 1951, *Papers*, 12:333–335; Diary, June 11, 1951, *Papers*, 12:340–342; DDE to WAH, June 12, 1951, *Papers*, 12:344–349.

39. Diary, June 11, 1951, *Papers*, 12:340. Also see DDE to WAH, June 30, 1951, *Papers*, 12:397–399.

40. The word "us" is actually underlined twice. Diary, July 2, 1951, *Papers*, 12:399–400.

41. DDE to Marshall, August 3, 1951, *Papers*, 12:457–463.

42. DDE to Paul Van Zeeland, September 11, 1951, *Papers*, 12:531–532.

43. DDE to Joint Chiefs of Staff, October 3, 1951, *Papers*, 12:592–595; DDE to Joseph Lawton Collins, December 20, 1951, *Papers*, 12:803–806. Also see DDE to Omar Nelson Bradley, October 31, 1951, *Papers*, 12:678–80, for Ike's efforts to obtain equipment.

44. DDE to Alfred Maximilian Gruenther, October 22, 1951, *Papers*, 12:661–665.

45. See, for instance, Diary, October 10, 1951, *Papers*, 12:629–630.

46. DDE to William Morrow Fechteler, December 10, 1951, *Papers*, 12:769–772. Also see DDE to Robert Abercrombie Lovett (hereafter RAL), December 13, 1951, *Papers*, 12:779–785.

47. Compare DDE to WAH, December 14, 1951, *Papers*, 12:788–790; Diary, December 15, 1951, *Papers*, 12:792–793; and DDE to RAL, December 19, 1951, *Papers*, 12:800–806.

48. Diary, December 21, 1951, *Papers*, 12:809–811.

49. DDE to RAL, January 2, 1952, *Papers*, 12:831–833. Also see DDE to Harry S. Truman, January 4, 1952, *Papers*, 12:839–843.

50. DDE to LDBC, December 27, 1951, *Papers*, 12:817–818.

51. DDE to Milton Stover Eisenhower, May 30, 1951, *Papers*, 12:304–306.

52. DDE to George Whitney, June 14, 1951, *Papers*, 12:351–353.

53. DDE to DeWitt Wallace, July 21, 1951, *Papers*, 12:430–431.

54. Diary, June 4, 1951, *Papers*, 12:321. For a different analysis and more detailed treatment of Eisenhower's decision to make a run for the presidency, see William B. Pickett, *Eisenhower Decides to Run: Presidential Politics and Cold War Strategy* (Chicago: Ivan R. Dee, 2000). See also Michael J. Birkner, "'He's My Man': Sherman Adams and New Hampshire's Role in the 'Draft Eisenhower' Movement," *Historical New Hampshire* 58 (2003): 5–25, and Douglass K. Daniel, "They Liked Ike: Pro-Eisenhower Publishers and His Decision to Run for President," *Journalism and Mass Communication Quarterly* 77, no. 2 (Summer 2000): 193–404.

55. Diary, June 5, 1951, *Papers*, 12:329.

56. DDE to George Whitney, June 14, 1951, *Papers*, 12:351–353.

57. DDE to Martin Withington Clement, July 21, 1951, *Papers*, 12:431.

58. DDE to Milton Stover Eisenhower, September 4, 1951, *Papers*, 12:520.

59. DDE to LDBC, September 27, 1951, *Papers*, 12:580–581.

60. DDE to RAL, May 28, 1952, *Papers*, 13:1238.

61. DDE to Harry S. Truman, April 2, 1952, *Papers*, 13:1154–1159.

62. Ibid.

63. DDE to LDBC, December 19, 1951, *Papers*, 12:798–800.

64. Ibid. Also see DDE to Sid Williams Richardson, December 26, 1951, *Papers*, 12:813–815.

65. DDE to George Arthur Sloan, January 29, 1952, *Papers*, 13:928–932; DDE to Clifford Roberts, February 9, 1952, *Papers*, 13:957–959; DDE to George Arthur Sloan, October 29, 1952, *Papers* 13:1404–1405.

66. See DDE to Milton Stover Eisenhower, June 10, 1952, *Papers* 13:1242.

67. For details on the political maneuvering at the Chicago Republican convention, see Jean Edward Smith, *Eisenhower in War and Peace* (New York: Random House, 2012), 516–519.

Ten. Pursuing Prosperity

1. Robert E. Baldwin, "The Changing Nature of U.S. Trade Policy Since World War II," in *The Structure and Evolution of Recent U.S. Trade Policy*, ed. Robert E. Baldwin and Anne O. Krueger (Chicago: University of Chicago Press, 1984), 5–32; Douglas A. Irwin, "The GATT in Historical Perspective," *American Economic Review* 85 (May 1995): 323–328. Devesh Kapur et al., *The World Bank: Its First Half Century, Volume 1, History* (Washington, DC: Brookings Institution Press, 1997), 1–14, 57–138. Also see Catherine Gwin, *U.S. Relations with the World Bank, 1945–1992* (Washington, DC: Brookings Institution Press, 1994), 195–207.

2. Many analysts focus primarily on productivity as the source of American economic growth in the twentieth century. See, for instance, Marc Levinson,

An Extraordinary Time: The End of the Postwar Boom and the Return of the Ordinary Economy (New York: Basic Books, 2016). Unfortunately, this leaves out the innovative goods and services that frequently drive the growth process, especially in the digital era.

3. Alvin H. Hansen, the distinguished Harvard economist, had been insisting since the late 1930s that the United States had entered a phase of "secular stagnation." See, for instance, his presidential address to the American Economic Association, "Economic Progress and Declining Population Growth," *American Economic Review* 29 (March 1939): 1–15. See also the following by Hansen: *Full Recovery or Stagnation?* (New York: W. W. Norton, 1938); *America's Role in the World Economy* (New York: W. W. Norton, 1945); and *Economic Policy and Full Employment* (New York: McGraw-Hill, 1947).

4. All of the information on the budget in this chapter is from Susan B. Carter et al., *Historical Statistics of the United States: Earliest Times to the Present*, vol. 5 (New York: Cambridge University Press, 2006); see esp. 102 on the deficits.

5. Michael J. Hogan, *The Marshall Plan: America, Britain, and the Reconstruction of Western Europe, 1947–1952* (New York: Cambridge University Press, 1987). See also Barry Eichengreen, *The European Economy Since 1945: Coordinated Capitalism and Beyond* (Princeton, NJ: Princeton University Press, 2007), esp. 52–130.

6. The conflicts had been fully elucidated in the debate over the Employment Act of 1946.

7. Phillip G. Henderson, *Managing the Presidency: The Eisenhower Legacy—from Kennedy to Reagan* (Boulder, CO: Westview Press, 1988) is an excellent study of Eisenhower's style of management. See also Bradley H. Patterson Jr., "Dwight Eisenhower's Innovations in the Structure and Operations of the Modern White House," *Presidential Studies Quarterly* 24, no. 2 (Spring 1994): 277–298.

8. John Kenneth Galbraith, *The Affluent Society* (Boston: Houghton Mifflin, 1958), 7–20. Galbraith labeled this collection of ideas "the conventional wisdom."

9. Installment buying was picking up in the 1950s, but many Americans, like Eisenhower, were wary of debt. See Alan Ehrenhalt, *The Lost City: Discovering the Forgotten Virtues of Community in the Chicago of the 1950s* (New York: Basic Books, 1995), esp. 59–85 and 104–110. Americans were, however, buying cars on the installment plan, as described in Sally H. Clarke, *Trust and Power: Consumers, the Modern Corporation, and the Making of the United States Automobile Market* (New York: Cambridge University Press, 2007), esp. part 3 on the mature market, 1945–1965.

10. Jean Edward Smith, *Eisenhower in War and Peace* (New York: Random House, 2012), 470; Ellis D. Slater et al., *The Ike I Knew* (Baltimore: Ellis D. Slater Trust, 1980), 3. On August 25, 1950, while thanking Ike for supplying

him with an abundant breakfast at an occasion in Denver, Slater commented on "the boys in Washington." He said, "Even with respect to taxes, the public condemns the [Truman] administration for not being more realistic."

11. DDE to George Arthur Sloan, March 6, 1950, *Papers*, 11:1003–1004. The Eisenhowers had spent an evening with Mr. and Mrs. Sloan in February 1950. Mrs. Sloan was the former Florence Lincoln Rockefeller.

12. DDE to Sloan, January 3, 1952, *Papers*, 12:836–838.

13. Ibid. Italics added.

14. See DDE to Sloan, January 29, February 8, and March 18, 1952, *Papers*, 13:928–932, 948–949, 1047.

15. DDE to Sloan, February 8 and 21, 1952, *Papers*, 13:948–949, 1007–1009.

16. See, for instance, DDE to Sloan, March 20, 1952, *Papers*, 13:1097–1104. Even here, however, Ike would not argue about "specific sums for any specific purpose." He had fought that battle too often as Chief of Staff. See also DDE to Sloan, March 25, 1952, *Papers*, 13:1118–1119.

17. William M. McClenahan Jr. and William H. Becker, *Eisenhower and the Cold War Economy* (Baltimore: Johns Hopkins University Press, 2011), 25–29, do an excellent job of introducing Ike's new team of advisors. The other two members of the council were Neil Jacoby, dean of UCLA's business school, and Walter W. Stewart, an economist affiliated with the Institute for Advanced Study at Princeton University and a frequent advisor to various government organizations. His expertise in banking was especially notable.

18. On price controls, see Hugh Rockoff, *Drastic Measures: A History of Wage and Price Controls in the United States* (New York: Cambridge University Press, 1984).

19. Dwight David Eisenhower, Annual Message to the Congress on the State of the Union, February 2, 1953. For Eisenhower's opposition to public power, see Wyatt Wells, "Public Power in the Eisenhower Administration," *Journal of Policy History* 20, no. 2 (2008): 227–262.

20. DDE, Diary, June 1, 1953, *Papers*, 14:265–267. Between 1952 and 1953, the budget deficit that worried Eisenhower had increased by more than 433 percent. For a monetary perspective on the "crisis" in early 1953, see Milton Friedman and Anna Jacobson Schwartz, *A Monetary History of the United States, 1867–1960* (Princeton, NJ: Princeton University Press, 1963), 612–620. For a more recent and substantially more favorable perspective, see Christina D. Romer and David H. Romer, "What Ends Recessions?," in *NBER Macroeconomics Annual 1994, Volume 9*, ed. Stanley Fischer and Julio J. Rotemberg, available at http://www.nber.org/books/fisc94-1; and the same authors' "The Evolution of Economic Understanding and Postwar Stabilization Policy," NBER Working Paper No. 9274, available at http://www.nber.org/papers/w9274. The authors comment on an "interesting evolution from a crude but fundamentally sensible model of how the economy worked in the

1950s, to more formal but faulty models in the 1960s and 1970s, and finally to a model that was both sensible and sophisticated in the 1980s and 1990s."

21. David A. Nichols, *Ike and McCarthy: Dwight Eisenhower's Secret Campaign Against Joseph McCarthy* (New York: Simon and Schuster, 2017) tells the full story. With the death in 1953 of Senator Taft and McCarthy's defeat in 1954, Ike's hold on the Republican Party was strengthened. It was, however, never complete.

22. On Ike and Congress see in particular Smith, *Eisenhower*, 581–601, and Jim Newton, *Eisenhower: The White House Years* (New York: Doubleday, 2011), esp. 120–125, 141–155, 179, 239–240, 258–259, 305–306. See also Ken Collier, "Eisenhower and Congress: The Autopilot Presidency," *Presidential Studies Quarterly* 24, no. 2 (Spring 1994): 309–325, and Henry Z. Scheele, "President Dwight D. Eisenhower and U.S. House Leader Charles A. Halleck: An Examination of an Executive-Legislative Relationship," *Presidential Studies Quarterly* 23, no. 2 (Spring 1993): 289–299.

23. The latter recession was more severe, with unemployment reaching a peak of 7.6 percent, but both the administration and the Fed refused to change course in any major way.

24. On Eisenhower and his relationships with Fed chairman William McChesney Martin, see McClenahan and Becker, *Eisenhower and the Cold War Economy*, 45–48, 57, 61–62, 64, 86, 95–96.

25. Robert Maranto, "The Administrative Strategies of Republican Presidents from Eisenhower to Reagan," *Presidential Studies Quarterly* 23, no. 4 (Fall 1993): 683–685, 694. See also Roger Biles, "Public Housing Policy in the Eisenhower Administration," *Mid-America* 81, no. 1 (Winter 1999): 5–25.

26. On the new highway system, see DDE to Gabriel Hauge, February 4, 1953, *Papers*, 14:23–25. "Our cities still conform too rigidly to the patterns, customs, and practices of fifty years ago. Each year we add hundreds of thousands of new automobiles . . . but our road systems do not keep pace with the need." The president asked Hauge to follow up with a study. For Eisenhower's subsequent discussion of the issue, see *Papers*, 15:1067; *Papers*, 16:1556–1557, 1733–1734. Congress passed the Federal Aid Highway Act of 1956, and Eisenhower signed the bill on June 29, 1956. See also Mark H. Rose's definitive account in *Interstate: Express Highway Politics, 1941–56* (Lawrence: Regents Press of Kansas, 1979). Ike's 1919 experience was with a cross-country military convoy that crept across the nation to California and gave him a good sense of just how bad America's roads were. For an interesting popular account with great pictures of the interstate road system, see Dan McNichol, *The Roads That Built America: The Incredible Story of the U.S. Interstate System* (New York: Barnes and Noble Books, 2003). On Eisenhower's more hesitant support for another infrastructure project, the St. Lawrence Seaway, see DDE, Memorandum to Legislative Leaders, *Papers*, 14:132–133. In 1954, the president

nevertheless signed the bill authorizing US participation with Canada in construction of the seaway.

27. Sally H. Clarke, *Regulation and the Revolution in United States Farm Productivity* (New York: Cambridge University Press, 1994).

28. On the battles over agricultural programs and an outcome that was depressing to Eisenhower and his long-embattled secretary of agriculture, Ezra Taft Benson, see Alan L. Olmstead and Paul W. Rhode, "The Transformation of Northern Agriculture, 1910–1990," in *The Cambridge Economic History of the United States*, vol. 3, *The Twentieth Century*, ed. Stanley L. Engerman and Robert E. Gallman (New York: Cambridge University Press, 2000), 693–742, and McClenahan and Becker, *Eisenhower and the Cold War Economy*, 113–151. For Eisenhower's perspective on this lost cause, see DDE to Ezra Taft Benson, November 14, 1959, *Papers*, 20:1739–1740; DDE to Ezra Taft Benson, August 22, 1960, *Papers*, 21:2056–2058; and DDE to Mary Conger, April 5, 1960, *Papers*, 20:1895–98: Eisenhower lamented the inability in the case of wheat farmers "to reach any agreement as to what is the appropriate function of government."

29. Most of Eisenhower's biographers include this famous quotation: see, for instance, Smith, *Eisenhower in War and Peace*, 554n.

30. J. Merton England, *A Patron for Pure Science: The National Science Foundation's Formative Years, 1945–57* (Washington, DC: National Science Foundation, 1982), 211–217. See Eisenhower's "Executive Order (10521) Concerning Government Scientific Research," Appendix 1, 353–355.

31. On "spillovers," see Richard N. Langlois and W. Edward Steinmueller, "The Evolution of Competitive Advantage in the Worldwide Semiconductor Industry, 1947–1996," in *Sources of Industrial Leadership: Studies of Seven Industries*, ed. David C. Mowery and Richard R. Nelson (Cambridge: Cambridge University Press, 1999), 19–78; see also 181, 275, and 206 in the same volume.

32. Timothy F. Bresnahan and Franco Malerba, "Industrial Dynamics and the Evolution of Firms' and Nations' Competitive Capabilities in the World Computer Industry," in *Sources of Industrial Leadership*, ed. Mowery and Nelson, 79–132, place the government purchases in their proper context. The government's role was important to a number of firms, including IBM, whose leader, Thomas Watson, was an enthusiastic Eisenhower supporter.

33. DDE to William Edward Robinson, August 4, 1954, *Papers*, 15:1228–1231. This letter gives an excellent guide to the systematic way Eisenhower approached the problems of presidential leadership: "I agree, of course, that I must learn enough about the underlying problems of each kind so that I can apply reasonable logic in reaching the decisions that I am compelled inescapably to make. But some of them require knowledge that goes far beyond basic principles. The only recourse is to determine those to which I should give really studious attention and treat these more exhaustively than those I may

more safely trust to instinct and to advisers. I suppose that the three most obvious classifications of the problem I am forced to consider are: (a) foreign affairs, (b) the domestic economy, and (c) domestic politics." He took special note of "*the farm problem,* itself consisting of 20 or 30 identifiable individual problems."

34. Langlois and Steinmueller, "The Evolution of Competitive Advantage," provide an excellent description of the exciting early years and the origins of Silicon Valley. See also Hyungsub Choi's detailed study "Manufacturing in Transit: Technical Practice, Organizational Change, and the Rise of the Semiconductor Industry in the United States and Japan, 1948–1960," Ph.D. dissertation, Johns Hopkins University, 2007, and Walter Isaacson, *The Innovators: How a Group of Hackers, Geniuses, and Geeks Created the Digital Revolution* (New York: Simon and Schuster, 2014).

35. Christophe Lécuyer, *Making Silicon Valley: Innovation and the Growth of High Tech, 1930–1970* (Cambridge, MA: MIT Press, 2006), 117–167, traces in meticulous detail the private sector innovations and the role that Stanford University and the US Department of Defense played in these complex developments. As Lécuyer makes clear, the prime actors in this entrepreneurial drama were in the firms, not in the public sector or at Stanford. See also Franco Malerba's international perspective in *The Semiconductor Business: The Economics of Rapid Growth and Decline* (London: Frances Pinter, 1985), and talented journalist T. R. Reid's *The Chip: How Two Americans Invented the Microchip and Launched a Revolution* (New York: Simon and Schuster, 1984).

36. For a good popular account of the impact of Sputnik, see Paul Dickson, *Sputnik: The Shock of the Century* (New York: Walker, 2001). See also Richard V. Damms, "James Killian, the Technological Capabilities Panel, and the Emergence of President Eisenhower's 'Scientific-Technological Elite,'" *Diplomatic History* 24, no. 1 (Winter 2000): 57–78.

37. On Sputnik, see Roger D. Launius, "Eisenhower and Space: Politics and Ideology in the Construction of the U.S. Civil Space Program," in *Forging the Shield: Eisenhower and National Security for the 21st Century*, ed. Dennis E. Showalter (Chicago: Imprint Publications, 2005), 151–182. See also James R. Killian Jr., *Sputnik, Scientists and Eisenhower: A Memoir of the First Special Assistant to the President for Science and Technology* (Cambridge, MA: MIT Press, 1977). As mentioned above, Paul Dickson gives a good account of the public and media response in *Sputnik*.

38. See, for instance, DDE to Neil Hosler McElroy, October 17 and 18, 1957, *Papers*, 18:496–497, 501–502. See also DDE to Charles Edward Potter, October 21, 1957, *Papers*, 18:503–505, on US scientific resources. Also see DDE to James Van Gundia Neel, November 1, 1957, *Papers*, 18:534–535.

39. In this same context, Eisenhower would request and Congress would provide support for a new National Aeronautics and Space Agency, would double

the budget for the National Science Foundation, and would pass the National Defense Education Act of 1958 to fund training in science and technology. As a measure of Ike's sense of the importance of ARPA (later DARPA), the president used General Andrew J. Goodpaster as his point man in the development of the new agency. On the National Defense Education Act, see Barbara Barksdale Clowse, *Brainpower for the Cold War: The Sputnik Crisis and National Defense Education Act of 1958* (Westport, CT: Greenwood Press, 1981).

40. It is important to note that while the government provided financial support for innovation and to some extent engaged in basic research, the entrepreneurship—that is the creative combination of capital, resources, labor, and novel ideas—took place overwhelmingly in the private sector. For a different view of that complex process, see Mariana Mazzucato, *The Entrepreneurial State: Debunking Public vs. Private Sector Myths* (London: Anthem Press, 2013).

41. The new companies were engaged in a wide range of economic activities. They included Hyatt Hotels, Food Lion, Budget Rent a Car, Amway, and the Playboy Club.

42. See, for instance, DDE to Russell Cornell Leffingwell, February 16, 1954, *Papers*, 15:903–904; DDE to Alice Liesveld, March 11, 1954, *Papers*, 15:947–48 ("I believe that the future of our country is still limitless, that America remains the 'land of opportunity' *for all who are ready to apply themselves to constructive goals*" [italics added]); DDE to Edward Everett Hazlett Jr., June 4, 1955, *Papers*, 16:1729–1731; DDE to Lewis Williams Douglas, September 30, 1956, *Papers*, 17:2297–98 ("We must find a way to foster a healthily growing, high-employment, peacetime economy while containing inflation. It is a new and challenging task").

43. There is a substantial body of literature on the performance of the economy and on the economic policies deployed in the postwar era. In addition to McClenahan and Becker, *Eisenhower and the Cold War Economy*, see Romer and Romer, "What Ends Recessions?," and Romer and Romer, "The Evolution of Economic Understanding." See also Dwight D. Eisenhower's annual Economic Reports to the Congress, 1953–1960.

44. See Burton I. Kaufman, *Trade and Aid: Eisenhower's Foreign Economic Policy* (Baltimore: Johns Hopkins University Press, 1982). More recently, McClenahan and Becker, *Eisenhower and the Cold War Economy*, give a thorough and perceptive analysis of the administration's problems, with analysis of the tension between its security concerns and its attempt to promote free trade.

45. DDE to Joseph William Martin Jr., June 29, 1953, *Papers*, 14:335–336. The matter at hand was the extension of the excess-profits tax. Eisenhower was determined to fight it out on this front: "We must move toward a balanced budget in a deliberate and orderly manner." The administration would first achieve that goal in 1956.

46. By January 1954, Ike's patience with his brother Ed was almost exhausted. "It is rather disturbing," he wrote, "to find one brother that seems always ready to believe that I am a poor, helpless, ignorant, uninformed individual, thrust to dizzy heights of governmental responsibility and authority, who has been captured by a band of conniving 'internationalists.'" DDE to Edgar Newton Eisenhower, January 27, 1954, *Papers*, 15:857–859.

47. DDE to Edgar Newton Eisenhower, November 8, 1954, *Papers*, 15:1386–1389. Ike added: "So how can you say I am getting 'bad' advice; why don't you just assume I am stupid, trying to wreck the nation, and leave our Constitution in tatters?"

48. DDE, Statement by the President upon Signing the Social Security Amendments of 1956, available at https://www.ssa.gov/history/ikestmts.html#1956a. In this regard, Eisenhower's policies were attuned to changes taking place in corporate America. See Christy Ford Chapin, "Corporate Social Responsibility and Political Development in the Health Insurance and Home Loan Industries," *Business History Review* 90, no. 4 (2016): 647–670. See also David Stebenne, "Social Welfare in the United States, 1945–1960," in *The Liberal Consensus Reconsidered: American Politics and Society in the Postwar Era*, ed. Robert Mason and Iwan Morgan (Gainesville: University Press of Florida, 2017), 108–126; and David Stebenne, *Modern Republican: Arthur Larson and the Eisenhower Years* (Bloomington: Indiana University Press, 2006), esp. 129–175.

49. Hugh Wilson, "President Eisenhower and the Development of Active Labor Market Policy in the United States: A Revisionist View," *Presidential Studies Quarterly* 39, no. 3 (September 2009): 519–548.

50. Don T. Martin, "Eisenhower and the Politics of Federal Aid to Education: The Watershed Years, 1953–1961," *Midwest History of Education Journal* 25, no. 1 (1998): 7–12.

51. The 1954 *Brown* decision (347 U.S. 483) overturned *Plessy v. Ferguson* (1896), which had allowed the states to establish separate (as they certainly were) but equal (as they clearly were not) schools.

52. Like Britain and Germany, the United States was running out of combat replacements. So Ike's action was prompted by a military problem, not a concern for racial justice.

53. Michael S. Mayer, "The Eisenhower Administration and the Desegregation of Washington, D.C.," *Journal of Policy History* 3 (1991): 24–41.

54. See David A. Nichols, *A Matter of Justice: Eisenhower and the Beginning of the Civil Rights Revolution* (New York: Simon and Schuster, 2007). For a different, substantially less positive interpretation of Eisenhower's position on African Americans' struggle for civil rights, see Newton, *Eisenhower*, 242–253. See also Smith, *Eisenhower*, 706–730, and Jeffrey R. Young, "Eisenhower's Federal Judges and Civil Rights Policy: A Republican 'Southern Strategy' for the 1950s," *Georgia Historical Quarterly* 77, no. 3 (Fall 1994): 536–565.

55. Nichols, *A Matter of Justice*, 169–281; Cary Fraser, "Crossing the Color Line in Little Rock: The Eisenhower Administration and the Dilemma of Race for U.S. Foreign Policy," *Diplomatic History* 24, no. 2 (Spring 2000): 233–264.

56. DDE, Annual Message Presenting the Economic Report to the Congress, January 20, 1960, available at www.presidency.ucsb.edu/ws/index.php?pid =11806. See also Ann Mari May, "President Eisenhower, Economic Policy, and the 1960 Presidential Election," *Journal of Economic History* 50 (June 1990): 417–427. The author concludes: "The Eisenhower presidency provides a compelling counterexample to the political business cycle hypothesis that presidents will manipulate the economy to enhance their re-election prospects. While Eisenhower engaged in highly contractionary policies upon entering office, he did not engage in significantly expansionary policies before the 1956 and 1960 presidential elections" (427). For another perspective on Ike's middle way, see Robert Mason, "'Down the Middle of the Road': Dwight D. Eisenhower, the Republican Party, and the Politics of Consensus and Conflict, 1949–1961," in *The Liberal Consensus Reconsidered*, ed. Mason and Morgan, 186–203.

Eleven. Pursuing Peace

1. On the long-running attempt of Republican senator John W. Bricker (Ohio) to amend the Constitution and limit the president's power to make treaties and establish executive agreements, see *Papers*, 14:74–75. Bricker did not abandon his effort until 1956. *Papers*, 16:2109–2111.

2. See, for instance, Eisenhower's cordial letter to General Franco of Spain, looking forward to "a new phase of friendship and cooperation not only between our military services but between our two nations." DDE to Francisco Franco y Bahamonde, September 5, 1953, *Papers*, 14:500–502.

3. DDE to Alfred Maximilian Gruenther, February 10, 1953, *Papers*, 14:39.

4. DDE to Churchill, April 7, 1953, *Papers*, 14:136–139; DDE to Charles Erwin Wilson, April 10, 1953, *Papers*, 14:160–161; DDE to Syngman Rhee, April 23, 1953, *Papers*, 14:166–167; and Diary, April 1, 1953, *Papers*, 14:172–174. On the problems of maintaining unity within his own political party, see Diary, May 1, 1953, *Papers*, 14:195–197.

5. DDE to William Phillips, June 5, 1953, *Papers*, 14:275–276.

6. Evan Thomas, *Ike's Bluff: President Eisenhower's Secret Battle to Save the World* (New York: Little, Brown, 2012), 14–15, 98–109.

7. DDE to Churchill, Chiang Kai-shek, May 5, 1953, *Papers*, 14:208–211.

8. DDE to Emmet John Hughes, December 10, 1953, *Papers*, 15:749.

9. Robert R. Bowie and Richard H. Immerman, *Waging Peace: How Eisenhower Shaped an Enduring Cold War Strategy* (New York: Oxford University Press, 1998), esp. 123–146 on Solarium and its immediate aftermath.

10. DDE to Gruenther, February 10, 1953, *Papers*, 14:39.

11. For an excellent history of the Eisenhower strategy and the manner in which the services responded to it, see Daun van Ee, "From the New Look to Flexible Response, 1953–1964," in *Against All Enemies: Interpretations of American Military History from Colonial Times to the Present*, ed. Kenneth J. Hagan and William R. Roberts (New York: Greenwood Press, 1986), 321–340. See also DDE, Diary, November 11, 1953, *Papers*, 14:671–672; DDE to Charles Erwin Wilson, January 5, 1955, *Papers*, 16:1488–1491; and DDE to Edward Everett Hazlett Jr., August 20, 1956, *Papers*, 17:2254–2257. Ike's Atoms for Peace program was closely linked to the new strategy. Martin J. Medhurst, "Atoms for Peace and Nuclear Hegemony: The Rhetorical Structure of a Cold War Campaign," *Armed Forces and Society* 23, no. 4 (Summer 1997): 571–593.

12. DDE to Errett Power Scrivner, June 30, 1953, *Papers*, 14:341–343. See also Donald Alan Carter, "Eisenhower Versus the Generals," *Journal of Military History* 71 (October 2007): 1169–1199.

13. DDE to Charles Erwin Wilson, January 5, 1955, *Papers*, 16:1488–1492.

14. Stephen E. Ambrose, *Eisenhower*, vol. 2, *The President* (New York: Simon and Schuster, 1984), esp. 85–96.

15. For a different tack on this question, see Thomas, *Ike's Bluff*, esp. 394–404.

16. DDE to Churchill, February 2, 1953, *Papers*, 14:18–19.

17. Burton I. Kaufman, *The Korean War: Challenges in Crisis, Credibility, and Command* (New York: Alfred A. Knopf, 1986), 287–348.

18. Diary, October 8, 1953, *Papers*, 14:570. Ike went on to write: "Trying to save South Korea is a little bit like trying to defend the basic rights of someone in court who insists on behaving in such fashion as to earn the contempt of the judge, the jury and all of the spectators."

19. DDE to Syngman Rhee, June 6 and 18, 1953, *Papers*, 14:278–282, 309–310.

20. DDE to Syngman Rhee, November 4, 1953, *Papers*, 14:638–640; DDE to Rhee, January 31, 1955, *Papers*, 16:1534–1536.

21. David Holloway, "Nuclear Weapons and the Escalation of the Cold War, 1945–1962," in *The Cambridge History of the Cold War*, ed. Melvyn P. Leffler and Odd Arne Westad (Cambridge: Cambridge University Press, 2010), 380–382.

22. Diary, December 10, 1953, *Papers*, 15:738–747.

23. David McIntosh, "In the Shadow of Giants: U.S. Policy Toward Small Nations: The Cases of Lebanon, Costa Rica, and Austria in the Eisenhower Years," *Contemporary Austrian Studies* 4 (1996): 222–279. See also Kenneth Lehman, "Revolutions and Attributions: Making Sense of Eisenhower Administration Policies in Bolivia and Guatemala," *Diplomatic History* 21, no. 2 (Spring 1997): 185–213.

24. Geoffrey Warner, "Eisenhower and Castro: US-Cuban Relations, 1958–60," *International Affairs* 75, no. 4 (1999): 803–817. See also Bevan

Sewell, "A Perfect (Free-Market) World? Economics, the Eisenhower Administration, and the Soviet Economic Offensive in Latin America," *Diplomatic History* 32, no. 5 (November 2008): 841–868.

25. See, for instance, DDE to Churchill, July 22, 1954, *Papers* 15:1207–11: "Colonialism is on the way out as a relationship among peoples. The sole question is one of time and method. I think we should handle it so as to win adherents to Western aims." See also DDE to Gruenther, November 30, 1954, *Papers*, 15:1413–1415.

26. See DDE to Paul Gray Hoffman, June 23, 1958, *Papers*, 19:952–960, for Eisenhower's lengthy explanation of his positions on events in Lebanon, Cyprus, France, and Indonesia.

27. See, for instance, DDE to John Foster Dulles, April 23 and 24, 1954, *Papers*, 15:1030–1031; DDE to Gruenther, April 26, 1954, *Papers*, 15:1033–1036; DDE to Churchill, July 8, 1954, *Papers*, 15:1170–1173. Also see Ambrose, *Eisenhower*, 2:100–101, 173–185, 204–211.

28. DDE to Ngo Dinh Diem, February 3, 1955, *Papers*, 16:1546–1549.

29. DDE to Churchill, February 24, 1953, *Papers*, 14:68–69; DDE to Muhammad Naguib, May 24, 1953, *Papers*, 14:244–245.

30. Steve Marsh, "The United States, Iran and Operation 'Ajax': Inverting Interpretative Orthodoxy," *Middle Eastern Studies* 39, no. 3 (July 2003): 1–38.

31. Steven E. Ambrose with Richard H. Immerman, *Ike's Spies: Eisenhower and the Espionage Establishment* (Jackson: University of Mississippi Press, 1999, orig. 1981), 189–214. In November 1954, Ike told his brother Edgar, "A year ago last January we were in imminent danger of losing Iran, and sixty percent of the known oil reserves of the world. You may have forgotten this. Lots of people have. But there has been no greater threat that has in recent years overhung the free world. That threat has been largely, if not totally, removed. I could name at least a half dozen other spots of the same character." DDE to Edgar Newton Eisenhower, November 8, 1954, *Papers*, 15:1386–1389. Ike's solution would last until 1979, when the Iranian Revolution overthrew the shah. See also Daniel C. Williamson, "Understandable Failure: The Eisenhower Administration's Strategic Goals in Iraq, 1953–1958," *Diplomacy and Statecraft* 17 (2006): 597–615.

32. See, for instance, Cole C. Kingseed, *Eisenhower and the Suez Crisis of 1956* (Baton Rouge: Louisiana State University Press, 1995), who concludes that Ike "was successful due to the force of his own personality, his bureaucratic skill, and his personal direction of an elaborate staff network that deferred all major decisions to the president before coordinating their execution" (154). In a more recent study, David A. Nichols, *Eisenhower 1956: The President's Year of Crisis: Suez and the Brink of War* (New York: Simon and Schuster, 2011), 286, comes to a similar conclusion: "By any standard, his was a virtuoso presidential performance—an enduring model for effective crisis management."

270   *Notes to Pages 200–204*

33. DDE to Churchill, November 27, 1956, *Papers*, 17:2412–2415, lays out Eisenhower's reactions stated diplomatically. He clearly was not happy to have first learned about the invasion in the newspapers.

34. DDE to Hazlett, November 2, 1956, *Papers*, 17:2355.

35. Jean Edward Smith, *Eisenhower in War and Peace* (New York: Random House, 2012), 686.

36. Shortly afterward the president exercised this new power, sending American troops into Lebanon. Peter L. Hahn, "Securing the Middle East: The Eisenhower Doctrine of 1957," *Presidential Studies Quarterly* 36, no. 1 (March 2006): 38–47.

37. DDE to Chiang Kai-shek, September 1, 1958, *Papers*, 19:1085–1086; Qiang Zhai, "Crisis and Confrontation: Chinese-American Relations During the Eisenhower Administration," *Journal of American-East Asian Relations* 9, nos. 3–4 (2000): 221–249.

38. DDE to Chiang Kai-shek, September 1, 1958, *Papers*, 19:1085–1086; DDE to Nikita Sergeyevich Khrushchev, September 29, 1959, and to Harold Macmillan, September 29, 1959; *Papers*, 20:1678–1683; DDE to Chiang Kai-shek, October 24, 1958, *Papers*, 19:1168–1170; and DDE to Chiang Kai-shek, January 12, 1961, *Papers*, 21:2245–2246.

39. Smith, *Eisenhower in War and Peace*, 543–544.

40. Nichols, *Eisenhower 1956*, 183ff., describes in exciting detail the intertwining of the Hungarian revolution and the Suez crisis. See also Chris Tudda, "'Reenacting the Story of Tantalus': Eisenhower, Dulles, and the Failed Rhetoric of Liberation," *Journal of Cold War Studies* 7, no. 4 (Fall 2005): 3–35; and Jim Marchio, "Resistance Potential and Rollback: US Intelligence and the Eisenhower Administration's Policies Toward Eastern Europe, 1953–56," *Intelligence and National Security* 10, no. 2 (April 1995): 219–241.

41. *Foreign Relations of the United States*, 1958–1960, vol. 8, *Berlin Crisis, 1958–1959*, ed. Charles S. Sampson (Washington, DC: Government Printing Office, 1993); David G. Coleman, "Eisenhower and the Berlin Problem, 1953–1954," *Journal of Cold War Studies* 2, no. 1 (Winter 2000): 3–34.

42. DDE, Memorandum for Files, February 27, 1959, *Papers*, 19:1378–1379.

43. DDE to Konrad Adenauer, September 28, 1950, and DDE to Khrushchev, September 28, 1950, *Papers*, 20:1676–1678.

44. Michael R. Beschloss, *MAYDAY: Eisenhower, Khrushchev, and the U-2 Affair* (New York: Harper and Row, 1986); R. Cargill Hall, "Clandestine Victory: Eisenhower and Overhead Reconnaissance in the Cold War," in *Forging the Shield: Eisenhower and National Security for the 21st Century*, ed. Dennis E. Showalter (Chicago: Imprint Publications), 119–149; R. Cargill Hall, "The Eisenhower Administration and the Cold War: Framing American Astronautics to Serve National Security," *Prologue* 27 (1995): 58–72.

45. Roger D. Launius, "Eisenhower and Space: Politics and Ideology in the Construction of the U.S. Civil Space Program," in *Forging the Shield*, ed. Showalter, 151–182.

46. Fred I. Greenstein, *The Hidden-Hand Presidency: Eisenhower as Leader* (New York: Basic Books, 1982) develops this tactic as a central theme in Ike's role as president.

47. As late as May 19, the president was lying about the incident, claiming, for instance, that the U-2 was a "civilian reconnaissance plane." DDE to Alberto Lleras Comargo, May 19, 1960, *Papers*, 20:1953–1954. In his customary manner, Ike tried to convert a negative—the collapse of the Paris meetings—into a positive result: "One good result of the failure of the conference was to bring the allies closer together." DDE to Macmillan, May 24, 1960, *Papers*, 20:1955–1956.

Twelve. The Wise Man

1. My thanks to Walter Isaacson and Evan Thomas for publishing their great book *The Wise Men: Six Friends and the World They Made* (New York: Simon and Schuster, 1986), a collective biography of six men who played crucial roles in defining America's position in the world during the immediate postwar years: Averell Harriman, Dean Acheson, George Kennan, Robert Lovett, John McCloy, and Charles Bohlen. George Marshall and Eisenhower came along too late to make that show, but clearly they were crucial to the reshaping of the containment policy and America's international role in the 1940s and 1950s.

2. On professionalism in America, see, for instance, the following sources: Paul J. Miranti, *Accountancy Comes of Age: The Development of an American Profession, 1886–1940* (Chapel Hill: University of North Carolina Press, 1990); Milton Friedman and Simon Smith Kuznets, *Income from Independent Professional Practice* (New York: National Bureau of Economic Research, 1954); Jane Eliot Sewell, *Medicine in Maryland: The Practice and Profession, 1799–1999* (Baltimore: Johns Hopkins University Press, 1999); Andrew Delano Abbott, *The System of Professions: An Essay on the Division of Labor* (Chicago: University of Chicago Press, 1988). Louis Galambos, *The Creative Society—and the Price Americans Paid for It* (New York: Cambridge University Press, 2012).

3. Here I am using the traditional distinction between dogma, which is the part of religious doctrine that does not change because it is a product of revelation, and doctrine, which is the body of rules and understandings in a religion. These rules and understandings are subject to change from time to time.

4. Had Eisenhower reflected on General Conner's long campaign on his behalf, he might have seen considerable evidence of cunning and an occasional touch of duplicity. He had, however, elevated Conner to such an exalted position that he was unlikely to associate his idol with Machiavellian skills. Judging by Ike's memoir, *At Ease: Stories I Tell to Friends* (New York: Doubleday, 1967), he did not see himself exercising those skills in his own military and political careers.

Index